CAPITALISM AND CONFRONTATION

CRITICAL READINGS

Edited by
Justin Paulson
Carlo Fanelli
Priscillia Lefebvre
Gülden Özcan

RED QUILL BOOKS

© Red Quill Books Ltd. 2012
Ottawa

www.redquillbooks.com
ISBN 978-1-926958-21-7

Library and Archives Canada Cataloguing in Publication

Capitalism and confrontation / edited by Justin Paulson ... [et al.].

Includes bibliographical references.
ISBN 978-1-926958-21-7

1. Global Financial Crisis, 2008-2009--Social aspects. 2. Global Financial Crisis, 2008-2009--Political aspects. 3. Capitalism. 4. Social movements. I. Paulson, Justin, 1974-

HB3717.2008C36 2012   330.9'0511   C2012-905728-2

QUILL BOOKS

RQB is a radical publishing house.
Part of the proceeds from the sale of this book will support student scholarships.

TABLE OF CONTENTS

PART I

PART II

ACKNOWLEDGMENTS

The "Capitalism and Confrontation" international conference at which many of these papers first appeared was held at Carleton University in 2010 and organized by the Critical Social Research Collaborative in Ottawa, Canada. It was sponsored by Carleton University's Faculty of Graduate Studies and Research, the Institute of Interdisciplinary Studies, the Institute of Political Economy, and the Departments of Geography & Environmental Studies, Law, Political Science, Social Work, and Sociology & Anthropology, as well as the Carleton University chapter of the Ontario Public Interest Research Group, the Carleton University Student Association, and the Canadian Union of Public Employees Local 4600. We are very thankful for their support.

The editors also wish to convey our immense thanks to Kate Keating and Margaret DeRosia, who tirelessly proofread and edited the manuscript and without whom this book would be in much poorer shape. We are grateful as well for the editorial assistance provided by Chris Dixon and Kirsten Francescone, and of course for the support and assistance of George Rigakos, Red Quill Books, and the anonymous reviewers whose feedback on the manuscript was essential to its improvement.

PART I

PART I

SOCIAL MOVEMENTS AND THE CRISIS

Justin Paulson, Carlo Fanelli, Priscillia Lefebvre and Gülden Özcan

It ought to be a truism that every economic crisis is at the same time also a social crisis. The one which began in 2008 feels particularly acute; this is partly a result of its roots in finance—and its consequent near-universal spread—and partly a result of the austerity imposed on most of us in order to pay for it. Those who pay (and suffer) the most during crisis are rarely those who cause it.

The universality of the crisis is important. A common populist line goes something like this: because the crisis began in finance (bad mortgages, complex derivatives, and the like), it ought to have stayed there, and indeed would have, if only it weren't for the hundreds of billions of dollars in public funds used to bail out the companies that got us into this mess. Would that it were so simple. But the financial sector—that part of the economy concerned with banking and the supply of credit—is not a neatly separated industry like cabinet-making or plumbing, nor is it a phantasm that creates profit by simply leeching off of the 'real' economy. Of course those sectors of the economy that are more directly concerned with, say, production or services are more tangible and more readily experienced, and so appear more 'real'; yet they are ultimately dependent on the smooth functioning of finance. From the standpoint of capital, production needs finance in order to keep moving and growing: when credit dries up (as it did in 2008), not only economic expansion but economic activity as such grinds to a halt. Capitalists never have the luxury of relating to finance as if it's in any way autonomous.

Finance is no less important from the workers' perspective. Our world is one in which the banks hold our mortgages and savings and process our paycheques, and in which pensions and retirement plans are tied up in the financial markets.[1] Were finance simply allowed to collapse, it would not be the capitalists first thrown out of their homes, but the working class—anyone without enough of a cushion to ride out the shock. In short, the crisis wrought by finance was *necessarily* a social crisis for us all; to 'let finance rot' would have forced untold numbers of workers to rot with it. To properly address the crisis, we need to begin with the recognition that the principal policy responses that raised so much ire—bailouts, public stimulus, and loose monetary policy—were insufficient but nevertheless necessary tools and an important counterweight to free-market fundamentalism. But who ultimately pays for them, and for the crisis as a whole—and what needs to be done to move past it—are other questions entirely. It is these latter questions that we ought to be grappling with.

Yet it has been oddly difficult for such questions to get posed in policy circles, at least in Europe and North America. Rather, because "we are all in it together," we are all expected, in the words of many a finance minister, to "share the pain." This is another way of saying we all need to take responsibility for capital's collapse during the crisis, and socialize capital's losses while expecting nothing in return. The existing and forthcoming struggles over austerity will highlight just how much is at stake—both for capital and for working people here and abroad.

The Crisis as Capitalism?

What is the relationship between crisis and capital as such?[2] The editors of this volume, and many of its contributors, are

---

1   For a more detailed workers' case in several recent contexts for not letting finance rot, see, e.g.: Doug Henwood, "How to Learn Nothing From Crisis," *Left Business Observer* 125 (2010): 1; Sam Gindin, "Beyond Wage Cuts, Beyond the Bailout," *The Windsor Star*, 20 November 2008, reprinted online at http://rppe.wordpress.com/2008/11/26/sam-gindin-beyond-wage-cuts-beyond-the-bailout/; and Leo Panitch, interview by Paul Jay, *The Real News*, 15 June 2011, http://therealnews.com/t2/index.php?option=com_content&t ask=view&id=31&Itemid=74&jumival=6919.

2   Certainly not all crisis is caused by capital itself; crisis can also be brought about by pressure from below. But this doesn't mean that social movements should rally behind economic collapse! Movement-created crises look very different—not least because they come packaged with a specific, alternative political project. Without an alternative political project organized across multiple scales of society, a worsening crisis may precipitate worsening austerity, and to the poor paying for the restoration of the rich.

sympathetic to the view that capitalism is one large unsolved crisis, for this is often the lived experience of the working class. David Harvey, for example, insists that capitalism never solves crises (whether precipitated by workers' struggles or overzealous investment bankers)—it just moves them around geographically.[3] And when the EZLN's Subcomandante Marcos spoke of neoliberalism as not a solution to the crisis, but rather "the crisis itself,"[4] surely this also rings true for those who most regularly experience neoliberal restructuring—the subjection of more and more of their lives to the forces of the free market—as an ongoing pattern of theft, displacement, and destruction. It is otherwise, however, for capital itself: indeed, from capital's perspective, crises *are* resolved when the rate of profit ticks upward, and they are never particularly dangerous for capital unless the rate of profit falls to zero. As an abstract system of value production that is mapped unevenly onto the real world,[5] capital may well be a never-ending series of *contradictions*, but that just means it has a propensity for crisis, not that it is reducible to crisis itself.[6]

But to adopt the perspective of capital here is, at some level, to split hairs: the point, for the essays that follow in this volume, is that for working people the world over, crisis doesn't fundamentally change the experience of capitalism so much as make those experiences sharper and more acute. Simply put, capitalism feels worse during crisis. It may be more useful then to bracket the profit rates and details of the credit crunch (as important as these may be) and instead think of crisis in terms of what it means for possibilities for resistance. More than turning points, large-scale crises of the kind we are living through now can be turning *periods*, not one

---

3   For his most recent elaboration of this point, see David Harvey, *The Enigma of Capital* (London: Oxford Univ. Press, 2010).

4   Subcomandante Marcos, "El Neoliberalismo es la Crisis Misma Hecha Teoría y Doctrina," communique of 17 March 1995, in EZLN, *Documentos y comunicados*, vol. 2 (México, D.F.: Ediciones Era, 1995), 256-268.

5   cf. Negt and Kluge: "Capitalism cannot avoid dirtying its hands with human beings. Herein lies its extreme instability." Oskar Negt and Alexander Kluge, *Public Sphere and Experience* (London: Univ. of Minnesota Press, 1993), 186.

6   cf. Leo Panitch and Sam Gindin, "Capitalist Crises and the Crisis This Time," in Panitch, Albo, and Chibber, eds., *Socialist Register 2011: The Crisis This Time* (Toronto: Fernwood, 2011) and Greg Albo, Leo Panitch, and Sam Gindin, *In and Out of Crisis: The Global Financial Meltdown and Left Alternatives* (Oakland: PM Press, 2010).

brief moment but a sustained length of time, a year or a decade, in which sharp opportunities are present for both capital and working people. Capital can (and typically will) try to use the crisis to reshape common sense according to its needs, and roll back whatever gains have been made by labour during a prior period. The cards are stacked in its favour; it takes a great deal of organization by the Left to present a real alternative and prevent such rollbacks and deepening entrenchment of class power. In this case, such organization was dreadfully absent at the onset of the crisis, particularly in the US and Canada, and some important turning points—such as the ability to socialize finance—were missed. But the crisis period, what McNally calls the "global slump,"[7] is far from over; battles over collective bargaining rights (especially in the United States) and austerity measures (everywhere) are just beginning. Situations of crisis of course demand that we think about new kinds of struggle, but also the renewed relevance of older ones. The essays in this volume highlight both. Social movements and academics have both spent far too much time declaring that we are in "new times"; we have to embrace new possibilities, but without fetishizing them.

So while it would be easy to entitle a volume such as this one "Crisis and Confrontation" rather than "Capitalism and Confrontation," that would miss the point. It is our aim instead to emphasize that while the particular financial instruments that drove the world economies off a cliff were historically specific (collateralized debt obligations, credit default swaps, and the like), the tendency to spread risk around—privatizing gains and socializing losses—is built into the logic of capital accumulation and capitalist production. Further, the crisis was not simply the result of free markets running amok in the absence of government intervention; fixing it, then, is not just a matter of invoking Keynes.[8] And indeed, the handling of crisis—how policymakers respond—puts the long-term tendencies of capital in sharp relief. Deficit reduction may be the norm in times of plenty, yet

---

7   David McNally, *Global Slump: The Economics and Politics of Crisis and Resistance* (Oakland: PM Press, 2010).

8   One protest sign photographed at Occupy Wall Street stated correctly: "The system isn't broken. It was BUILT this way." The 'Occupy' protests represent a new kind of movement spawned by the crisis and the inability of the political status quo in the United States to solve it; they remain in their infancy as this book goes to press.

capital is entitled to use every tool of the state and public as a crutch in times of need, repeatedly bailing itself out of the mess it is in, while denying to labour those same tools in order to enrich life. The opportunity costs are astonishing; few economists questioned the necessity of the bailout of AIG, while nationalization of US health insurance companies or the banks, or free post-secondary tuition, etc., remains—puzzlingly—"too costly."

We also want to emphasize that while confrontation with some aspect of capitalism does happen (and it's inconceivable to imagine that during crisis it wouldn't),[9] all else being equal it is as likely to be reactionary as transformative. There is no intrinsic reason to simply expect people's responses to be progressive, absent sustained mobilization toward that end. History offers far too many examples of fight-back from the Right; there is no shortage of right-wing, liberal, neoliberal and otherwise capitalist responses to acute social and economic crisis that claim to take the side of working people against finance, bankers, or "big government." Sometimes the mantle of class struggle is simply a mask for a cynical power grab (as seems to be the case with much of the American "Tea Party"), but it can be genuinely populist too. In times of recession and depression, many a worker has cast in her or his lot with the Right, leading to retrenchment at best, and fascism at worst. The only responses to the crisis that have a shot at being socially and economically transformative are those that conceive of their antagonism as being with *capital*, not just a momentary glitch in the system.

Austerity and Retrenchment

At the onset of the crisis, it became commonplace to declare the "end of neoliberalism." This would seem to be a remarkable turnaround. Neoliberalism was, after all, preparing to celebrate thirty years of being "the only alternative" in capitalism! But as an edifice neoliberalism seemed to have been cracked wide open by the crisis. There could be no return to free market fundamentalism—or so

---

9   This point appears uncontroversial. A diverse list of research papers compiled by *The Economist* from a rather broad spectrum of academic sources, governments, and think tanks, finds general agreement that the sudden growth of inequality tends to be an engine of unrest. ("Unrest in Peace," *The Economist*, 22 October 2011, 94).

it was thought. Neoliberalism was supposed to be "dead but dominant"—still there, zombie-like, in practice (so long as nothing
had yet replaced it), but no longer believed in theory. There was
soon a headlong rush into public spending (although temporary),
and even the governor of the Bank of England suggested turning banks into public utilities.[10] Three short years later, and the
remarkable turnaround was most remarkable for not happening
at all; the only playbook among central bankers today is a *deepening* of neoliberalism. Thus the headlong rush now—especially
in Europe, but also in North America—is to slash public spending, engage in further and rapid privatization of public services
and resources, fret about inflation, and muzzle organized labour.
As always, policy responses are uneven: the UK is currently at
the forefront of the new austerity, running what amounts to a
huge social experiment in upward wealth redistribution; the US
Federal Reserve, unusually enough, seems to be (smartly) playing
the laggard in terms of austere monetary policy, while US policymakers are torn between a needed stimulus package and the
ideological drive to reign in public spending. Canada has forged
its own course—keeping monetary policy loose while shrinking
the size of the public service and most vociferously going after
unions and the right to strike. And so it seems that all the headlines and academic talks proclaiming neoliberalism's demise
were quite premature. Of course, this isn't to say that the cracks
aren't continuing to appear, or even that large numbers of people
aren't challenging capital in the wake of the crisis. As Slavoj Zizek
recently remarked:

> There is no lack of anti-capitalists today. We are even
> witnessing an over-load of critiques of capitalism's horrors:
> newspaper investigations, TV reports and best-selling
> books abound on companies polluting our environment,
> corrupt bankers who continue to get fat bonuses while
> their firms are saved by public money, sweatshops where
> children work overtime. There is, however, a catch to

---

10   Mervyn King, "Speech by Mervyn King, Governor of the Bank of England,
      to Scottish Business Associations, Edinburgh, on Tuesday 20 October 2009,"
      http://www.bankofengland.co.uk/publications/speeches/2009/speech406.
      pdf.

all this criticism, ruthless as it may appear: what is as a rule not questioned is the liberal-democratic framework within which these excesses should be fought.[11]

Indeed, the most significant debates in the pages of *The Economist* and *The New York Times* from 2008-2011 have been between orthodox neoliberals and Keynesians, not between capitalism and non-capitalist alternatives. And by early 2011, austerity had already appeared as the new normal.

Neoliberalism is hardly a monolith: its ideological and material shape has varied across different spaces and scales since the 1970s. Yet the variations of neoliberalism, both in ideology and in practice, have always constituted a set of intensive, "class-war" approaches to existing problems of accumulation and growth.[12] The austerity drive is most readily understood as one of these proposed solutions, rooted in the twin fundamentalisms of deficit-busting and inflation-busting.[13] Public sector austerity makes the providers of the bailout and stimulus pay twice: first as a loan to the private sector (with the attendant opportunity cost), and again when it is forced to eat the cost while those bailed out resume their profitability. This leads to some remarkable juxtapositions—as when the UK government decided to allow banks to recover all their losses from the financial crisis at the same time that it slashed more than a hundred billion dollars from public spending. Of course, there were street protests when Barclays admitted paying only 1% of its 2009 profit of 11.9 billion pounds in taxes.[14] But, as Thatcher proclaimed, "there is no alternative"—or, as Britain's chancellor of the exchequer remarked of the austerity program, "there is no plan B."[15] Neoliberalism's greatest strength would appear to be the lack of credible alternatives.

---

11 Slavoj Zizek, "A Permanent Economic Emergency," *New Left Review* 64 (2010): 87. The 'Occupy' protests may finally be breaking out of this pattern; at this stage it is too early to tell.

12 cf. David Harvey, *A Brief History of Neoliberalism* (London: Oxford Univ. Press, 2005). See also *In and Out of Crisis*.

13 This is despite the general absence of significant inflation outside China.

14 "Protestors besiege Barclays after 'shocking' revelation over tax," *The Guardian Weekly* 25.02.11, 13.

15 "George Osborne on spending review: there is no plan B," *The Guardian*, 21 October 2010. Accessed at http://www.guardian.co.uk/politics/2010/oct/21/george-osborne-spending-review-there-is-no-plan-b on 22 October 2010.

The UK is not alone in being saddled with public sector austerity. Greece, Ireland, California, Wisconsin, Ontario, Latvia—the list goes on and on.[16] At the beginning of 2011, the *New York Times* reported that the ideology of austerity was even crossing party lines in the US:

> The dismal fiscal situation in many states is forcing governors, despite their party affiliation, toward a consensus on what medicine is needed going forward... The prescription? Slash spending. Avoid tax increases. Tear up regulations that might drive away business and jobs. Shrink government.[17]

In some cases the prescription includes cutting taxes – not sales or even income tax, but business and property taxes. How did we get from the end of neoliberalism to such dramatic retrenchment? When the horizons of possibility are so heavily restricted, neoliberal common sense may be questioned only to take up its dominant role once again. It would surely be more productive for social movements—especially labour—to use the crisis in order to demand an *expansion* of the public sector and public services, not least to meet the increased needs of the swelling ranks of the unemployed and underemployed. But instead the Left is stuck fighting against cutbacks, which is too often a losing battle, especially when the ideological playing field is so heavily stacked against it.

The stakes are higher than they might appear. The trillions of dollars in spending to aid banks and private corporations should have plainly demonstrated that public spending is, in fact, possible. After we were told for decades that there isn't enough money for schools, or for parks, or for health care, it is quite apparent now that this was a lie—not theoretically, but practically. So if it is

---

16 One of the best assessments of the austerity push in the UK, Ireland, Greece, and the US is in Greg Albo and Bryan Evans, "From Rescue Strategies to Exit Strategies: The Struggle Over Public Sector Austerity," in Panitch, Albo, and Chibber, *Socialist Register 2011*, 291-301. For a Canadian assessment, see Stephen McBride and Heather Whiteside, *Private Affluence and Public Austerity* (Toronto: Fernwood, 2011).
17 Monica Davey, "Budget Worries Push Governors to Same Mind-Set," *New York Times* 17 January 2011, accessed at www.nytimes.com on 17 January 2011.

common sense that the public should be starved of resources in order to support private corporations, what's to prevent people from reversing the equation? What's to keep them from insisting on billions or trillions of dollars for free and universal public education and healthcare, improved parks, carbon dioxide reductions, and a general increase in living standards (with all of this paid for by holding down or skimming off the wages and benefits of the private sector)? The imposition of public sector austerity to pay for the private-sector rescue, then, is not merely class warfare, but ideologically crucial from the standpoint of capital; it ensures the continued disciplining of labour, and of the public in general.

In this regard, austerity may not even work as an exit strategy to the crisis. Historically, the question of solutions has been principally a political one; socializing capitalist losses is a rather old and successful form of top-down class struggle. So one could think of this round of public sector austerity as simply a technocratic solution in the arsenal of capital, as it frequently has been in the past. But in this case, it is difficult to envision how. Austerity is not a response to the crisis at all, but to the bailouts and stimulus packages throughout the wealthy countries that for three years eased the crisis. It was that bailout and stimulus that staved off collapse; credit (both public and private) flowed again and unemployment was stunted, but there is little evidence that capital has recovered in any sustainable way. To argue for austerity at this point in the slump, then, is a bit like arguing that a breathing tube should be removed from a patient on life-support simply because the patient is not dead. From a practical standpoint, reining in the purse-strings in favour of the resumption of free-market orthodoxy ought to appear as lunacy, even to a capitalist. But austerity functions in this case less to save capitalism than to destroy labour, or at least force it into a permanent cycle of defensive struggles. The danger for social movements is that they will be stuck fighting on these terms, always a step behind.

Simply put, the Left has been, in many cases, late to the party; as opportunities have arisen in the crisis, it has not been well-enough organized on the right scales in order to present (or force through) credible alternatives for restructuring social life. When credit markets froze and the banks began to collapse, Hayekian and Friedmanite ideologies of small government and market solutions—in which the private sector is perceived to do everything right while the public sector is bloated, inefficient, and ineffective—were called into question to the point of no longer being common sense. But until they are actually *replaced*, restoration and intensification will remain the most likely outcome. Actual replacement will require active resistance with consistent demands, emphasizing the shared experience of capitalist failures and celebration of successful points of struggle, while enlarging the horizon of alternatives.

Popular Responses to the Crisis

Confrontation and resistance are indeed occurring. Most of the essays collected for this volume were written before the meltdowns, bailouts, and explosion of popular movements in Greece, the UK, and Ireland, and all of them were drafted prior to the emergence of Occupy Wall Street. As the push for austerity intensifies, it is not at all surprising to see it spawning further struggles. Indeed, as this book goes to press, the austerity push has begun to backfire in places as disparate as Greece and Wisconsin, as some of the largest popular mobilizations in a generation have come out in a sustained way to oppose the cuts, and the New York Times reports that "almost half of the public thinks the sentiment at the root of the Occupy movement generally reflects the views of most Americans."[18]

But defensive struggles are only a start. Resistance that does not take the offence can only at best reassert the status quo; at worst, it is destroyed. Fortunately, both the crisis writ large and the battles over austerity offer opportunities that social movements *can* take up: to rethink the role of government, public resources, and social solidarity; to rethink the agents of working-class resistance (unions? parties? something new?); and to rethink (and reclaim) concepts of democracy and internationalism from markets and capitalist globalization. With no apparent end in sight to the global slump, movements have an extended opportunity to think big—to restructure the economy, in "green" ways certainly, but also in more socialized ways. The cracks in free market fundamentalism are being papered over, but they won't be fully repaired until the material economy is repaired

---

18   Jeff Zelaney and Megan Thee-Brenan, "New Poll Finds a Deep Distrust of Government." *The New York Times*, 26 October 2011. Online at http://www.nytimes.com/2011/10/26/us/politics/poll-finds-anxiety-on-the-economy-fuels-volatility-in-the-2012-race.html.

as well. In the meantime, despite all turning points that have already been missed, neoliberalism remains vulnerable to any credible alternatives, including non-capitalist ones.

Movements need to rethink themselves as well. As demonstrated by several of the essays here, while organized labour is leading the struggle in some parts of the world, it is far from obvious that we can expect the same on a large scale in North America. Decades of defensive fights that were often lost, alongside a growing Thatcherite fatalism, created a union culture built more on accommodation than confrontation. (Ironically, the austerity drive may be breathing new life into US unions, mobilizing workers by threatening their organizations' very existence.) But the practical resources of organized labour remain crucial to popular struggles, especially in countries without significant Left political parties around which social movements can coalesce. At the same time, community groups often suspicious of organized labour—for its historic whiteness, patriarchy, homophobia and xenophobia—have been spearheading resistance to neoliberal restructuring at the local level, sometimes with a well-formed class politics, sometimes without, but almost always starved of resources. We are finally beginning to see new alliances form between unions and working-class community groups as a way of moving beyond defensive, bounded and sectoral struggles. If this process continues, it may represent a turning point.

Related to this is the obvious but oft-neglected requirement of solidarity in the face of the crisis. The impulse to look out for oneself only in light of worsening conditions has to be resisted at all levels, if we are to come out of the crisis with anything but a stronger neoliberalism. Solidarity is important between struggles in various parts of the world not only in the sense of supporting each other but also in so far as they can learn from each other, as several of the essays here make clear. But we often forget how crucial solidarity is within even the most local class struggles. For example, if providers of public services (in Canada, these are typically members of public service unions) and service users (most often the poor, immigrants, First Nations, people of colour, the elderly, and so on), so easily pitted against each other, instead work together for the expansion and improvement of services, then the resistance to austerity can be transformed into an offensive struggle. It is transformations of this kind that might lead to a struggle that can actually be won.

The Plan of the Book

Most of the essays collected here were first presented in 2010 at the "Capitalism and Confrontation" international conference at Carleton University, organized by the Critical Social Research Collaborative. The conference aimed to bring together a broad spectrum of theoretical perspectives and examples of confrontation (from the top and from the bottom), not only in Canada but also in the United States, South America, South Africa, Turkey, South Asia, and East Asia. The chapters that follow offer original analyses of the crisis—both in its specific, contingent dimensions and in relation to broader capitalist processes—and of a variety of forms of resistance to it. The papers are written from a variety of scholarly, political, and activist perspectives, and together challenge the dominant accounts of the crisis and the trajectory of economic and social recovery. The range of contexts is global; North American readers will likely be familiar with some of the struggles and contexts presented in this book, but not all. We hope these struggles and contexts will be read not as disconnected pieces but as elements that make up a larger picture of the multidimensional operations of global capital, the financial crisis, and burgeoning resistance.

In Part 1, Lebowitz and Fanelli start us off with reflections on the Marxian legacy, and how Marx (and Engels) can help frame the current conjuncture. Since 2008, even more orthodox publications such as *The Economist*, *The Financial Times*, and *Foreign Affairs* have suggested Marx remains relevant after all; but in what ways? It's well and good to acknowledge that Marx understood the nature of crisis. But what about getting out of it? And can we learn from Marx without resorting to dry "Marxology"? These essays address such questions. Lebowitz challenges us to look to Marx for a better understanding of the nature of socialism, which he argues is coterminous with human and social development. His contribution allows us to postulate socialism as a real (neither imagined nor utopian) alternative to the crisis; he echoes Hugo Chávez's exhortation that we need to "re-invent" socialism, first in principle and then in deed. It is worth asking to what extent we need to re-invent popular movements as well, and Fanelli's essay does precisely this, arguing that while the labour movement remains crucial to the confrontation of capital, it is in dire need of its own re-invention and renewal.

The set of essays in Part 2 addresses the depth of the crisis while often pointing toward innovative opportunities for resistance. Kokallaj explores the environmental degradation stemming from neoliberal governance, and how we might think about the conditions for and agents of a democratic eco-governance in its place. Spronk's contribution focuses on the interconnectedness of three erstwhile-separate crises in the South: the food crisis, the financial crisis, and the climate crisis. We cannot and should not, she argues, treat these as separate issues—neither in understanding the nature of the crisis, nor in thinking about resistance. From a policymaking perspective, any progressive, non-neoliberal trajectory out of the crisis needs to address all three crises as one.

The chapters by Fowler, Coşar & Özman, Lefebvre, and Cobbett are all specific case studies of neoliberal politics, governance, and even war; in most cases these processes predate the financial crisis but have, they argue, been amplified by it. Fowler's assessment of the Canadian Autoworkers paints a bleak picture of organized labour's capitulation to capital's terms at the deepest part of the crisis in 2009. On the other side of the world, Coşar and Özman analyze the course of privatization in Turkey since 1980, with a specific examination of the privatization of TEKEL, the state tobacco and alcohol corporation. In this case as well, we see the weakness of organized labour playing a role, but also hints of other possible 'cracks' in the neoliberal edifice. While the Thatcherite hegemony proclaiming "there is no alternative" has played a key role in marginalizing labour struggles in much of the world, especially since the collapse of "actually existing socialism," Lefebvre's chapter offers a window into a different part of the neoliberal toolkit: overt violence. Her essay provides an overview of Philippine labour struggles, in which organizers face regular and brutal repression. Such situations exemplify Fredric Jameson's reminder that the underside of contemporary capitalist culture is "blood, torture, death, and terror,"[19] and highlight the urgent need for international solidarity among those fighting for progressive alternatives to capital. Cobbett's chapter looks to South Africa—once considered a beacon of hope against capital—and the inability of the governing ANC to

---

19   Frederic Jameson, *Postmodernism, or, The Cultural Logic of Late Capitalism* (Durham: Duke Univ. Press, 1991), 5.

provide basic services and infrastructure on account of the enduring state-capital relationship. The ANC's adoption of neoliberalism has made it impossible, she argues, to undo the social and economic fragmentation that was the legacy of apartheid.

Part 3, the final set of essays, presents case studies of resistance. Wark, Macdougall, and Brons begin with the role of anarchism and anarchists in anti-capitalist organizing. Their essay dispels a number of misconceptions about anarchist organization and is, we believe, crucial for understanding some of the most vital and energetic currents of struggle today. Pandey's chapter on eco-feminist alternatives to capitalist globalization insists that our search for alternatives to capital should not look merely in capital's own toolkit, but can rather be rooted in traditional knowledges that "can be perfectly scientific and are capable of being deployed in the present context as alternatives." Her case study is the ecofeminist movements of the Indian Himalayas, and it parallels nicely the similar possibilities we have seen arising out of the indigenous movements of Meso- and South America that are closer to home. John Clarke brings us back to Canada with a focused chapter on the resistance to Ontario's cuts to its social assistance programs, a resistance that has been gaining traction under the leadership of the Ontario Coalition Against Poverty. Stephanie Ross closes the collection with an analysis of the Greater Toronto Workers' Assembly. A nascent attempt to forge a working-class alliance between organized labour and diverse community groups in Canada's largest city, the Assembly faces challenges that are a microcosm of the challenges facing all those who are trying to chart a course out of the existing marginalization of the Left. If workers and community organizers are indeed able to solidify their capacities to work together in Toronto to prevent the re-entrenchment of neoliberalism and public austerity, there will surely be important lessons for those struggling elsewhere for a fair, just, and sustainable future built out of the wreckage of the crisis.

EIGHT THESES ABOUT MARX AND SOCIALIST ALTERNATIVES

Michael A. Lebowitz

This chapter seeks to clarify common misconceptions about Marx and the nature of socialism. Through a close reading of Marx's work over a 30-year period, Marx's concept of socialism is understood to be internally consistent, and coextensive with human and social development achieved through revolutionary practice. If capitalism, with all its crises, is to be finally transcended, Lebowitz argues that the 'socialist principle' must be at the root of a new politics.

1. For Marx, the whole point of socialism was human development.

From the outset of his work, Marx rejected the preoccupations of the political economists of his time and envisioned a 'rich human being'—one who has developed his capacities and capabilities to the point where he is able "to take gratification in a many-sided way," "the rich man profoundly endowed with all the senses."[1] "In place of the wealth and poverty of political economy," Marx proposed, "come the rich human being and rich human need. The rich human being is simultaneously the human being in need of a totality of human manifestations of life—the man in whom his own realisation exists as an inner necessity, as need."[2]

---

1   This chapter is a revised version of a paper presented at the Universidad Autónoma Metropolitana, Xochimilco, Mexico in October 2009. The arguments are developed more fully in Lebowitz, *The Socialist Alternative: Real Human Development* (New York: Monthly Review, 2010).

2   Karl Marx, *Economic and Philosophical Manuscripts of 1844*, in Marx and Engels, *Collected Works*, vol. 3 (New York: International Publishers, 1975), 302, 304.

It was not only the young Marx, however, who spoke so eloquently about rich human beings. In the *Grundrisse*, Marx continued to stress the centrality of the concept of rich human beings. "When the limited bourgeois form is stripped away," he asked, "what is wealth other than the universality of individual needs, capacities, pleasures, productive forces etc., created through universal exchange?"[3] In continuing to envision a rich human being, "as rich as possible in needs, because rich in qualities and relations... as the most total and universal possible social product," Marx revealed his understanding that real wealth is the development of human capacity.[4]

Grasping this concept is essential if we are to understand the perspective from which Marx proceeded: real wealth is the development of human capacities, the development of human potential. Rather than thinking of a being with simple needs and simple productive powers, Marx looked to the "development of the rich individuality which is as all-sided in its production as in its consumption."[5] This is what Marx's conception of socialism was all about: the creation of a society that removes all obstacles to the full development of human beings. In contrast to a society where the worker exists to satisfy the need of capital for its growth, he looked to what he called in *Capital* "the inverse situation, in which objective wealth is there to satisfy the worker's own need for development."[6]

In that society of associated producers, each individual is able to develop his full potential: i.e., the "absolute working-out of his creative potentialities," the "complete working out of the human content," the "development of all human powers as such the end in itself."[7] In socialism, the productive forces would have "increased with the all-round development of the individual, and all the springs of co-operative wealth flow more abundantly."[8] The result, in short, would be the production of rich human beings.

How, though, are rich human beings produced? How do we ensure that all people have the opportunity for the full development of their potential?

---

3   Karl Marx, *Grundrisse* (New York: Vintage, 1973), 488.
4   Ibid., 409.
5   Ibid., 325.
6   Karl Marx, *Capital*, vol. 1 (New York: Vintage, 1977), 772.
7   Marx, *Grundrisse*, 488, 541, 708.
8   Karl Marx, *Critique of the Gotha Programme*, in Marx and Engels, *Selected Works*, vol. 2 (Moscow: Foreign Languages Publishing House, 1962), 24.

2. The key to the development of our capacities is revolutionary practice.

'Revolutionary practice' is the simultaneous changing of circumstances and human activity or self-change. Marx introduced this concept in the context of criticizing Robert Owen's idea that you can change people by giving them gifts. That was the essence of the utopian socialism of his time—that if we change the circumstances for people (for example, by creating new structures, new communities, and the like, and inserting people into these), they will be themselves different people. And Marx said, no, you are forgetting something rather important: you are forgetting really existing human beings. You are forgetting that it is they who change circumstances and that they change themselves in the process.

Further, who is this 'we' that would change circumstances for people? This idea that we can change circumstances for people and thus change them, Marx noted, divides society into two parts— one part of which is superior to society. Indeed, is there a group of people at the top of society who will change circumstances for us? A group that knows how to build socialism for us? A group that knows enough to bestow that gift upon those whom they consider to know nothing? You are forgetting, Marx remarked, something else rather important: that "the educator must himself be educated."[9]

3. It is essential to understand that the key link for Marx is this combination of human development and practice.

Make the key link of human development and practice our starting point and there is a simple answer to the question of how the development of human capacity occurs: we develop through all our activities. As the French Marxist Lucien Sève commented, "Every developed personality appears to us straight away as an enormous accumulation of the most varied acts through time," and those acts play a central role in producing human 'capacities'—"the ensemble of 'actual potentialities,' innate or acquired, to carry out any act

---

9   Karl Marx, "Theses on Feuerbach," in Marx and Engels, *Collected Works*, vol. 5 (New York: International Publishers, 1975).

whatever and whatever its level."[10]

Thus, in all their activities, people produce in themselves the potentialities to carry out other acts that reproduce and expand their capabilities. "Every kind of consumption," Marx pointed out, "in one way or another produces human beings in some particular aspect"; thus, when "attending lectures, educating his children, developing his taste, etc.," the worker expands his capacities in different dimensions.[11] In short, the worker explicitly pursues his "own need for development" when he uses his time away from the organized workplace "for education, for intellectual development, for the fulfillment of social functions, for social intercourse, for the free play of the vital forces of his body and his mind."[12]

But people also transform themselves when their own development is not their preconceived goal (In this case, it is an unintended consequence of their activities). "The coincidence of the changing of circumstances and of human activity or self-change"—this, after all, is the essence of Marx's view of "the self-creation of man as a process." Marx was most consistent on this point when talking about the struggles of workers against capital and how this revolutionary practice transforms "circumstances and men," expanding their capabilities and making them fit to create a new world.[13]

Marx, though, did not at all limit his view of this process of self-change to the sphere of political and economic struggle. In the very act of producing, "the producers change, too, in that they bring out new qualities in themselves, develop themselves in production, transform themselves, develop new powers and new ideas, new modes of intercourse, new needs and new language."[14] The worker as outcome of his own labour, indeed, enters into Marx's discussion in Capital of the labour process; there the worker "acts upon external nature and changes it, and in this way he simultaneously changes his own nature."[15]

---

10 Lucien Sève, *Man in Marxist Theory and the Psychology of Personality* (Sussex: Harvester Press, 1978), 304, 313.
11 Marx, *Grundrisse*, 90-91, 287; see also Michael A. Lebowitz, *Beyond CAPITAL: Marx's Political Economy of the Working Class*, 2nd ed. (New York: Palgrave Macmillan, 2003), 66-72.
12 Marx, *Capital*, vol. 1, 772, 375.
13 See Lebowitz, *Beyond CAPITAL*, 178-83.
14 Marx, *Grundrisse*, 494.
15 Marx, *Capital*, vol. 1, 283.

In short, every labour process inside and outside the formal process of production (that is, every act of production, every human activity) has as its result a joint product: both the change in the object of labour and the change in the labourer herself.

4. The spectre of socialism haunts Marx's Capital.

Once we understand Marx's consistent focus upon human development, it is clear that the very premise of his Capital is the concept of a society in which the development of all human powers is an end in itself. The "society of free individuality, based on the universal development of individuals and on the subordination of their communal, social productivity as their social wealth"[16] is the spectre that haunts Marx's *Capital*. Can we doubt at all the presence of this other world oriented to the human end-in-itself from *Capital*'s opening sentence? We are immediately introduced to the horror of a society in which wealth appears not as real human wealth but, rather, as "an immense collection of commodities."[17] Think of the condemnation implied there for a writer who is so clear that real wealth is human capacities!

Further, can we doubt at all that socialism is Marx's premise when without any logical development in this supremely logical work, Marx suddenly evokes a society characterized not by the capitalist's impulse to increase the value of his capital but, rather, by "the inverse situation in which objective wealth is there to satisfy the worker's own need for development"?[18] In fact, that 'inverse situation' is precisely the perspective from which Marx persistently critiques capitalism. After all, he comments that in capitalism means of production employ workers; and he describes that as "this inversion, indeed this distortion, which is peculiar to and characteristic of capitalist production." But an inversion and distortion of what? Simply, an inversion of the "relation between dead labour and living labour" in a different society, one in which the results of past labour are "there to satisfy the worker's own need for development."[19]

---

16   Marx, *Grundrisse*, 158.
17   Marx, *Capital*, vol. 1, 125.
18   Ibid., 772.
19   Ibid., 425.

If we read *Capital* with the purpose of identifying the inversions and distortions that produce truncated human beings in capitalism, then we can get a sense of Marx's idea of what is "peculiar to and characteristic of" production in that 'inverse situation' in socialism. We understand that all means for the development of production are not necessarily "means of domination and exploitation of the producers" but that this is a 'distortion': that in socialism, we would be liberated and not enslaved by our own products. We begin to understand the necessary conditions for producing rich human beings by considering Marx's account of their negation in capitalism.

What are the characteristics of socialist production that we can discover in *Capital*? What kind of production has as its joint product not the crippled human beings who are the result of capitalist relations of production but "the totally developed individual, for whom the different social functions are different modes of activity he takes up in turn"?[20] What kind of activities are essential to produce this rich human being whose "own realisation exists as an inner necessity, as need?"

Given the 'dialectical inversion' peculiar to capitalist production that cripples the body and mind of the worker and alienates from her "the intellectual potentialities of the labour process," it is clear that to develop the capacities of people the producers must put an end to "the enslaving subordination of the individual to the division of labour and therewith also the antithesis between mental and physical labour."[21] It is no accident that Marx indicated in *Capital* that the "revolutionary ferments whose goal is the abolition of the old division of labour stand in diametrical contradiction with the capitalist form of production."[22]

Head and hand must be reunited. For the development of rich human beings, the worker must be able to call "his own muscles into play under the control of his own brain."[23] Expanding the capabilities of people requires both mental and manual activity. Not only does the combination of education with productive labour make it possible to increase the efficiency of production;

---

20   Ibid., 617-18.
21   Marx, *Critique of the Gotha Programme*, 24.
22   Marx, *Capital*, vol. 1, 619.
23   Ibid., 643.

this is also, as Marx pointed out in *Capital*, "the only method of producing fully developed human beings."[24] Here, then, is the way to ensure that "the productive forces have also increased with the all-around development of the individual, and all the springs of co-operative wealth flow more abundantly."[25]

5. To understand Marx's concept of socialism, we need to understand his distinction between the Being and Becoming of an organic system.

In capitalism as an organic system, "every economic relation presupposes every other in its bourgeois economic form, and everything posited is thus also a presupposition, this is the case with every organic system."[26] Furthermore, that is what Marx demonstrated in *Capital*. He showed how capitalism was a system of reproduction, one which tends to reproduce all its premises. That is, it reproduces its property relations and its relations of production. And this is the case with every organic system.

However, there is a very big difference between an organic system, one that produces its own premises and thus rests upon its own foundations, and the 'becoming' of such a system. We will never understand Marx's conception of socialism or what he had to say about economic systems in general if we don't grasp the essential distinction between the 'Becoming' of a system and its 'Being': between the historical emergence of a particular form of society and the nature of that society once it has developed upon its own foundations.

A new system does not drop from the sky. It never produces its own premises at the outset. Rather, when a new system emerges, it necessarily inherits premises from the old. Its premises and presuppositions are 'historic' ones, premises that are produced outside the system. And insofar as those historic premises are from outside the system, they cannot be a basis for understanding an organic system "in which all the elements coexist simultaneously and support one another."[27]

---

24 Ibid., 614.
25 Marx, *Critique of the Gotha Programme*, 24.
26 Marx, *Grundrisse*, 278.
27 Karl Marx, *The Poverty of Philosophy*, in Marx and Engels, *Collected Works*, vol. 6 (New York: International Publishers, 1976), 167.

For example, Marx noted that if you want to understand the modern city, you don't do it by discussing the flight of serfs to the cities. That is "one of the *historic* conditions and presuppositions of urbanism [but]... not a *condition*, not a moment of the reality of developed cities." Similarly, we should not talk about things like how "the earth made the transition from a liquid sea of fire and vapour to its present form." We should talk about the earth and capitalism now—not those "presuppositions of their becoming which are suspended in their being."

The historic presuppositions of capitalism took many forms, among which were individual savings acquired from various sources. However, the dependence of capitalism upon original savings, Marx stressed, belongs "to the *history of its formation*, but in no way to its *contemporary* history, i.e. not to the real system of the mode of production ruled by it."[28] Once capitalism exists, then capital "itself, on the basis of its own reality, posits the conditions for its realization." In short, you have real capital when capital produces its own premises, when it no longer rests upon historic presuppositions.

Thus to understand capitalism as a system, we must look at how the system is reproduced, how it "creates its own presuppositions... by means of its own production process." We look at how capital "no longer proceeds from presuppositions in order to become, but rather it is itself presupposed, and proceeds from itself to create the conditions of its maintenance and growth."[29] That, as we have seen, is how Marx proceeded: by examining capitalism as an organic system and by demonstrating that capital is the result of the exploitation of workers and is the workers' own product turned against them. Once he had identified the essential elements in capitalist relations of production as capital and wage-labour, then he could focus upon the preconditions for the initial emergence of each. *Theory, in short, guides the historical inquiry.* Our method, Marx noted, "indicates the points where historical investigation must enter in"; understanding the nature of capitalism as an organic system "point(s) towards a past lying behind this system."[30]

But see, he stressed, how bourgeois economists obscured the distinct nature of capital by "formulating the conditions of its becoming as the conditions of its contemporary realization;

28   Marx, *Grundrisse*, 459.
29   Ibid., 460.
30   Ibid., 460-61.

i.e., presenting the moments in which the capitalist still appro-priates as not-capitalist—because he is still becoming—as the very conditions in which he appropriates as *capitalist*."[31] This completely distorts the nature of capitalism. By treating capital as if it *remains* based upon historic presuppositions like indi-vidual savings, the capitalist relation of production (and, thus, capital's dependence upon exploitation of the wage-labourer) disappears. *This is why Marx explicitly distinguished between the accumulation of capital within capitalism as a system and the 'original accumulation' —and why the former must come first in our analysis.*

If we fail to distinguish between the being and the becoming of an organic system, we don't understand the elements in the *com-pleted* system. For example, there is an essential difference between money as it emerges historically and all the sides of money within capitalism as an organic system, and the same distinction is true of the commodity. Stated another way, when we consider the elements *historically*, we are looking at the elements in their flawed and defec-tive state—where they are not yet produced in their appropriate form. "How, indeed," Marx asked in 1847, "could the single logical formula of movement, of sequence, of time, explain the structure of society, in which all relations coexist simultaneously and support one another?"[32]

Every new system as it emerges is inevitably defective: it is "in every respect, economically, morally and intellectually, still stamped with the birth marks of the old society." This under-standing is at the core of a dialectical perspective. As Hegel put it, the "new world is perfectly realized as little as the new-born child"; it realizes its potential "when those previous shapes and forms... are developed anew again, but developed and shaped within this new medium, and with the meaning they have thereby acquired."[33] Marx understood such development as the process of becoming: "the process of becoming this totality forms a moment of its process, of its development." And how does this development occur? "Its development to its totality

---

31   Ibid., 460.
32   Marx, *The Poverty of Philosophy*, 167.
33   G.W.F. Hegel, *The Phenomenology of Mind* (New York: Harper Torchbooks, 1967), 75-76, 81.

consists precisely in subordinating all elements of society to itself, or in creating out of it the organs which it still lacks. This is historically how it becomes a totality."[34]

But how precisely does a new system become? Beginning with the defects it inherits, those characteristics of the old society, *how does it subordinate all elements of society to itself and create the organs which it still lacks* in order to rest upon its own foundations? How does socialism develop into an organic system in which all its premises are results of the system?

6. It is a distortion of Marx to conceive two separate stages after capitalism, each with its own specific principle.

What is socialism? For many people schooled in the texts of the twentieth century, the following propositions essentially hold:

- Socialism involves the replacement of the private owner-ship of the means of production by state ownership.
- Socialism is the first stage after capitalism and is succeeded by the higher stage, communism.
- Development of the productive forces is the condition for communism.
- The principle of distribution appropriate to socialism and the development of productive forces is in accordance with one's contribution.
- In short, socialism in this conception is the stage in which you develop productive forces and thereby prepare the way for the higher stage. Further, an important characteristic of the socialist stage is the place of material incentive, the application of the 'socialist principle' of 'From each accord-ing to his ability, to each according to his work.'

The Soviet Constitution of 1936 offers a classic version of this vision of socialism. According to Article 11, socialism is a society in which economic life is "determined and directed by the state national economic plan with the aim of increasing the public wealth, of steadily improving the material conditions of the work-ing people and raising their cultural level...." Article 12 reads that

---

34   Marx, *Grundrisse*, 278.

"In the U.S.S.R. work is a duty and a matter of honor for every able-bodied citizen, in accordance with the principle: 'He who does not work, neither shall he eat.'" The principle applied in the U.S.S.R. is that of socialism: 'From each according to his ability, to each according to his work.'"[35]

The immediate source of this concept of two stages and a specific 'socialist principle' was Lenin. Reading Marx's distinction in *The Critique of the Gotha Programme* between the new society as it initially emerges and that society once it has produced its own foundations, Lenin labelled these as two separate stages, socialism and communism. And he asked in *State and Revolution*, what would be the character of the state after capitalism? His answer was that a state would be unnecessary in the higher stage of communism. However, a state would clearly be required within socialism. Why? *Because until such time as it was possible to distribute products in accordance with needs, and until such time as it was possible to allow people to choose whatever activities they wished, a state was necessary.*

The state was necessary within socialism, Lenin argued, in order to apply the rule of law as "regulator (determining factor) in the distribution of products and the allotment of labour among the members of society." Indeed, he insisted, until the higher stage, "the strictest control by society and by the state over the measure of labour and the measure of consumption" would be essential. "He who does not work, neither he shall not eat" was one principle that would be applied strictly, as would "the other socialist principle: 'An equal amount of products for an equal amount of labour.'"

Furthermore, this need for the state to regulate "the quantity of products to be received by each" would continue until the socialist stage brought about "an enormous development of productive forces." The latter would be the "economic basis for the complete withering away of the state" and the development of communism. "To each according to his needs" would be possible as a basis of distribution for people only "when their labour becomes so productive that they will voluntarily work according to their ability."[36]

---

35 Soviet Constitution of 1936, http://www.departments.bucknell.edu/russian/const/36cons01.html.
36 V.I. Lenin, *The State and Revolution* (Peking: Foreign Languages Press, 1965), 114-15.

But how did this conception of two stages ("stages of economic ripeness") and of the specific socialist principle relate to Marx's view? In his *Critique of the Gotha Programme*, Marx did indeed distinguish between a communist society "as it has developed on its own foundations" and one "just as it emerges from capitalist society; which is thus in every respect, economically, morally and intellectually, still stamped with the birthmarks of the old society from whose whom it emerges." Furthermore, he explicitly recognized that it was "inevitable" that the latter society "when it has just emerged after prolonged birth pangs from capitalist society" would be characterized by 'defects.'

However, this conception of two stages distorts Marx's perspective. In Marx's understanding, there was *one organic system*—a system that necessarily emerges initially from capitalism with *defects*. Like every organic system, that system is in the process of *becoming*; it is a system that begins not with premises that it itself has produced but, rather, with *historical* premises, *inherited* elements. Accordingly, like other organic systems in the process of becoming, like capitalism itself, socialism must go beyond what it has inherited to produce its own premises; it has to generate premises in their *socialist* economic form.

Once socialism does produce its own premises, then we can say that the system "has *developed* on its own foundations." This process of development is the process of becoming the organic system of socialism: "its development to a totality consists precisely in subordinating all elements of society to itself, or in creating out of it the organs it still lacks. This is historically how it becomes a totality."

Socialism, in short, must subordinate the defects it inherits—not transform them into a principle that must be enforced by the state. But how do you build the new society based upon a defect? Indeed, it is by means of the designation of separate stages of socialism and communism that an alien principle is smuggled into a Marxist conception of socialism.

7. Building upon self-interest undermines the development of socialism.

Marx was very clear in his *Critique of the Gotha Programme* in describing socialism as it emerges from capitalist society as "in every respect, economically, morally and intellectually, still stamped with the birth marks of the old society from whose womb it emerges." Characteristic of socialism as it emerges was a particular 'defect'—an 'inevitable' defect—and that defect is revealed by the continued existence of an exchange relation: "[A]ccordingly, the individual producer receives back from society—after the deductions have been made—exactly what he gives to it." It is an exchange not of commodities in which "the producers do not exchange their products"), but it is an exchange of one's labour with society: "[T]he same amount of labour which he has given to society in one form he gets back in another."[37]

To grasp the significance of Marx's identification of this relation as one of exchange, it is important to recognize how deeply he felt about exchange relations. In his earliest comments about political economy, he stressed that its starting point was the premise that we are separate, that the community of human beings is at its core a relationship of separate property owners. This is how political economy views society, he proposed: it "starts out from the relation of man to man as that of property owner to property owner."[38]

When we produce in this relationship, Marx observed, "I have produced for myself and not for you, just as you have produced for yourself and not for me." In other words, I am not producing for you as another human being. "That is to say, our production is not man's production for man as a man, i.e., it is not social production." Rather, its logic is "Give me that which I want, and you shall have this which you want." And, he noted that "since our exchange is a selfish one, on your side as on mine, and since the selfishness of each seeks to get the better of that of the other, we necessarily seek to deceive each other." We struggle against each other, and "the victor is the one who has more energy, force, insight, or adroitness."[39]

How different it is if we relate to each other as human beings. If we are part of the human family, then if another has a need, I would want to help. When we relate to each other as owners, however, another's need does not induce me to help. On the contrary, another's need gives me power over him or her. The other's needs make that person dependent on me: "Far from being the means

37   Marx, *Critique of the Gotha Programme*, 23-24.
38   Karl Marx, "Comments on James Mill," in Marx and Engels, *Collected Works*, vol. 3 (New York: International Publishers, 1975), 217.
39   Ibid., 225-26.

which would give you power over my production, they are instead
the means for giving me power over you." At the same time, however, my needs give you power over me. We struggle against each
other because we are, in fact, separate self-seekers.[40]

What kind of people are produced in this relationship that
begins with "the separation of man from man?" Very clearly, people
who remain alienated from each other, from our activity and from
our own products. Indeed, we are the property of our own products, we are in "mutual thralldom to the object." And there is no
obvious escape from inside this relation. If I were to say to you that
I have a need, "it would be recognized and felt as being a request,
an entreaty, and therefore a humiliation, and consequently uttered
with a feeling of shame, of degradation."[41]

Marx never moved away from this view of the exchange relation. In
the *Grundrisse*, he wrote that in exchange, despite "the all-round dependence of the producers on one another," those producers are separate
and isolated; there is "the total isolation of their private interests from
one another." What exists, accordingly, is "the connection of mutually
indifferent persons." And "their mutual interconnection—here appears
as something alien to them, autonomous, as a thing." In the "recipro-
cal and all-sided dependence of individuals who are indifferent to one
another," the connection of people exists as a relation "external to the
individuals and independent of them"; it is, in fact, a power over them.
Our own social product, this connection of "mutually indifferent individuals," drives us and gives us impulse. The market is our connection
as mutually indifferent individuals, and it is a power over us.[42]

This is the context in which to understand Marx's critique of the
cooperative factories that emerged in the mid-nineteenth century.
These cooperative factories, he said, demonstrated that workers
do not need capitalists; they were in this respect a great advance,
"the first examples of the emergence of a new form." But that new
form was emerging "within the old form." The cooperatives were
reproducing "all the defects of the existing system." They did not go
beyond profit-seeking and competition. While combining workers
on a new basis and abolishing the opposition between capital and
labour, this cooperative production remained an isolated system

40   Ibid., 225, 228.
41   Ibid., 227.
42   Marx, *Grundrisse*, 156-58.

"based upon individual and antagonistic interests," one in which the associated workers had "become their own capitalist," using the means of production to "valorize their own labour."[43]

Individual and antagonistic interests, too, marked the experience in the self-managed enterprises of Yugoslavia, which were oriented toward maximizing income per member of each individual enterprise. About these Che Guevara, noted in 1959, each firm was "engaged in violent struggle with its competitors over prices and quality." And he commented that this was a real danger because this competition could "introduce factors that distort what the socialist spirit should presumably be."[44]

Let us come back now to Marx's comments in the *Critique of the Gotha Programme* about the defect in socialism as it first emerges. "The same principle," he noted, "prevails as in the exchange of commodity-equivalents: a given amount of labour in one form is exchanged for an equal amount of labour in another form." What we see here is the continuation of 'bourgeois right': the claims of individual producers upon society's output are determined not by the individual producers' membership in society, but rather are proportional to the labour they supply."[45] Marx explicitly called this a 'defect'; it was a defect in the relation of distribution—a relation often described as distribution in accordance with work (or contribution).

Yet as Marx pointed out, it was a 'mistake' of the Gotha Programme itself to stress "so-called distribution." Relations of distribution, after all, are only the 'reverse side' of relations of production; they cannot be treated "as independent of the mode of production." *So precisely what is the relation of production that generates this particular distribution rule?* This brings us to a question that, despite much invocation of the phrase 'bourgeois right,' has not been asked often enough: precisely what is the relation of production that generates this particular distributor role?" The relation of production that underlies this specific relation of distribution involves *production by private owners of labour-power.* Despite the common ownership of the means of production, labour-power remains here private property:

---

43   Karl Marx, *Capital*, vol. 3 (New York: Vintage, 1981), 571. See also Lebowitz, *Beyond CAPITAL*, 88-89 and 215.

44   Carlos Tablada, *Che Guevara: Economics and Politics in the Transition to Socialism* (Sydney: Pathfinder, 1989), 111-12.

45   Marx, *Critique of the Gotha Programme*, 23-24.

> The capitalist mode of production... rests on the fact that the material conditions of production are in the hands of non-workers in the form of property in capital and land, while the masses are only owners of the personal condition of production, of labour power.[46]

Common ownership of the "material conditions of production," thus, is only a *partial* passage beyond the "narrow horizon of bourgeois right." Insofar as producers relate to each other as the "owners of the personal condition of production, of labour power," each producer or group of producers demands a *quid pro quo* for the expenditure of her activity. Each seeks to maximize income for a given quantity of labour (or to minimize labour for a given income). "Give me that which I want, and you shall have this which you want," after all, implies its opposite: if I don't get the equivalent, you shall not have what you want. As separate owners of labour-power, the interests of society do not guide the activity of producers.

And what is the effect of this defect of private ownership of labour-power and self-interest? *Inequality.* Marx pointed out that an exchange of equivalents by which a producer is entitled to receive "the same amount of labour which he has given to society" is a *right of inequality* that "tacitly recognizes unequal individual endowment and thus productive capacity as natural privileges." The only thing that matters in such a social relation is how much labour an individual has contributed. But how could this be accepted as a just relationship in a socialist society? *It is an entirely one-sided perspective!* Unequal individuals are considered "from one *definite* side only, for instance, in the present case, are regarded *only as workers* and nothing more is seen in them, everything else being ignored."[47]

In short, just like the political economy that Marx criticized in his earliest writings, the conception of distribution according to contribution looks at the producer "only as a worker[...] It does not consider him when he is not working, as a human being."[48] Unlike many of his followers, this was a perspective that Marx always rejected. Indeed, precisely because differences in ability imply no differences in needs, *The German Ideology* argued that "the false

---

46 Ibid., 23, 25.
47 Ibid., 23-24.
48 Marx, *Economic and Philosophical Manuscripts*, 241.

tenet, based upon existing circumstances, 'to each according to his abilities,' must be changed, in so far as it relates to enjoyment in its narrow sense, into the tenet, *'to each according to his need'*; in other words, a *different form* of activity, of labour, does not justify *inequality*, confers no *privileges* in respect of possession and enjoyment."[49]

As we can see, Marx was very critical of the inequality that flows from this 'defect'; however, he vastly *understated* the inequality that emerges as the result of the self-oriented activity manifested in the social relation of exchange. People differ in far more than the 'individual endowments' to which he pointed. Producers also possess different particular means of production. And insofar as those means of production are possessed by self-seeking producers (even with common ownership and worker management), the result of this differential access to particular means of production will tend to be that some owners of labour-power are able to secure benefits from which other members of society are excluded—that is, for the rule of distribution to become "to each according to his contribution and that of the means of production he possesses."

And that was precisely what occurred in Yugoslavia. Some workers had access to much better means of production than others, and the unemployed had access to no means of production. Growing inequalities in Yugoslavia were the product of monopolies: the ability to exclude others from particular means of production. Rather than social property, what existed was *group property*. "Although social property may be legally established," the leading Yugoslav economist, Branko Horvat noted, "this difference in incomes or the relative size of nonlabour income in privileged industries reflects the degree of privatization of social property."[50]

Return then to the question of the becoming of socialism as an organic system. Socialism inherits defects from capitalism and its development into a new organic system "consists precisely in subordinating all elements of society to itself, or in creating out of it the organs which it still lacks." And the defect it especially must subordinate is that 'right of inequality' that views members of this society "only as workers and nothing more is seen in them, everything else being ignored." This

---

49   Karl Marx and Friedrich Engels, *The German Ideology*, in Marx and Engels, *Collected Works*, vol. 5 (New York: International Publishers, 1976), 537-38.

50   Branko Horvat, *The Political Economy of Socialism* (Armonk, NY: M.E. Sharpe, 1982), 238.

one-sided conception, Marx recognized, does not look upon producers as human beings. So how can you build the new society by relying upon self-interest and the desire of owners of labour-power for an equivalent return for their activity? How can you make the defect inherited from capitalism a principle to be enforced by the state?

This is precisely the point made by Che Guevara in his "Man and Socialism in Cuba":

> The pipe dream that socialism can be achieved with the help of the dull instruments left to us by capitalism (the commodity as the economic cell, individual material interest as the lever, etc.) can lead into a blind alley. And you wind up there after having travelled a long distance with many crossroads, and it is hard to figure out just where you took the wrong turn.[51]

In fact, that reliance upon "the dull instruments left to us by capitalism" does more than merely "lead into a blind alley." To build upon material self-interest is to build upon an element from the old society; and, it points backward. It points back toward capitalism.

8. The key link between human development and practice points to a different socialist principle.

Once we recognize the importance of the key link and understand that every process of activity, every process of production, generates a joint product, then it should be clear that the people produced in an exchange relation are not those who will build a new socialist society. After all, what kind of people are built where self-interest is the dominant principle? What are the joint products of that process?

To build the new society, as Che Guevara knew, it is necessary, simultaneous with new material foundations, to build new socialist human beings. And that means that the relations within which people act must be those which produce those new people. Those are relations of a communal society, where productive activity is not undertaken out of self-interest and where there is not an exchange of things but an exchange of activity for communal needs and purposes.

---

51   Tablada, *Che Guevara*, 92.

For Marx, it was the expansion of what a person is entitled to "in his capacity as a member of society" that marks the development of the new society. "That which is intended for the common satisfaction of needs," he pointed out, "such as schools, health services, etc... grows considerably in comparison with present-day society and it grows in proportion as the new society develops."[52] This portion grows as we look upon others as human beings— where we move away from viewing people from "one definite side only," where they are "regarded only as workers and nothing more is seen in them, everything else being ignored."

That is the socialist principle: producing for the needs of others as members of a human society. It is a principle that must increasingly subordinate the defects inherited from capitalism; and it is a principle that does not distinguish between a lower and a higher stage—because there is only one system.

We are left here, though, with a problem of terminology. If we reject the idea of two separate stages and a specific 'socialist principle' and replace it with the idea of a single organic system that is in the process of becoming, then what should we name that society? Socialism? Communism? Or something else? Marx generally called it communism, especially in his mature work, and I have followed Marx in this respect in the past. However, I no longer think this is the appropriate terminology to use in the twenty-first century.

The term 'communism' communicated something different when Marx wrote in the nineteenth century. Communism was the name Marx used to describe the society of free and associated producers: "an association of free men, working with the means of production held in common, and expending their many different forms of labour-power in full self-awareness as one single social labour force." But very few people think of communism that way now. In fact, people hardly think of communism as an economic system, as a way in which producers organize to produce for the needs of all. Rather, communism is now viewed as a political system; in particular, as a state that stands over and above society and oppresses working people.

In *State and Revolution*, Lenin called attention to Engels' refusal to use the term 'Social-Democrat' because "at that time the Proudhonists in France and the Lassalleans in Germany called

---

52   Marx, *Critique of the Gotha Programme*, 23-24.

themselves Social-Democrats."[53] Engels' decision was a political one based on concrete circumstances. The same logic applies, I think, to anyone at this time more interested in social transformation than scholasticism. We need to understand how the experience of the twentieth century has grasped the minds of the people who must be reached. As President Chávez indicated in his speech at the 2005 World Social Forum, we have to 're-invent' socialism. That is another reason to stress the term that the young Marx employed when describing "the goal of human development, the form of human society": *socialism*.

---

53   Lenin, *State and Revolution*, 95, 117.

RENEWING WORKING CLASS POLITICS: MARX AND ENGELS' CHALLENGE TO THE LABOUR MOVEMENT

Carlo Fanelli

As workplace concessions deepen and collective bargaining rights appear increasingly fragile, this chapter draws on Marx and Engels in the search for a social movement politics that can steer us out of the crises of capital. In comparing and contrasting how the extraction of surplus-value differs in its pre-capitalist and capitalist forms, and the subsequent challenges encountered in an earlier era of trade union organizing, the argument in this chapter is that a renewed labour and social justice movement must revive the theoretical and political promise of a working class politics. To do so means challenging the very existence and legitimacy of capitalism.

As organized bodies with the explicit aim of improving the work and living conditions of their members, labour unions have rarely been as isolated and marginalized as they are today.[1] As the immediacy of the Great Recession recedes and governments around the world look to drastically cut the public stimulus spending that salvaged the making of global capitalism, labour unions are

---

1   Bill Fletcher Jr. and Fernando Gasparin, *Solidarity Divided: The Crisis in Organized Labor and A New Path Toward Social Justice* (Berkeley: UC Press, 2008); David Camfield. *Canadian Labour In Crisis* (Halifax: Fernwood, 2011); Thom Workman, *If You're In My Way I'm Walking: The Assault on Trade Union Freedoms Since the 1970s* (Halifax: Fernwood, 2009).

increasingly being ostracized as public enemy number one.[2] While parts of North America and Western Europe experienced a punctuated and uneven 'class compromise' in the immediate decades following WWII, this edifice began to crack increasingly in the mid-1970s, and has been gradually chipped away at ever since. In response to the mounting attacks against trade union freedoms there has been a resurgence of literature aimed at renewing the labour movement as a subject of academic interest and progressive political intervention.[3] This article proposes that a renewed labour movement is dependent upon a reignited class project, which by its very nature is anti-capitalist.

Given the focus of workplace concessions and attacks against the public provision of social services, this chapter revisits the work of Marx and Engels in an effort to shed some light on the progressive potential and political limitations of trade union organizing as an end in itself.

In exploring some of the insights gleaned from an earlier era of labour organizing, community and workplace activists may be better able to confront the limitations of existing organizational capacities and perhaps reveal some new and creative strategies for contesting the power of capital. In what follows, I explore how the extraction of surplus value differs in its feudal and capitalist forms. Second, I consider the arguments put forth by Marx and Engels regarding the progressive potential and structural limitations of unionization given market imperatives. Third, I argue that a renewed working class politics means simultaneously working to build the capacities of the entire union to

2   For a critical introduction see Carlo Fanelli, Chris Hurl, Priscillia Lefebvre and Gülden Özcan, eds., *Saving Global Capitalism: Interrogating Austerity and Working Class Responses to Crises, Alternate Routes 22* (Ottawa, ON: Red Quill Books, 2011); Leo Panitch, Greg Albo and Vivek Chibber, eds., *The Crisis This Time, Socialist Register 2011* (London: Merlin Press, 2011); Bryan Evans and Ian Hussey, eds., *Organizing for Austerity: The Neoliberal State, Regulating Labour and Working Class Resistance*, special issue of *Socialist Studies* 7, no. 1/2 (Spring/Fall 2011).

3   Pradeep Kumar and Christopher Schenk, eds., *Paths to Union Renewal: Canadian Experiences* (Peterborough, ON: Broadview Press, 2006); Vanessa Tait, *Poor Workers' Unions: Rebuilding Labor From Below* (Cambridge, Massachusetts: South End Press, 2005); Lowell Turner, Harry C. Katz and Richard W. Hurd, *Rekindling the Movement: Labor's Quest for Relevance in the 21st Century* (New York: Cornell University Press, 2001); Kate Brofenbrenner, Sheldon Friedman, Richard W. Hurd, Rudolph A. Oswald and Ronald L. Seebeer, eds., *Organizing to Win: New Research on Union Strategies* (New York: Cornell Univ. Press, 1998); see also the special issue "Reorganizing Unions" in *Studies in Political Economy* 74 (2004), http://spe-journal.ca.

fight back against concessionary demands; developing a movement inside the union that pushes for enhanced democratic participation and control; a radically feminist, antiracist, class struggle-oriented political praxis that engages with the struggles of the broader community; and educational efforts intent on building a cadre of workers and activists that embody intellectual understanding and are active.

The Extraction of Surplus Value: Feudal Versus Capitalist Class Exploitation

The analysis presented here begins with a *denaturalization* of capitalism. Beginning with the decline of the laws and protection provided by the fall of the old Roman Empire, a feudal hierarchy soon came to dominate the western European political landscape. At the bottom of the hierarchy were serfs or peasants who owed their allegiance to noblemen, who in turn owed their allegiance to an overlord, and so it went up the chain of authority until reaching its apogee in the form of the king. Absent an enforceable system of legal and juridical means, custom and tradition, including the threat of violence, were the dominant social relationships mediating the extraction of the social surplus. While serfs tended to the land and agriculture producing the means of subsistence, lords lived off of the labour of the serfs who farmed their fields and paid taxes in kind in exchange for protection.[4]

Generally, in feudal societies the direct producers often remained in control or at least possession of their means of production and conditions of labour, ensuring that the means of life were sheltered from the forces of the market. The transfer of surplus-value most often took the form of political or 'extra-economic' forms of extraction such as through customary norms, traditions, bonds, as well as political, military and religious forms of tax and tribute.[5] In other words, the

---

4   E.K. Hunt and Mark Lautzenheiser, *History of Economic Thought: A Critical Perspective*, 3rd ed. (New York: M.E. Sharp, 2011).

5   For example, Marx argued, "Under these conditions, the surplus-labour for the normal landowner can only be extracted from them by extra-economic compulsions, whatever the form this might assume." (*Capital*, vol. 1, 926.) More recently, see George Comninel, *Rethinking the French Revolution* (London: Verso, 1987); Ellen Mieksins Wood, *The Origin of Capitalism: A Longer View* (New York: Monthly Review Press, 2002); and David McNally, "Inequality, The Profit-System and the Global Crisis," in *Bankruptcies & Bailouts*, ed. Julie Guard and Wayne Antony (Halifax: Fernwood, 2009), 32-42.

coercive mechanism was generally outside the realm of the economic as the nature of the transaction was by and large independent of the process of production.[6]

For capitalism to become ever more dominant, though, the economic self-sufficiency of the feudal manor had to be broken down; that is, undermined or, as in most cases, destroyed. This required bringing market forces to the countryside, which would remove traditional rights and security over the means of subsistence, and replace it with the vagaries of the market. The transition from feudal to capitalist forms of appropriation entailed transforming labourers into wage workers by dispossessing them of their land, labour and resources. Peasant revolts through the 14th to 16th centuries were dealt with through violent social conflicts.[7] War and disease led to depopulation and labour shortages. Formerly communal lands were thus unilaterally turned into private property and thereby commodified. As Hunt and Lautzenheiser note: "The early sixteenth century is a watershed in European history. It marks the vague dividing line between the old, decaying feudal order and the rising capitalist system. After 1500, important social and economic changes began to occur with increasing frequency, each reinforcing the other and all together ushering in the system of capitalism."[8]

Capitalism, on the other hand, is unique in the sense that appropriation generally takes place through economic or market-induced means. This is not to say that political, customary or military forms of appropriation do not influence market transactions in capitalist societies—of course they do—but rather that the distinct system of market dependence means that the requirements of life are embedded in a political and economic framework in which competition and profit maximization permeate all aspects of social life. As Marx put it: "Direct force, outside economic conditions is still used but only in exceptional circumstances. In the ordinary run of things,

---

6   As Marx noted: "The extent to which the worker ('a self sustaining serf') can obtain a surplus over what we would call wages in the capitalist mode of production depends, other things being equal, on the proportion in which his working time is divided between labour time for himself and statue-labour for the landlord." Karl Marx, *Capital*, vol. 3 (London: Penguin, 1991), 926.

7   Michael Perelman, *The Invention of Capitalism: Classical Political Economy and the Secret History of Primitive Accumulation* (Durham: Duke Univ. Press, 2000).

8   Hunt and Lautzenheiser, 17.

the laborer can be left to the 'natural laws of production,' i.e., to his dependence on capital, a dependence springing from and guaranteed in perpetuity by the conditions of production themselves."[9] As a result, while the extraction of surplus-value in feudal societies was often a very tangible or direct political relationship of exploitation (serfs certainly knew that lords and such exploited them), what makes class domination specifically capitalist is the intangible exploitation embedded in market forces.

In other words, class exploitation is obscured since there is no direct transfer of surplus-value and no rent, tax or tribute directly paid to one's exploiters. Instead, a historically unique form of labour servitude increasingly takes hold, securing workers to both a wage and capital. Impersonal market mechanisms ensure that wage workers are in a perpetual state of insecurity, while the ever-present fear that capital will at any moment abandon them, leaving them without a job or alternative recourse to live, permeates their everyday lived experiences. Although capitalist class relations have the unique ability to give the impression—as Marx put it—that workers are "free agents of production," and in actuality, market dependence is an instituted compulsion: capital has a choice while the working class does not.[10]

The 'Progressive Aspects' of Unionization

In the middle to late 1800s, Marx and Engels were witnessing a major turning point in the history of civilization. As more workers left or were forced from the countryside, great numbers increasingly migrated to cities becoming wage dependent earners. "This migration to the cities meant more labour for the capitalist industries, more men for the armies and navies, more men to colonize new lands, and more potential consumers, or buyers, of products."[11] Accordingly, the new capitalist class slowly but surely displaced the nobility as the dominant social actors in the new socioeconomic system. "By the sixteenth

---

9   Karl Marx, *Capital*, vol. 1 (London: Penguin, 1990), 899.
10 Critical of capitalist apologists who argued that "their contract with the Master was settled by mutual convention," Marx wrote: "the silent compulsion of economic relations sets the seal on the domination of the capitalist over the worker." (Ibid.)
11 Hunt and Lautzenheiser, 17.

century, the handicraft type of industry, in which the craftsman owned the workshop, tools and raw materials and functioned as an independent, small-scale entrepreneur, had been largely replaced in the exporting industries by the putting-out system."[12] As the putting-out system developed, merchant-capitalists increasingly came to own the tools, machinery and buildings, and would hire workers to complete the finished products. Increasingly, then, workers no longer sold a finished product to merchants but rather their capacity to labour for a given amount of time. Consequently, capitalist control increasingly took hold of the process of production, thereby displacing workers and guilds, as the market and monetary profits replaced custom/tradition in determining what, where, and when production would occur.

The growing reserve army of labourers in cities like London and Manchester, for example, threatened skilled crafts workers' ability to withhold their labour, but also led to a growing concentration of workers in industrial factories. As workers increasingly became dependent on capital in order to gain access to the means of life, labourers increasingly began to organize themselves into 'combinations' (unions) based upon their trades and skills in an effort to resist rampant exploitation. For Marx and Engels the combination of workers represented an initial attempt on the part of labour to defend themselves against capital and market forces. As such, Marx and Engels argued that "not only were unions legitimate but necessary."[13] While trades unions were important for sporadic and episodic "guerilla fights" between capital and labour, for Marx and Engels they were still more important as *"organized agencies for superseding the very system of wage labour and capital rule."*[14] In other words, the freedom of association, to collectively

---

12 Hunt and Lautzenheiser, 13. The putting-out system can generally be understood as a form of subcontracting. The merchant-capitalist would provide an independent craftsman with the raw materials and necessary resources, and than pay him a fee to work the materials into finished products. It is important to note here that crafts works were still by and large completed in independent workshops.

13 Of course, such an assertion is in itself hardly revolutionary. But placed in historical context, apart from the aristocracy and bourgeoisie that were intent on restricting labour's ability to unite, Marx and Engels encountered a good many progressives who were also hostile, if not unsympathetic, of workers' rights to organize collectively.

14 Karl Marx, "Instructions for the Delegates of the Provisional General Council," 1866, http://www.marxists.org/archive/marx/iwma/documents/1866/instructions.htm#06. (Italics in the original.)

bargain on behalf of and in accordance with their coworkers, was for them a fundamental *potentiality* that under definite social conditions embodied an emancipatory force capable of transcending social relations of servitude. As Engels elaborated:

> [unions]...feel bound to proclaim that they, as human beings, shall not be made to bow to social circumstances, but social circumstances ought to yield to them as human beings; because silence on their part would be a recognition of the social conditions, an admission of the right of the bourgeoisie to exploit the workers in good times and let them starve in bad ones... But what gives these unions and the strikes arising from them their real importance is this, that they are the first attempt of the workers to abolish competition.[15]

In their attempts to mitigate the corrosive effects of unbridled competition, emerging industrial unions increasingly began struggling over demands for improved wages, workplace health and safety standards, a shorter working day, an end to child labour, respect for prison labor, the collection of workplace statistics and basic legislative safeguards. They were joined by political parties, radicals and social justice activists. Placing the context of growing labour activism in perspective, Engels wrote:

> It is, in truth, no trifle for a working man who knows want from experience, to face it with wife and children, to endure hunger and wretchedness for months together, and stand firm and unshaken through it all. What is death...in comparison with gradual starvation, with the daily site of a starving family, with the certainty of future revenge on the part of the bourgeoisie...[16]

Labor organizing spread through the European strike waves of the late 1860s to middle 1870s, reaching its apex in the Paris Commune

15   Frederick Engels, *The Condition of the Working Class in England* (1845), Ch. 10, http://www.marxists.org/archive/marx/works/1845/condition-working-class/ch10.htm.
16   Ibid.

of 1871. As a consequence, unions increasingly began to develop a counterculture of resistance that served as a guiding framework for programmatic demands, popular educationals and collective strategizing. For instance, workers often separated by trade, language, skill, ethnicity and religion came together in makeshift community centres that sought to break down prescribed sociocultural, political and economic barriers by meeting, sharing resources and experiences, and collectively strategizing ways of moving forward. These 'labour temples,' many of which sprang up throughout western Europe and, later, the US and Canada, were often built by volunteer and/or unemployed labour and financed largely by individual donations.[17] Of course, the state responded with severe repression and crackdowns. As these nodal points of community participation faded from view, often incorporated into official union structures through the late nineteenth and early twentieth centuries, the sociocultural values and political skills of an earlier era of organizing working class communities were increasingly lost. Nevertheless, the emphasis was on overcoming employer and state efforts intent on dividing and separating workers in order to socially and politically defeat them. For these reasons, Marx and Engels suggested that unions had the potential to become "schools of socialism."

As capitalist and state militancy intensified, Marx and Engels argued that although organizing waged workers at the point of production was necessary, failing to carry such political momentum forward beyond the workplace could potentially impede future gains. This meant at every opportunity turning seemingly 'economic' or workplace advancements into political openings that could translate gains for a small number of workers into larger ones for the benefit of the class as a whole.[18] Increasingly, however, this failed to happen. While crafts workers' unions and industrial unions became larger and to some extent better organized at

17   Goeff Eley, *Forging Democracy: The History of the Left in Europe 1850-2000* (New York: Oxford University Press, 2002); Howard Kimeldorf, *Battling for American Labor: Wobblies, Craft Workers and the Making of the Union Movement* (Berkeley and Los Angeles: University of California Press, 1999); Charles Lipton, *The Trade Union Movement in Canada 1827-1959*, 3rd edition (Toronto: NC Press, 1973).
18   Certainly improved wages were important but would amount to little more than "*better payment for the slave,* and would not win either for the worker or for labour their human status and dignity." Karl Marx, *The Economic and Philosophic Manuscripts of 1844* (New York: International Publishers, 2001), 118-119.

the point of production, these gains at times undermined the collective capacity-building potential of the class as a whole. Many of the benefits that accrued to the male-dominated organized sectors of the working class came at the expense of those people—including non-unionized workers—who were excluded because of race or gender. This dynamic played a dual role: first, in fermenting internal working class resentment aimed at a so-called "labour aristocracy"; and second, in leading some unionized sectors into an alliance with capital and liberal/social-democratic political parties who believed that such improvements were permanent. This further atomized the working class as against the interests of capital. Rather then developing the capacities of union workers as class organizations, unions were increasingly becoming less "points of attack" or "agencies of organization" for the working class, than centres of capitalist class collaboration.

As a consequence, Marx and Engels became increasingly concerned with what they saw as the growing opportunism and trenchant economism of elected union executives. For instance, they wrote of "venal trade union leaders" who in finding employment within the liberal party were able to deliver working class votes.[19] This worked to depoliticize the growing militancy of trade unions, as well as tilt the balance of class forces in favour of capital. Writing of the perverse ability of labour unions to draw votes from a constituency whose class interests were largely hostile to the party they were supporting, Marx and Engels anticipated to a significant extent the gradual integration, discipline and, when necessary, expulsion of the more militant and radicalized trade union activists. Lured by the competition for self-preservation among workers, significant numbers of trades unionists moved away from building the union as part of asserting the interests of the working class, and instead gravitated towards the preservation and betterment of their own memberships. This was accompanied by the increasing entanglement of labour unions with officially social democratic political parties that accepted the logic of capital and thereby an electoral landscape that marginalized extra-parliamentary and extra-judicial actions in

---

19　Reflecting on this point, Marx wrote: "When I denounced them [trade union leaders] at the Hague Congress I knew I was letting myself in for unpopularity, calumny, etc, but such consequences have always been a matter of indifference to me…in making that denouncement I was only doing my duty." Karl Marx, "Letter to Kugelman," 1874, http://www.marxists.org/archive/marx/works/1874/letters/74_05_18.htm.

favour of incrementalism, unionism as an end in itself and liberal conceptions of representative democracy.[20]

Writing in response to the development of social democratic trade unionism, Engels concluded that "[t]he trade union movement among all the big, strong and rich trade unions has become more an obstacle to the general movement than an instrument of its progress."[21] Here Engels is drawing attention to a detached 'labour aristocracy,' in addition to reproaching trade unions for closing their doors to the 'unskilled,' an action that impeded the formation of an independent working class political initiative.[22] In protecting their marginally advantaged tradecrafts at the expense of the unorganized and unwaged majority, unions were essentially paving the way for their own decline.

Seeking to reorient the trajectory of unionism in the favour of the working class as a whole, Marx, speaking to the General Council of the First International, argued: "The poorer workers…remain outside the trade union for a long time, and the poorest of all never belong to them. *The trade unions by standing alone are powerless— they will remain an aristocratic minority.*"[23] They warned, in other words, that when unions focus exclusively on workplace gains, particularly those economic in nature, this can inadvertently arouse working class resentment. Furthermore, they argued that this was a trap since it allotted capital and the state the ammunition to suggest that "privileged" unionized workers gained at the expense of their non-unionized counterparts.[24] Instead, as Marx

---

20   John Kolasky, *Prophets & Proletarians: Documents on the Rise and Decline of Ukrainian Communism in Canada* (Edmonton: Canadian Institute of Ukrainian Studies Press, 1990); David Jay Bercuson, *Confrontation at Winnipeg: Labor, Industrial Relations and the General Strike* (Montreal: McGill-Queen's Press, 1990); Martin Upchurch, Graham Taylor and Andrew Mathers, *The Crisis of Social Democratic Trade Unionism in Western Europe: The Search for Alternatives* (Surrey: Ashgate Publishing, 2009); Norman Penner, *From Protest to Power: Social Democracy in Canada, 1900-Present* (Toronto: James Lorimer & Co., 1992); John H Kautsky, *Social Democracy and the Aristocracy* (New Brunswick, New Jersey: Transaction Publishers, 2002).

21   Frederick Engels, "Letter to Caffiero," 1871, http://www.marxists.org/archive/marx/works/1871/letters/71_07_16.htm.

22   Kenneth Lapides, ed., *Marx & Engels on the Trade Unions.* (New York: Praeger, 1987).

23   Lapides, 82. Emphasis added.

24   This would also bolster views that unions represented a market rigidity that impeded economic equilibrium and the proverbial law of supply and demand This rationale was taken to extreme proportions by Milton Friedman and Rose Friedman, *Free to Choose: A Personal Statement* (Orlando, Florida: Harcourt Books 1990).

and Engels repeatedly emphasized, neither protective legislation from the "great trade union of the ruling class" (i.e. the state), nor the resistance of the trade unionists alone abolished the main thing that had to be eliminated: "The capital-labour relationship, which the antagonism between the capitalist class and the wage-working class always generates anew."[25] On the whole, therefore, while trade unions could bargain within the system, they could not escape the political and economic contradictions that stymied their continual expansion owing to their class exploitation.

Challenging the Labour Movement

Given that the trade union movement was failing to live up to its emancipatory potential, Marx and Engels emphasized the need to challenge "wage-slavery." While economic freedoms and limited political liberties were no doubt important, as were the improvements in working conditions for those organized, which also helped raise the basic legislative floor for others, for them the benefits accrued through unionization and legislation would always be under attack, temporary and conjunctural. As long as social relations of capital were dominant and the imperatives of cut-throat competition, labour rationality, and profit maximization were the most essential features of society, they understood that the working class would remain in a position of modern-day serfdom. Consequently, Marx and Engels stressed that the labour movement alone was incapable of abolishing the root cause of the workers' distress. Unless unions made an effort to broaden their aims and advocate on behalf of and in accordance with all of society's oppressed, unions risked degenerating into almost reactionary enclaves of privilege, upholding the manifest divisions of the working class and stunting its political potential. Rather than applying palliatives, they must cure the malady. "*The unions must convince the world at large that their efforts, far from being narrow and selfish, aim at the emancipation of the downtrodden millions.*"[26] In this sense, if unions were to become a progressive force of movement, rather than reactionary, even if defensive, opportunists, this meant building unions as expressions of working class unity.

---

25 Lapides, 161.
26 Karl Marx, "Instructions for the Delegates." Emphasis added.

Marx and Engels had a scathing contempt for those "who openly claim that the workers are too ignorant to emancipate themselves, but must first be emancipated from the top down, by the philanthropic big and petty bourgeois."[27] On this note, Marx and Engels were vehemently critical of doctrinal sectarians and "narrow-minded" trade union leaders that sought to put their goals and ambitions above those of the working class as a whole: "It is far more important that the movement should spread...than that it should start and proceed, from the beginning, on theoretically correct grounds. There is no better road to theoretical clearness of comprehension than by one's own mistakes *durch schaden warden* [to learn by bitter experience]."[28] Rather, for them, the challenge facing trade unions was to go about actively building the political and organizational capacities of not only its membership, but the class as a whole.[29] As they argued in the *Communist Manifesto*: "The real fruit of their battle lies not in the immediate result, but in the ever-expanding union of workers. This union is helped on by the improved means of

---

27 Karl Marx and F. Engels, "Strategy and Tactics of the Class Struggle," letter to the SPD leadership, 1879, http://www.marxists.org/archive/marx/works/1879/09/17.htm.

28 Frederick Engels, "Letter to Wischnewetsky, 1886, http://www.marxists.org/archive/marx/works/1886/letters/86_12_28.htm.

29 In a revealing paragraph from the "General Rules" drafted for the International Workingmen's Association, Marx (with guidance from Engels) wrote: "That the emancipation of the working classes must be conquered by the working classes themselves, that the struggle for the emancipation of the working classes means not a struggle for class privileges and monopolies, but for equal rights and duties, and the abolition of all class rule; That the economical subjection of the man of labor to the monopolizer of the means of labor—that is, the source of life—lies at the bottom of servitude in all its forms, of all social misery, mental degradation, and political dependence; That the economical emancipation of the working classes is therefore the great end to which every political movement ought to be subordinate as a means; That all efforts aiming at the great end hitherto failed from the want of solidarity between the manifold divisions of labor in each country, and from the absence of a fraternal bond of union between the working classes of different countries; That the emancipation of labor is neither a local nor a national, but a social problem, embracing all countries in which modern society exists, and depending for its solution on the concurrence, practical and theoretical, of the most advanced countries; That the present revival of the working classes in the most industrious countries of Europe, while it raises a new hope, gives solemn warning against a relapse into the old errors, and calls for the immediate combination of the still disconnected movements." And thereby declared: "That all societies and individuals adhering to it will acknowledge truth, justice, and morality as the basis of their conduct toward each other and toward all men, without regard to color, creed, or nationality; That it acknowledges *no rights without duties, no duties without rights*." Karl Marx, "General Rules," 1864, http://www.marxists.org/archive/marx/works/1864/10/27b.htm.

communication that are created by modern industry, and that place the workers of the different localities in contact with one another."[30] To challenge the power of capital more than revolutionary slogans and appeals to solidarity were needed. "The trade unions ought not to forget that they cannot continue to hold the position they now occupy unless they really march in the van of the working class."[31] Therefore, "it is necessary that our aims should be thus comprehensive to include every form of working activity."[32]

What's more, they argued that the social democratic party-trade union nexus was rife with contradictions. Social democratic parties had no interest in challenging the logic of capital or the democratic limitations of the capitalist state, and trade unions were increasingly suffering from a lack of transparency between an elected and accountable executive and its rank and file members. Likewise, they were critical of those that sought to trivialize or disregard the essential role of women's social reproduction and unpaid labour, which was to be central to any working class movement. For instance, as Engels argued, "equal wages for equal work to either sex is until abolished in general demanded…It is my conviction that real equality of women and men can come true only when the exploitation of either by capital has been abolished and private housework has been transformed into a public industry."[33] As Marx added, "Anyone who knows anything about history knows that great social changes are impossible without the feminine ferment."[34] For Marx and Engels the recognition of the simultaneously classed, gendered and racialized underpinnings of production and reproduction were central to developing the political capacities of the working class.[35] Furthermore, recent scholarship has been central in continuing to dismantle

30 Karl Marx and Friedrich Engels, *The Communist Manifesto* (London: Penguin, 2002).

31 Frederick Engels, "Trade Unions," 1881, http://www.marxists.org/archive/marx/works/1881/05/28.htm.

32 R. Landor, "Interview with Karl Marx," 1871, http://www.marxists.org/archive/marx/bio/media/marx/71_07_18.htm.

33 Frederick Engels, "Letter to Gualliame-Schack," http://www.marx.org/archive/marx/works/1885/letters/85_07_05.htm.

34 Karl Marx, "Letter to Kugelmann in Hanover," 1868, http://www.marxists.org/archive/marx/works/1868/letters/68_12_12.htm.

35 Frederick Engels, *The Origin of the Family, Private Property and the State* (New York: International Publishers, 2001). For further reading see the fine collection by Janet Sayers, Mary Evans and Nanneke Redclift, eds., *Engels Revisited: Feminist Essays* (London: Routledge, 1987).

notions that Marx and Engels were exclusively class-based thinkers that neglected other forms of identity and oppression. Rather, as Kevin Anderson has recently reminded us, "Marx's mature social theory revolved around a concept of totality that not only offered considerable scope for particularity and difference, but also made those particulars – race, ethnicity or nationality – determinants for the totality."[36] While Marx and Engels emphasized the transcendence of class privileges, they were critically aware that intersecting axes of oppression would not be mechanically resolved with the abolition of class rule. They were apprehensive, however, about a politics based on differences alone and sought the means through which the diversity of the working class could be transformed by means of a class project that genuinely acknowledged and addressed these differences while recognizing their social and political interdependencies.

It is in this context that they argued unions not be "too exclusively bent upon the local and immediate struggles with capital... they must now learn to act deliberately as organizing centres of the working class in the broad interest of its *complete emancipation.* They must aid every social and political movement tending in that direction."[37] They must, in short, become "affiliated societies" to be used as "centres or points of attack" in the struggle of labour against capital. For Marx, this meant that trade unions emphasize a regular cooperation between the employed and unemployed in order to destroy or weaken the ruinous effects of this "natural law" of capitalist production against the working class.[38] This required extending gains beyond the workplace and genuinely reflecting on the limitations of economic gains alone, which meant being ready to substitute membership gains for social and political ones that extended to the unorganized and unwaged. "Instead of the conservative motto, a fair day's wage for a fair day's work, they ought to inscribe on their banner the revolutionary watchword *abolition of the wage system.*"[39] All in all, if organized labour was going to have

---

36 Kevin B. Anderson, *Marx at the Margins: On Nationalism, Ethnicity and Non-Western Societies* (Chicago: University of Chicago Press, 2010). Recall, too, Marx's adage "that labor cannot emancipate itself in white skin where in black it is branded."

37 Karl Marx, "Instructions for the Delegates," sec. 6.

38 Karl Marx, *Capital*, vol. 1, 793.

39 Karl Marx, *Value, Price & Profit* (1865), ch. 3, http://www.marxists.org/archive/marx/works/1865/value-price-profit/ch03.htm.

a progressive future, it would need to be anchored in a politics that oriented its struggles toward the emancipation of the working class as a whole and therefore the abolition of class privileges.

Renewing Working Class Politics

Far from creating a crisis of neoliberal legitimacy or capitalism, the capitalist classes have emerged emboldened and recalcitrant in the midst of the Great Recession.[40] In fact, a reinvigorated attack by the capitalist class, led in many instances by legislative and political acts by the state, is emerging unconcealed in its efforts to undermine unions' collective bargaining rights. Paradoxically, however, despite a significant economic downturn that should have put labour and activists on the offensive, many are more atomized and alienated than at any point since WWII. The dilemma, as outlined by Marx and Engels more than a century ago, is for organized labour to move to the anti-capitalist Left or risk increasingly becoming an impediment to rather than an instrument of a renewed working class politics. The failure to do so may regrettably amount to an historic class defeat.

Our exposition of Marx and Engels has thus far revealed that trade unions did not begin nor evolve into class organizations but were from the very beginning sectionalist associations. Considered in historical perspective, the political heights of the trade union movement, particularly those in Europe, Canada and the US, lasted all but three decades after WWII before witnessing the movement's gradual diminution of power.[41] As such, in many ways, class polarization is in 2011 akin to that of the 1920s.[42] Given the context of the current crisis, existing private sector unions are increasingly being threatened and cajoled into workplace concessions. The same is true in the public

40   Greg Albo, Sam Gindin and Leo Panitch, *In & Out of Crisis: The Global Financial Meltdown and Left Alternatives* (Oakland: PM Press, 2010); David McNally, *Global Slump: The Politics and Economics of Crisis and Resistance* (Oakland: PM Press, 2010); David Harvey, *The Enigma of Capitalism, and the Crises of Capitalism* (London: Oxford University Press, 2010).

41   Fletcher Jr. and Gasparin, 2008; Camfield, 2011; Workman, 2009; Susan Fernie and David Metcalf, eds., *Trade Unions: Resurgence or Demise? The Future of Trade Unions in Britain* (London: Routledge, 2005).

42   McNally, 2010; Harvey, 2010; Armine Yalnizyan, *The Rise of Canada's Richest 1%* (Ottawa: Canadian Centre for Policy Alternatives, 2010).

sector where governments of all stripes are seeking to strip away hard won collective bargaining rights. Undocumented and immigrant workers often fare much worse.[43] Despite continuing concerns over, on the one hand, the lack of democratic participation, mobilization and decision-making power by many unions' rank-and-file workers and, on the other, unaccountable and insular executive committees, if ever a privileged set of workers did exist, they are increasingly a thing of the past as the downward convergence of wages, working conditions and benefits harmonizes ever lower. Bearing this in mind, should unions strive to regain their once prominent role in society, they need to take the risks of organizing working class communities and fighting back while they still have *some* capacity to do so, or risk continuing along the several decades-long union impasse and decline in general living standards.

Of course, this is not the place for a detailed overview of debates about class. It is worth noting, however, that for Marx and Engels classes are not a thing, a partition where neatly demar-cated typologies, iron-like, clearly separate the producers from the appropriators. Classes do not exist independent of the changing historical circumstances and social relations in which they arise. For Marx and Engels, the "Lazarus-layers" of the working class are constantly shifting and redefining themselves, displacing past relationships and recreating them anew. In other words, as Braver-man reminded us more than three decades ago, "classes, the class structure, the social structure as a whole, are not fixed entities,

---

43 D.W. Livingstone, Dorothy E. Smith and Warren Smith, *Manufacturing Meltdown: Reshaping Steel Work* (Halifax: Fernwood Publishing, 2011); Carlo Fanelli and Priscillia Lefebvre, "The Ottawa and Gatineau Museum Workers' Strike: Precarious Employment and the Public Sector Squeeze," in *Uniting Struggles: Critical Social Research in Critical Times*, eds. Fanelli and Lefebvre (Ottawa: Red Quill Books), 121-146; Aziz Choudry, Jill Hanley, Steve Jordan, Eric Shragge and Martha Stiegman, *Fight Back: Workplace Justice for Immigrants* (Halifax: Fernwood Publishing, 2009). On the degra-dation of labour more generally see: Ursula Huws, *The Cybertariat: Virtual Work in a Real World* (New York: Monthly Review Press, 2003);Vivian Shalla and Wallace Clement, eds., *Work In Tumultuous Times: Critical Perspectives* (Montreal: McGill-Queen's University Press, 2007); Andrew Jackson, *Work and Labour in Canada: Critical Issues* (Toronto: Canadian Scholars' Press, 2005); Ann Duffy, Daniel Glenday and Norene Pupo, eds., *Good Jobs, Bad Jobs, No Jobs: The Transformation of Work in the 21st Century* (Toronto: Harcourt Brace Canada, 1997); Dave Broad and Wayne Antony, eds., *Capitalism Rebooted: Work, Welfare, and the New Economy* (Halifax: Fernwood, 2006).

but an ongoing process, rich in change, transition and variation, and incapable of being encapsulated in formulas, no matter how analytically proper such forms may be."[44] Moreover, the concept of the working class never precisely delineated a specific body of people but was rather an ongoing expression for a social and historical process.[45] Of course, in analytical terms the working class can certainly be defined based on its relationship to the means of production and those who must sell their labour-power in order to live (a diverse majority of people). But a broadly defined working class politics is about all labourers and their families, their paid and unpaid experiences, and the ways in which intersecting axes of oppression simultaneously influence other dimensions of social life. In other words, it is necessary to do away with the notion that class oppression is experienced only when one works for a wage or participates in paid employment. Rather class oppressions penetrate deeply into the very fabric of social life and includes the waged, unwaged and those denied a change to work because their skills are apparently unproductive or of inferior efficiency. The working class is constantly changing not only in terms of how it sees itself but also in its relationship to others within the class.

Unfortunately, as Marx and Engels alluded to in the *Communist Manifesto*, the inability to cultivate a socialistic class-consciousness and concrete relationships between workers and their communities has played a significant role in augmenting class fragmentation. Rather than fighting their true enemies—the capitalist class and state that supports them—the tendency among the working class has been to fight the enemies of their enemies.[46] This is a common and widespread phenomenon. How can public sector unions demand a pay raise when the private sector is getting battered? Is this why my taxes keep getting

---

44 Harry Braverman, *Labour and Monopoly Capital: The Degradation of Work in the Twentieth Century* (New York: Monthly Review Press, 1998), 282.

45 David R. Roediger, *Working Toward Whiteness: How America's Immigrants Became White* (Cambridge, Massachusetts: Basic Books, 2005); Jane L. Collins, *Gender, Labor, and Power in the Global Apparel Industry* (Chicago: University of Chicago Press, 2003); Kris Paap, *Working Construction: Why White Working-Class Men Put Themselves And the Labor Movement in Harm's Way* (Ithaca: Cornell University Press, 2006).

46 As Marx and Engels put it: "At this stage, therefore, the proletarians do not fight their enemies, but the enemies of their enemies, the remnants of absolute monarchy, the landowners, the non-industrial bourgeois, the petty bourgeois." (Marx and Engels, 2002, 229.).

raised? Are unions to blame for Z company moving elsewhere to take advantage of "competitive" wages? We often hear that "unionized workers should be happy they have a job at all; someone who's unemployed will do it for half the wage." This fragmentation is not without cause. Yet a "necessary condition for the existence of capital is the ability to divide and separate workers—in order to defeat them. Rather than a contingent, incidental characteristic... this is an inner tendency of capital."[47] What's more, many of these concerns speak to the sheer brutality of capitalism, which places workers in a perpetual competition with one another. In other words, given the structural antagonisms central to the production and reproduction of social life, in coming to terms with the inhumanity, irrationality and illogicality of capitalism new questions may arise and discussions emerge seeking an alternative way of organizing society.

Given the scale and scope of what labour unions and the working class are collectively up against, organizing solely around specific issues and particular constituencies, as impressive and energetic as it may be, cannot add up to the kind of strength, organization and structure that is needed to bring about all-encompassing change. Indeed, recalling the historical significance of labour temples discussed earlier, we see the emergence of innovative organizational forms in promising developments such as the Greater Toronto Workers' Assembly, budding community and workplace fight backs, the Arab Spring upheavals and recent Occupy protests.[48] To conclude, labour unions remain the largest, most organized, resourced and stable institutions—institutions of a class "in itself"

---

47   Michael Lebowitz, *Beyond Capital: Marx's Political Economy of the Working Class*, 2nd edition (Hampshire, England: Palgrave Macmillan, 2003), 122. (See also Chapter 2 of this volume.) Or, as Marx put it: "This antagonism among the proletarians of England is artificially nourished and kept up by the bourgeoisie. It knows that this split is the true secret of the preservation of its power." Cited in Kevin Anderson, "Not Just Capital and Class: Marx on Non-Western Societies, Nationalism and Ethnicity," *Socialism and Democracy* 24, no. 3 (2010): 20.

48   See Ross, Chapter 13 in this volume; also Herman Rosenfeld and Carlo Fanelli, "A New Type of Political Organization? The Greater Toronto Workers' Assembly," MRzine, http://mrzine.monthlyreview.org/2010/rf050810.html; Michael D. Yates, ed., *Wisconsin Uprising: Labor Fights Back* (New York: Monthly Review Press, 2012); and Keith Gessen, Astra Taylor, Eli Schmitt, Nikil Saval, Sarah Resnick, Sarah Leonard, Mark Greif, and Carla Blumenkranz, eds., *Occupy! Scenes From Occupied America* (London: Verso, 2011).

but not yet "for itself"—fighting against the rule of capital. Many have undertaken extraordinary initiatives in their workplaces and communities. The challenge is to further embed, that is, extend and deepen, these initiatives within a broader anti-capitalist, socialist framework. A renewed labour movement must begin with the recognition that capitalism is a criminal system incompatible with nature and the interests of the overwhelming majority of the earth's inhabitants. Revitalizing the theoretical and political promise of a working class politics remains a crucial step in realizing the possibility of creating a better world without capitalism.

PART II

PART II

(RE)CONCEPTUALIZING ECO-GOVERNANCE: AN INTEGRATED GRAMSCIAN-POLANYIAN APPROACH TO POLITICAL ECOLOGY

Alda Kokallaj

This chapter synthesizes Gramscian and Polanyian perspectives on human society and nature in order to develop an original approach to political ecology and eco-governance. Polanyi and Gramsci are understood to fill the lacunae in each other's approaches to understanding the ways in which society and nature are mutually constituted. This allows us a new way to theorize both the environmental degradation stemming from neoliberal governance, and how we might think about the conditions for and agents of a democratic eco-governance in its place.

The financial crisis of the late 2000s brought about the worst economic recession since the Great Depression. This economic recession gave rise to a series of demonstrations around the world that questioned economic inequality, corporate greed and democratic foundations of political authority. As the movement has brought together people of a variety of political orientations, environmental concerns have come to constitute an important aspect that brings together economic inequality with socio-ecological justice. These crises highlighted the extent of economic inequality in society, which has jointly raised awareness of how ecological degradation affects social classes differently. The ecological crisis that we now face is multifaceted: climate change, deforestation, soil degradation, species extinction, global energy security and the environmental consequences associated with that very need to fuel economic growth. As the demonstrations against corporate greed have revealed, thinking about inclusion and more democratic forms of governance has become a necessity. Also, the environmental crises remind us that any emerging shape of democratic governance will be incomplete if our (human) impact on the environment and our relationship with nature and the environment are not addressed.

This chapter explores theoretical propositions about the possibility of a democratic eco-governance and brings to light calls for democratic eco-governance even in sites that are considered unconcerned with environmental degradation/risks. It introduces an integrated Gramscian-Polanyian approach and assesses how that can help us to understand dynamics towards democratic eco-governance. Neither Gramsci nor Polanyi has developed a theory that addresses the society-nature relation or a theory of democracy *per se*.[1] Moreover, none of these theoreticians wrote from the perspective of a political ecologist. Nonetheless, a growing body of literature draws on each of the thinkers separately to make sense of the resistance of environmental movements and their efforts for a more socially and environmentally just political order. Although political ecology has its foundations in the disciplines of Geography and Environmental Studies, in connection to Political Science, political ecology is concerned with the fair distribution of benefits and risks of social cooperation in a communicative context. In this context, the wealth/risk production and distribution are performed in such a way that would reflect all the actors, regardless of how they are structurally situated and affected.[2]

One of the concerns of political ecologists is that issues related to environmental decision making, preservation and degradation are increasingly governed by the tenets of neoliberal governance. This entails the shift of the responsibility from the government to a multiplicity of actors, which can be public or private. Some scholars have questioned the neoliberal forms of environmental governance as undemocratic as they are exercised by non-elected

1   Sue Golding, *Gramsci's Democratic Theory: Contributions to a Post-Liberal Democracy* (Toronto: Univ. of Toronto Press, 1992).
2   Robyn Eckersley, *The Green State: Rethinking Democracy and Sovereignty* (Cambridge: MIT Press, 2004).

bodies.[3] This pattern has become apparent in conservation projects as well as pipeline and energy development projects in the developing world. There is a growing body of green democratic theory that grapples with the meaning of environmental democracy, by focusing especially on the normative and procedural aspects that would constitute it.[4] But how and where can we identify and locate the sites of resistance/struggle that demand inclusiveness, participation and the expression of daily experiences with environmental degradation, water and air pollution, soil erosion and the like, as they connect to other experiences elsewhere and to broader political issues? My contention is that an integrated Gramscian-Polanyian approach can be of valuable help in that respect.

This chapter rests on two premises. First, struggles related to nature/environment are essential to any discussion about political predictions. Nature has emerged as the realm that performs a double role. On the one hand there are calls for nature to be counted as an actor in governance and on the other, nature emerges as the locus where lay people, without direct access to governance, can gain it through vocalizing their environmental concerns. Hence nature emerges as a political space where civil society, regardless of class, gender, race and ethnicity, may raise its voice and exercise agency. Second, the foundation of Gramsci's and Polanyi's thought and some of their concepts present us with a toolkit that is helpful in understanding where the agency for democratic eco-governance lies and how that would be realized. From Polanyi's thought I take the notion of nature as an agent that provokes social resistance, the notion of society as an agent of change and the notion of counter-movement as the process of change. From Gramsci's thought I take the notion of civil society as a site of consent and contestation, and the expanded notion of

---

3   cf. Murray Low, "Cities As Spaces of Democracy: Complexity, Scale and Governance," in *Spaces of Democracy: Geographical Perspectives on Citizenship, Participation and Representation,* ed. Clive Barnett and Murray Low (London: Sage, 2004), 129–146; Matthew Himley, "Geographies of Environmental Governance: The Nexus of Nature and Neoliberalism," *Geography Compass* 2, no. 2 (2008): 433–451; Shannon Logan and Gerda R. Wekerle, "Neoliberalizing Environmental Governance? Land Trusts, Private Conservation and Nature on the Oak Ridges Moraine," *Geoforum* 39 (2008): 2097–2108; and Jamie Peck and Adam Tickell, "Neoliberalizing Space," *Antipode,* 34, no. 3 (2002): 380-404.

4   See, e.g., Laurie Adkin, ed., *Environmental Conflict and Democracy in Canada* (Vancouver: UBC Press, 2009).

intellectuals to help me identify the unorganized but concerned resistance. The integrated Gramscian-Polaniyan approach comes to life by seeing these notions in concert. This chapter maintains that although Gramsci and Polanyi did not write as political ecologists, by integrating concepts from their work we can start to build a potent political ecology. The following sections answer three questions: first, is it possible to think of an integrated Gramscian-Polaniyan approach; second, what would this approach look like; and third, what are some practical illustrations of it?

Convergences in Gramsci's and Polanyi's Thought

Is it possible to think of an integrated Gramscian-Polaniyan approach? The end of the Cold War and the advancement of neoliberal globalization have allowed for an expansion of the scholarship inspired by Gramsci's and Polanyi's work. Their thought shares several commonalities. First, the idea of change is at the center of their thought. They are among the scholars that not only provide an analysis of how change could happen, but also a strategy for change. Second, in both their frameworks, events are not understood in isolation; instead an event informs and is in turn informed by history. This understanding allows for concepts that are not fixed but continuously in flux, making them useful for understanding practical problems. Third, ontologically both theorists see collective agency as creating structures.[5]

Despite the similarities in their thought, the two thinkers are seldom considered together. Burawoy offers an exception in that he links Gramsci's and Polanyi's thought to argue for a Sociological Marxism.[6] He achieves this aim by analyzing the notion of society as developed by each of the thinkers. He calls Polanyi's concept of society "active

---

5   Robert W. Cox and Bjorn Hettne, eds., *International Political Economy: Understanding Global Disorder* (Halifax: Fernwood, 1995); see also Mitchell Bernard, "Ecology, political economy and the counter-movement: Karl Polanyi and the second great transformation," in Stephen Gill and James H. Mittelman, *Innovation and Transformation in International Studies* (New York: Cambridge Univ. Press, 1997), 77-78.

6   Michael Burawoy, "For a Sociological Marxism: The Complementary Convergence of Antonio Gramsci and Karl Polanyi." *Politics & Society* 31, no. 2 (2003): 193-261.

society," which implies that as capitalist expansion threatens society, the society becomes active and imposes restrictions on market expansion. From Gramsci he takes the insight that civil society serves as the realm in which the state is supported but at the same time provides the terrain for challenging capitalist hegemony and potentially moving beyond.[7] He argues that for Polanyi, the battle between society and market is like a battle between good and evil. Burawoy's contribution in linking the two thinkers is limited to the theoretical realm, but it provides an assessment of the two thinkers as connected on a broad scale.

This chapter builds on Burawoy's contribution, developing it further by discovering how the works of these two thinkers complement each other when placed in the specific context of political ecology. Such engagement with the two thinkers can deepen the theoretical discussion about their constructs and our understanding of theoretical sites for eco-governance. As well, it can help to identify partakers in eco-governance and develop strategies of involvement in eco-governance. A Gramscian political ecology as a body has not yet been developed, even though Gramsci's notions of hegemony, historic bloc and civil societies have been used extensively in the field of environmental politics[8], and other works have focused on the elements of resistance and the shaping up of a counter movement. It has been argued that a lack of Gramscian political ecology is mainly because Gramsci's writings do not explicitly "express an ecological awareness or specifically be concerned with environmental problems."[9] Similarly Polanyi, despite his discussion of society's reaction to the commodification of nature, does not develop a social thought directed specifically to the environmental problems of the time. Thus, I suggest that it is more theoretically enriching and politically fruitful if we focus on an integrated Gramscian-Polanyian political ecology, rather than separately

---

7   Pat Devine, "The Continuing Relevance of Marxism," in Sandra Moog and Rob Stones, eds., *Nature, Social Relations and Human Needs: Essays in Honour of Ted Benton* (London: Palgrave Macmillan, 2008).

8   David L. Levy and Peter J. Newell, "Business Strategy and International Environmental Governance: Toward a Neo-Gramscian Synthesis," *Global Environmental Politics* 2, no. 4 (November 2002): 84-101; see also Levy and Newell, eds., *The Business of Global Environmental Governance* (Cambridge: MIT Press, 2005).

9   Benedetto Fontana, "The Concept of Nature in Gramsci," *The Philosophical Forum* 27, no. 3 (Spring 1996), 238. cf. John Bellamy Foster, *The Ecological Revolution: Making Peace with the Planet* (New York: Monthly Review Press, 2009).

developing *a* Gramscian and *a* Polanyian political ecology. The following section discusses how an integrated Gramscian-Polanyian framework to political ecology would be constituted.

An Integrated Gramsci-Polanyi Framework for Political Ecology

An integrated Gramscian-Polanyian approach can be valuable in identifying and locating the sites of resistance that demand inclusiveness, participation and the expression of daily experiences with environmental degradation and related social concerns. In this section, I will explore specific concepts in their thought that help not only to perform this task, but also to delineate the integrated framework for political ecology.

Polanyi's work goes to the heart of what shapes contemporary debates on humanity's relation to nature, and nature's relation to humanity. For him, "Man and nature are practically one in the cultural sphere. [While] markets for labor, land, and money are easy to distinguish[...] it is not easy to distinguish those parts of a culture, the nucleus of which is formed by human beings, their natural surroundings, and productive organizations, respectively."[10] An understanding of Nature is found also in Gramsci, although less prominent. In the section 'What is Man?' from "The Study of Philosophy," he writes that 'man' cannot be understood in isolation but through relationships. For Gramsci,

> [t]he humanity, which is reflected in each individuality is composed of various elements: 1. the individual; 2. other men; 3. natural world. But the latter two elements are not as simple as they might appear. The individual does not enter into relations with other men by juxtaposition, but organically, in as much, that is, as he belongs to organic entities which range from the simplest to the most complex. Thus Man does not enter into relations with the natural world just by being himself part of the natural world, but actively, by means of work and technique.[11]

---

10   Karl Polanyi, *The Great Transformation: The Political and Economic Origins of Our Time* (Boston: Beacon Press, 2001), 169-170.
11   Antonio Gramsci, *Selections From The Prison Notebooks*, ed. and trans. Quintin Hoare and Geoffrey Nowell Smith (New York: International Publishers, 1971), 352.

Although Gramsci discusses nature, that alone does not provide an outline for environmental politics today, but it provides the bases for understanding the integral connection that exists in the society-nature complex.[12] It is at this particular point that we can turn to Polanyi, who dedicates a good portion of his work to the reaction of society when nature is *commodified*. Gramsci's discussion of nature, then, provides us with the bases for understanding the integral connection that exists in the society-nature complex. Alone, however, it does not provide us with an outline for environmental politics today; therefore, Gramsci's perspective on nature and the environment must be complemented with that of Polanyi. Although there is a lacuna in each of these theoretical perspectives, by recasting the works of both thinkers in terms of political ecology they can combine to greater effect—and can spark ideas more useful for contemporary environmental politics—than when examined in isolation.

Polanyi argues that commodification is a utopia, and once land, labor and money are separated from the social fabric, it is then that society will react. This for him is a movement of self-preservation on the side of society as it tries to protect itself from market advancement. While Polanyi elaborates extensively on the reaction of society to the disembeddedness of the three elements, he does not discuss where in the society the agency of change lies. He is indeed interested in change and his work speaks to understanding change, yet society as an agent of change is not a well theorized concept. Although Polanyi extensively discusses the market, he does not delve into the elements that constitute society and how different groups in society connect to form a strategy for resistance to the market.

This shortcoming in Polanyi's conceptualization became particularly evident during my field research experience. My field research focused on the shape of environmental governance in post-communist transition countries, and it aimed to identify spaces of resistance

---

12   cf. *Geoforum* 40, no. 3 (2009), esp. Michael Ekers, Alex Loftus and Geoff Mann, "Gramsci Lives!"; Kiran Asher and Diana Ojeda, "Producing nature and making the state: Ordenamiento territorial in the Pacific lowlands of Columbia"; Abdurazack Karriem, "The rise and transformation of the Brazilian landless movement into a counter-hegemonic political actor: A Gramscian analysis"; and Alex Loftus, "Intervening in the environment of the everyday." See also Fontana, "The Concept of Nature in Gramsci."

to energy projects that have destructive eco-social implications. The energy projects under study were the Baku-Tbilisi-Ceyhan pipeline passing through Azerbaijan and Georgia and Vlora Thermo Power Plant (VTPP) in Albania. In all three countries, people were dissatisfied with neoliberal policies employed to achieve the transition to market economies, and they were concerned by the environmental implications of these projects. Their reaction, which was widespread, was vocalized in daily discussions and their criticisms were echoed by a sympathetic media. When interviewed, community members and civil society groups in all three countries expressed their serious concerns about national parks, mineral water resorts, soil degradation due to oil spills, deforestation, disappearance of arable land, air pollution, sea pollution and the threat to tourism in general. Although these energy projects directly affect the population and the nature on which they rely for their well-being and that of future generations, their environmental resistance cannot be characterized as society's resistance in the sense that Polanyi predicts. Such settings cast doubt on Polanyi's notion of society that, faced with concrete situations, emerges as a romanticized and even reified view of society.

It is at this point that Gramscian constructs can fill the lacuna that exists in Polanyi's work. With Gramsci's concept of civil society, we can develop Polanyi's notion of reified society by providing a more elaborated understanding of an agent of change. For Gramsci civil society occupies the realm "between state and market and outside of the private sphere of family and friendship."[13] Gramsci's concept of civil society is employed here for the nuances that characterize it. In Gramscian terms civil society cannot be understood as monolithic or as completely supporting or rejecting a point of view or an event. Instead, for him the realm of civil society is one where politics happen. It is the realm of contestation and consent at the same time. The vibrant and fluid nature of Gramsci's concept of civil society makes it a compelling tool to be employed in analyses of resistance.[14]

---

13   Ronnie Lipschutz, "Power, Politics and Global Civil Society," *Millennium: Journal of International Studies* 33, no. 3 (2005): 757. See also Lipschutz and James K. Rowe, *Globalization, Governmentality and Global Politics: Regulation for the Rest of Us?* (New York: Routledge, 2005), 51.

14   David Forgacs, ed., *The Antonio Gramsci Reader: Selected Writings 1916-1935* (New York: NYU Press, 2000); Robert W. Cox with Michael Schechter, *The Political Economy of a Plural World: Critical Reflections on Power, Morals and Civilization.* (London: Routledge, 2002).

In adaptations of this notion as a tool, one to understand and analyse resistance, we run the risk of presenting civil society as a unified bloc, as a set of institutions or as a "romanticised" space that furthers a common cause, i.e., environmental preservation. However, many civil society activists find themselves in situations along the Gramscian terms, where civil society is a contestable terrain. This was illustrated in both case studies: the BTC pipeline and the VTPP. Civil society activists, when questioned about the coherence of the resistance to the projects, pointed out that there were groups involved in the campaign that were engaged in furthering other sets of private interests. For instance, some individuals would view their involvement with civil society activities as a venue for acquiring consultancy contracts with the Multilateral Development Banks instead.[15] Another problem with the use of the civil society concept as a unified agent that fights for the public good is that it conflates the state with civil society. Indeed, several of the civil society activists that I interviewed had previously occupied state positions or were affiliated with state institutions. This raises questions about the independence of civil society when considered as a total whole.[16]

In order to address this challenge, probing further into the Gramscian toolkit and looking at the notion of intellectuals can be helpful. For Gramsci an intellectual is anyone whose function in society is primarily that of organizing, administering, directing, educating or leading others. Gramsci is concerned both with the analysis of those intellectuals who serve the dominant social group and also with the problem of how to form intellectuals of the subaltern social groups who will be capable of opposing and transforming the existing social order. Those intellectuals that emerge from the subaltern group itself and that aim at transforming the existing social order for Gramsci are organic intellectuals.[17] For Gramsci all men are intellectuals, but not all men perform the function of an intellectual in society. An intellectual is not defined only by eloquence, but also by "active participation in practical life, as constructor, organizer,

---

15 Interviews with civil society activists were conducted by the author in Georgia (May 2010), Azerbaijan (June 2010), and Albania (July 2010).

16 James Mittelman, "Globalization and Environmental Resistance Politics," *Third World Quarterly* 19, no. 5 (December 1998): 847-872.

17 Gramsci, in Forgacs, ed., *The Antonio Gramsci Reader*, 300.

'permanent persuader'..."[18] By recasting the notion of an intellectual to mean one who does "mental work" or is engaged in "activity of using the brain," Gramsci envisages a situation in which intellectual activity is expanded—and thus more people become involved in activities of organizing, deliberating and leading. This acknowledgment encourages a process of democratization, which may inhibit the formation of bureaucracies and encourage participation not only of elitist 'traditional intellectuals' who are conventionally seen as holding special privileges and knowledge, but also of 'organic' ones.[19]

This conception of intellectual activity expands our understanding of civil society beyond the mainstream. Conventionally, civil society is understood as institutionalized, organized and possessing administrative or scientific expertise, i.e., NGOs, media, universities, and businesses. Gramsci's conception of intellectual work as mental work allows for broadening of the concept of civil society in a way that it connects back to the role played by society in the double movement as conceptualized by Polanyi. Thus, by employing notions from both thinkers it is possible to arrive at an integrated model that is more complete. Through Polanyi's conception of the man-nature relation it is possible to augment the humanity-nature relation lacking in Gramsci's thought. And by relying on Gramsci's notion of organic intellectuals and civil society we are able to unpack Polanyi's very agent of the double-movement by making it more historically, culturally and spatially identifiable.

Many scholars have warned that Gramsci's concepts should be used with caution outside the Western context. Indeed, most influential works in political ecology and international political economy have employed Gramsci's concepts within the Western context where there is a thick civil society and the lines that separate it from the state and corporate business can be delineated more clearly. Carrying out research in post-communist countries, where civil society is a recent development and moderately thin, raises the challenge of how to capture existing voices of resistance. How can we avoid dismissing these voices as insufficiently vocal, and also encourage further participation and dialogue that would lead to thickening of civil society? These

---

18   Ibid., 321.
19   Ibid., 425.

dynamics can be addressed by the integrated Gramscian-Polaniyan framework, which allows for capturing the layers of civil society that are weakly (or not fully) crystallized.

Like the society that Mittelman researched in Eastern Asia, the civil society in the three post-communist countries where I conducted my research can be classified in five layers. The first three layers can be easily identified, but two others are eclipsed and unorganized. With regard to environmental activism the first layer consists of international environmental organizations and other international non-governmental organizations such as Friends of the Earth, World Wildlife Fund, Bank Information Center and CEE Bankwatch Network. The second layer consists of regional NGO coalitions like the umbrella coalition, the Caucasus Environmental NGO Network (CENN). The third layer consists of civil society coalitions within each country that are located in capital cities with representatives in other cities around the country. The fourth layer consists of those organizations that implement projects. The fifth layer consists of unorganized masses; it is the one that is overlooked in the post-communist settings.[20] One distinguishing characteristic of 'the fifth layer' is that while apparently passive, it is not uninterested or unconcerned in the face of environmental degradation and potential environmental risks resulting from energy projects.

In this respect especially, the Gramscian-Polanyian approach with the notion of intellectuals characterised by "active participation in practical life, as constructor[s], organizer[s], 'permanent persuader[s]'…"[21] opens up a theoretical and political space to include individuals and groups in society that are not necessarily organized at all times, but that possess local knowledge and are concerned with the environmental and health effects of development projects. Indeed, in both case studies—the BTC pipeline and the VTPP—this layer of civil society was mobilized and demanded participation in discussions around the environmental and social implications of the two projects. Another distinguishing feature of this layer of civil society that became apparent during my field research was that in line with Polanyi's idea of the double movement, the local communities—fisherman, farmers, local residents, and land owners in Albania, Georgia

---

20   Mittelman, 858.
21   Gramsci, in Forgacs, ed., *The Antonio Gramsci Reader*, 300.

and Azerbaijan—were mobilized when the threat of environmental risks was severe and apparent.

What this signifies for environmental politics is that the drawbacks of environmental degradation or health concerns are not exclusively the realm of trained experts: the knowledge and perspectives of lay people who have been in constant interaction with the ecosystem have as much of an important contribution to make. Local knowledge and participation are crucial elements of democratic eco-governance. As Lipschutz argues, what distinguishes environmental change and degradation is that they take place mostly at the microlevel. Moreover, the decisions made at the local level are important in the practical and political sense as decisions made at the supra-local level would not reflect the local conditions.[22] Precisely for dealing with such situations an integrated Gramscian-Polanyian approach is important for it allows for research that probes deeper in settings where civil society is shaped differently, but certainly is *not* inexistent.

Although none of the two thinkers developed a theory of democracy *per se,* they put together the concepts necessary for us to discern their vision for a democracy that is not hierarchical but participatory and socially centered. Gramsci and Polanyi make important contributions in providing a vision of democracy, and through the notions of 'organic intellectuals' and active society they start us thinking about democratic eco-governance. However, a concrete model of democratic eco-governance is not fleshed out by either of the theorists. Another body of literature that grapples with principles, theorizing and procedural requirements of ecological citizenship, deliberative democracy and green state moves the conversation of democratic eco-governance forward. Adkin, for instance, argues that the "normative and deliberative approaches to ecological democracy are *embedded* in counter-hegemonic politics..." and suggests that "[i]nsofar as democratic counter-hegemonic movements can constitute historical blocs, possibilities are opened for democratising reforms and the strengthening of communicative rationality."[23]

---

22 Lipschutz, "From Place to Planet: Local Knowledge and Global Environmental Governance," *Global Governance* 3 (1997): 95.
23 Laurie Adkin, "Ecology, Citizenship, Democracy," in *Environmental Conflict and Democracy in Canada*, 13. See also John S. Dryzek and David Schlosberg, eds., *Debating the Earth: The Environmental Politics Reader*, 2nd ed. (New York: Oxford Univ. Press, 2005), and Robyn Eckersley, *The Green State.*

Thus, Gramsci's and Polanyi's thought encourages us to follow theoretical pathways of green democratic theory, and, in combination the two streams of thought can help to articulate a clearer theorization of democratic eco-governance as well as a fuller understanding of political struggles for democratic eco-governance.

Conclusion

This chapter has provided an integrated Gramscian-Polanyian approach for political ecology as a means of understanding the conditions and agents that can bring about democratic eco-governance. In the face of increased environmental degradation that is (de)regulated by neoliberal governance, the works of Antonio Gramsci and Karl Polanyi can assist this work. Notwithstanding the importance of their works taken separately, this paper has maintained that an integrated Gramscian-Polaniyan approach can be fruitful for methodological, theoretical and political purposes.

The first part of this paper focused on a discussion of the importance of the two thinkers for the contemporary social thought and the similarities in their thought. The second part presented the Gramscian-Polanyian framework and, by using experiences from field research in three post-communist countries as illustrations, it showed that the framework is methodologically useful in order to identify the locus of action and change in specific projects that involve environmental degradation, being it of the local or supra-local scale. Theoretically, it is interesting to engage the two theoreticians in the light of political ecology. While attempts have been made by scholars to situate Gramsci's and Polanyi's thought (independently) in environmental politics, or use their concepts to make sense of environmental movements, they can complete each other, particularly in relation to capitalism's effect on nature and socio-political responses to that effect. Politically, it is important for democratic eco-governance to be identified at the scale where the crisis takes place. This has implications for linking it to other similar cases in what Lipschutz calls "networks of knowledge-based relations," and altogether would result in challenging the hierarchy and the structures responsible for environmental degradation.

Polanyi concludes *The Great Transformation* by upholding society as the guardian of freedom. Today, while faced with a threat of planetary dimensions, the emphasis on *the social* becomes even more important. To paraphrase John Bellamy Foster, a genuine ecological answer is one that is based on social agency. Social agency may take a progressive or regressive trajectory, and it is in this respect that Gramsci's and Polanyi's thought informs us that any successful political project requires constant struggle and involvement of all.

THE TRIPLE CRISIS: FOOD, FINANCE AND CLIMATE CHANGE

Susan Spronk

> While most analyses of the global recession have focused their
> attention on North America, Europe, China and Japan, the crisis has
> also been having a major impact upon the Global South. This chapter
> addresses the "triple crisis" related to food prices, climate change, and
> finance, situating in historical perspective the ways in which many in
> Latin America and the Caribbean have dealt with some form of crisis
> for decades—and what a progressive policy agenda should look like.

When the global financial crisis broke out in the fall of 2008, daily headlines were replete with stories of a grim economic situation: bank failures, steep job losses and a crisis of consumer confidence in the world's largest market economies in the North. As the global credit system ground to a halt, the western media fixated on the effects of this "economic nuclear winter" on western consumers. History suggests, however, that the worst tolls of economic crises have usually been visited upon the peoples of the South. Indeed, many countries of the South have experienced one crisis after another since the 1980s. This chapter describes the "triple crisis" of 2007-2008 related to food prices, climate change and the financial crisis, which are the result of the transformation to the state and economy that have taken place during the neoliberal era.

Inter-linkages between the Crises: Food, Fuel and Finance

Neoliberalism, a model of economic and social management with its origins in Pinochet's Chile, was implemented by Reagan and Thatcher in the North and by IMF and World Bank-mandated structural adjustment programs in the South.[1] These programs mandated fiscal discipline, budget austerity, privatization of public goods, devaluation of local currencies, and the lowering of tariffs and other protectionist measures. This new form of economic management has fundamentally transformed the production and consumption patterns in the global South, reorienting economic production apparatuses outwards instead of inwards, a process that has deepened the impact of crises that originate from outside one nation's borders.[2] In short, neoliberal structural adjustment programs have pushed many formerly protected markets into the world economy, making them more vulnerable to the booms and busts cycles that characterize capitalist growth.

The vulnerability associated with integration into the market economy was brought into relief with the dramatic hike in world food prices in 2007-2008. The Food and Agricultural Organization (FAO) of the United Nations reported that between January 2007 and June 2008 the international prices of wheat and rice rose 74 and 166% respectively, a 30-year high.[3] Thousands of people took to the streets in "food rebellions" in places such as West Bengal and Haiti as basic staples became unaffordable.[4] During what has been called the "tortilla crisis" 45,000 people marched in Mexico City in January 2007 protesting the fact that the average person was spending 30% of their income on tortillas as the price climbed 50% within one year.[5]

Conventional explanations of the global food crisis of 2007-2008 blame the hike in prices on high oil prices and investor speculation on basic grains.[6] As oil prices peaked at $145 per barrel in July 2008,

1   David Harvey, *A Brief History of Neoliberalism* (New York: Oxford University Press, 2005).
2   Philip McMichael, *Development and Social Change: A Global Perspective*, 4th ed. (Los Angeles: Pine Forge Press, 2008).
3   George Rapsomanikis, "The 2007–2008 Food Price Swing: Impact and Policies in Eastern and Southern Africa," (Rome: Food and Agricultural Organization of the United Nations, 2009).
4   Eric Holt-Giménez, Raj Patel, and Annie Shattuck, *Food Rebellions!: Crisis and the Hunger for Justice* (Oakland: Food First Books, 2009).
5   Hepzibah Muñoz, "Corn Crisis and Market Discipline: The Limits of Democracy in Mexico," *Relay* March/April 2007.
6   Food and Agricultural Organization, "Price Surges in Food Markets," in *Economic and Social Perspectives* (Food and Agricultural Organization of the United Nations, 2010).

an increasing amount of cereals previously used for food or animal feed was diverted to the production of ethanol. While in the early 2000s, about 20 million tons of US maize was used for the production of ethanol, by 2007, this amount had jumped to 80 million tons. An internal World Bank report leaked to *The Guardian* estimated that biofuels drove up international food prices by as much as 75% (not 3% claimed by the US government) as global demand drove up prices despite increases to supply.[7]

As critical scholars have noted, however, while the immediate trigger of the crisis was rising fuel prices, it has much deeper historical roots in the restructuring of the world food system under foreign aid and neoliberal structural adjustment policies that have fostered increasing dependency in the global South.[8] In other words, the real issue is the fact that many countries of the global South have become more dependent on the international market for provision of their basic foodstuffs as they have lost the ability to produce and distribute their own food to the local population.

Since the 1950s, agricultural products produced by large agribusiness in the North have been "dumped" in Southern markets. Global food aid programs such as US Public Law 480 have managed to build a market for surpluses produced in advanced capitalist countries in the post-colonial countries of the global South. PL 480 was based upon four principles: find an outlet for the mounting tons of surplus agriculture commodities; promote American geo-political interests to combat communism; establish and develop humanitarian assistance programs; and create new markets abroad for US agricultural products.[9] As a researcher with Food First put it, "Sixty years of US food aid has only achieved success with two of its four original goals: dumping surpluses and cornering markets. Meanwhile, an estimated 90% of the world's farmers who work an average 2 hectares each can't compete with the bottom barrel prices of subsidized American grains."[10]

7   Aditya Chakrabortty, "Secret Report: Biofuel Caused Food Crisis: Internal World Bank Study Delivers Blow to Plant Energy Drive," *The Guardian*, July 8 2008.

8   Walden F. Bello, *The Food Wars* (London: Verso, 2009); Philip McMichael, "The World Food Crisis in Historical Perspective," *Monthly Review* 61, no. 3 (2009): 32-47.

9   Richard Ball and Christopher Johnson, "Political, Economic, and Humanitarian Motivations for PL 480 Food Aid: Evidence from Africa," *Economic Development and Cultural Change* 44, no. 3 (1996): 515-537.

10   Shoshana Perrey, *Food Aid in Africa: A Profitable Business* (Food First, 2009), http://www.foodfirst.org/en/node/2675.

During the neoliberal period, these tendencies toward food dependency set in train during the previous centuries were made worse, as the hollowing out of government supports for small agricultural producers mandated by neoliberal austerity policies further devastated rural economies in many regions. In the era of stronger state control in the 1970s and even the early 1980s, domestic food markets in the developing world were often in the hands of state marketing boards and cooperatives. These institutions would guarantee floor prices, and provide fertilisers and seeds. They also controlled import volumes, redistributed food where there were production shortfalls, and purchased commodities from cooperatives. Under the IFI-mandated adjustments of the 1980s and 1990s, these institutions have been dismantled. Under the auspices of the WTO and other trade agreements, tariff protections have been removed, pushing all producers into the international market. Countries such as the Philippines and Gambia, which at one point were nearly self-sufficient with respect to rice production, become dependent on imports from other countries. As less expensive imported food flooded into countries, many people quit farming and abandoned systems that had worked in their cultures for centuries.[11] As small holder agriculture producing for local markets has became unviable economically, there has been a net migration from rural to urban areas worldwide in a process dubbed "depeasantization" and an increasing concentration of capital in food production.[12]

The reorientation of the global system of production toward external markets engendered by neoliberalism is also linked to the second crisis, the 'fuel crisis,' the ultimate outcome of which is climate change. Of course, more narrowly conceived, the fuel crisis refers to the rising price of crude. The hike in oil prices in the summer of 2008 increased the import bill of many developing

---

11   Walden Bello, *Dilemmas of Domination: The Unmaking of the American Empire* (New York: Metropolitan Books, 2005).

12   Farshad Araghi, "Global Depeasantization: 1945-1995," *The Sociological Quarterly* 36 (1995): 337-68; Deborah Fay Bryceson, Cristóbal Kay, and Jos E. Mooij, *Disappearing Peasantries?: Rural Labour in Africa, Asia and Latin America* (London: Intermediate Technology Publications, 2000); Fred Magdoff, John Bellamy Foster, and Frederick H. Buttel, *Hungry for Profit: The Agribusiness Threat to Farmers, Food, and the Environment* (New York: Monthly Review Press, 2000).

nations, leading to balance of payments problems. But again, the problem with the global system of production based upon petroleum goes much deeper than the temporary shortfalls created by price fluctuations of commodities in international markets. The problem again can be illustrated by the global food system.

Thanks to the expansion of international trade in recent decades, food now travels a great distance from the location where it is grown to the location where it is consumed. Unlike the previous generation, citizens of the North can now eat strawberries from Mexico and asparagus from Peru in January. In the mid-1990s, researchers at the Leopold Center for Sustainable Agriculture of Iowa counted the "food miles" of food that arrived at the Chicago O'Hare International Airport terminal, finding that on average it traveled 2,429 km to get to Iowa destinations in 1998, a 22% increase over 1981. This average distance was 33 times greater than the 45-mile average distance traveled by food items in a local farm-to-institution program in Iowa and used 4 to 17 times more fuel.[13] Indeed, the neoliberal mantra of "export or die" has produced what Larry Elliot of *The Guardian* once described as the "chocolate biccie paradox." In 2004, the UK exported 17,240 tonnes of chocolate biscuits, which passed en route 17,590 tonnes of chocolate biscuits that came from countries like France and Germany.[14]

The drive for export that has intensified under neoliberal structural adjustment policies has also contributed to the problem of overproduction, discussed in greater detail below, contributing to the collapse of commodity prices. The case of coffee is paradigmatic. When the International Coffee Agreement, an organization established in the early 1960s to raise prices, collapsed under the weight of neoliberalism in 1989, so did prices. In the push to pay back IMF and World Bank-mandated structural adjustment loans, more and more countries sought to increase the production of coffee for export, flooding the market. New coffee-producers such as Vietnam joined the fold in the 1980s and 1990s, displacing older producers such as Colombia and Brazil.[15] In turn, the depressed

13　Mark Xuereb, "Food Miles: Environmental Implications of Food Imports to Waterloo Region," (Waterloo, ON: Region of Waterloo, Public Health, 2005), 5.
14　Larry Elliot, "The Chocolate Biccie Paradox," *The Guardian*, April 15 2006.
15　Gavin Fridell, *Fair Trade Coffee: The Prospects and Pitfalls of Market-Driven Social Justice* (Toronto: Univ. of Toronto Press, 2007).

conditions for traditional export crops and continual drive for foreign exchange earnings has pushed some coffee producers into fostering the production of "non traditional exports," such as snow peas in Kenya, which find their way to grocery store shelves in the North, adding yet more "food miles" to North American and European diets and exacerbating the problem of climate change.[16]

When we compare the effects of the global financial crisis and the consequences of climate change, we see a similarity: those who are most likely to suffer the consequences of climate change are the least responsible for its making. The Intergovernmental Panel on Climate Change has reported that we are already seeing the consequences: in the increased frequency and intensities of cyclones and hurricanes in the Pacific Ocean, the Indian Ocean, the Caribbean; in the increased intensity and frequency of droughts in mid-continents in Africa, Asia, Latin America; in the increased incidence of floods in the major river deltas in Asia and Africa and other parts of the world; and the melting of ice caps at the northern and southern poles and glaciers around the world. Over the last century, it has been estimated that global temperatures have risen by 0.7°C. Researcher Norman Myers estimated that by 2050 up to 200 million people—or one out of every 45 people—will be forced to migrate due to the erosion of coastal areas, droughts, and conflict.[17] Highly populated island states such as Indonesia and the Philippines and drought-prone regions in sub-Saharan Africa are particularly vulnerable. The recent civil conflict has been dubbed one of the world's first climate change wars. To help avert catastrophe, Jubilee South is lobbying the international community to adopt green technologies and to establish a fund to help vulnerable countries adapt to climate change, aiding with displacement of populations if necessary.

The upshot of all this is once the financial crisis broke in global North in the summer of 2008, many countries of the South were already feeling a squeeze due to higher fuel and food costs, which

16 S. E. Mannon, "Risk Takers, Risk Makers: Small Farmers and Non-Traditional Agro-Exports in Kenya and Costa Rica," *Human Organization* 64, no. 1 (2005): 16-27.
17 Cited in Oli Brown, "Climate Change and Forced Migration: Observations, Projections and Implications," *A background paper for the Human Development Report* (Geneva: United Nations Development Program, 2007), 5.

themselves are symptoms of longer-term dependency on imports. While the effects of the collapse of the sub-prime mortgage market were felt immediately in countries whose banking systems were tightly tied into the North American and European markets, such as the transition countries of eastern Europe, the ripple effects are going to be felt later in the global South compounding earlier imbalances. As Jomo K.S., United Nations Assistant Secretary-General for Economic Development in the United Nations Department of Economic and Social Affairs (DESA), put it in a recent interview, the impact of the crisis on the global South is an indication of globalization's "devastating success."

There are three main mechanisms by which the current crisis is being transmitted to the South: remittances, international trade, and development finance.[18] Remittances have become an important source of income for many households in the global South, particularly in Latin America, the region of the world where remittances have been amongst the highest given the integration of Mexico in the North American economy. While remittances have slumped in Asia and Africa, Latin American saw the sharpest decline due to the contraction of the US economy. In Latin America, remittances declined 15% in 2009, which was the first time that a drop has been registered since statistics started being collected in 2000.[19] Such a decline is likely to have an important economic impact in that region, where remittances are estimated to have outstripped the amount of foreign direct investment (FDI) by a third and official development assistance (ODA) by a factor of ten.[20] World trade, on the other hand, saw its sharpest decline in 70 years, contracting by 12% in 2009.[21] In Asia, the contraction has meant a significant slowdown in industrial production. In Latin America and Africa, where export growth has mainly been driven by the boom in primary

---

18   Jose Antonio Ocampo, "The Impact of the Global Financial Crisis on Latin America," *Cepal Review* 97 (2009): 9-32.

19   InterAmerican Development Bank, "IDB Sees Turning Point in Remittances to Latin America and the Caribbean" (2010), http://www.iadb.org/news-releases/2010-05/english/idb-sees-turning-point-in-remittances-to-latin-america-and-the-caribbean-7109.html.

20   Ibrahim Awad, "The Global Economic Crisis and Migrant Workers: Impact and Response," (Geneva: ILO, 2009), 35.

21   WTO, *Trade to Expand by 9.5% in 2010 after a Dismal 2009, WTO Reports* (World Trade Organization, 2010); available from http://www.wto.org/english/news_e/pres10_e/pr598_e.htm.

commodities, the fall in commodity prices has meant a tightening of state budgets. In terms of development finance, the costs of borrowing have increased dramatically as international banks have hiked interest rates. The IMF has used the opportunity to restore its legitimacy, which was badly damaged by the way that it handled the Asian flu of the late 1990s. Callable capital has tripled in 2009 to more than $750 billion to help countries deal with balance of payments shocks. The World Bank is also set to triple its lending from 2009-2012. Such influxes of capital will do little, however, to address the deep-seated ills at the base of the international economic system.

Solutions to the Crises: Toward a Progressive Agenda

Ultimately, the solution to the global financial crisis depends very much on what the problem is defined to be. The imperialist powers of North America and Europe have chosen to see the problem narrowly as lack of liquidity and have bailed out the banks. As critical Marxist scholars have pointed out, by contrast, the most recent financial crisis is best understood as the intensification of one of the central contradictions of global capitalism: the crisis of overproduction.[22]

Overproduction is the tendency for capitalism to build up, in the context of heightened inter-capitalist competition, tremendous productive capacity that outruns the population's capacity to consume owing to income inequalities that limit popular purchasing power. As economic historian Robert Brenner has documented, since the Second World War, new manufacturing powers entered the world market, starting with Germany, Japan and the USA, followed by the Newly Industrializing Countries (e.g. South Korea, Taiwan and Brazil), and then the "workshop of the world": China.[23] Each of these new competitors produced consumer goods for export at cheaper and cheaper prices. In order to stem the erosion

22   Walden F. Bello, "The Capitalist Conjuncture: Over-Accumulation, Financial Crises, and the Retreat from Globalisation," *Third World Quarterly* 27, no. 8 (2006): 1345-1367; Robert Brenner, "The World Economy at the Turn of the Millennium toward Boom or Crisis?," *Review of International Political Economy* 8, no. 1 (2001): 6-44.
23   Brenner, "The World Economy."

of profitability, producers strove to introduce new technologies and to intensify production, which only made the problem of over-production worse. Capitalists then cut back on production, thus reducing employment, and suppressed wages, which increased social inequality throughout the neoliberal era. The end result has been flagging aggregate demand, a problem that found its tempo-rary solution in the encouraging of public and private borrowing, most recently in the housing market. Indeed, up to half of the US's GDP growth between 2000 and 2005 was fuelled by the housing market as the real, productive economy flagged.[24] In this sense, financialization of the economy was one of the "escape routes" for capital in the face of flagging profitability in the 1970s. In the narrow sense, it worked; profit rates have been restored under a regime of "jobless growth" fuelled mainly by consumer debt.[25]

In the global North, there are many ideas on the Left on how to address the crisis of overproduction—from work-time reduction to various ideas about green conversion, the traditional ideas on the Left on expansion of the social sector.[26] These measures also apply to the global South, but problems at the international level must also be addressed. In the short-term, necessary steps include the reform of governance of the international financial system, an international audit of odious and illegitimate debt and payment moratorium, and the encouragement of equitable taxation systems. One of the most important demands to emerge in the international NGO community in recent years is the closing of tax havens. Chris-tian Aid has estimated that developing countries lose $160 billion in tax revenue a year due to secrecy jurisdictions, which represent 3% more than global aid flows.[27]

Solving the problem of overproduction will ultimately entail moving beyond reformist reforms to a new agenda calling for the

---

24 Robert Brenner, "Robert Brenner: A Devastating Economic Crisis Unfolds," *Green Left Weekly*, January 25, 2008; available from http://www.greenleft.org.au/node/38913.
25 Leo Panitch and Martijn Konings, "Myths of Neoliberal Deregulation," *New Left Review*, no. 57 (2009): 67-83.
26 Gregory Albo, Sam Gindin, and Leo Panitch, *In and Out of Crisis: The Global Financial Meltdown and Left Alternatives* (Oakland, Calif.: PM Press, 2010).
27 Fraser Reilly-King, et al., "What's Missing in the Response to the Financial Crisis?," (Ottawa, Canada: Halifax Initiative, North-South Institute, Univ. of Ottawa, 2010), 3-4.

re-orientation of the production system itself and the democratization of the economy and society. The Climate Justice Action group,
a coalition of civil society organizations mobilized around the
climate summits, has put forward one of the most comprehensive
statements that aims to address the problems of over-production
and the petroleum-based economy, outlining six long-term goals:

- Leave fossil fuels in the ground
- Re-assert peoples' and community control over production
- Re-localize food production
- Massively reduce over-consumption, particularly in the
  North
- Respect indigenous and forest peoples' rights
- Recognize the ecological and climate debt owed to the
  peoples of the South and make reparation.

While these goals may seem lofty, the "slow food" and commu-
nity-supported agriculture movements that are blossoming in the
global North and the "food sovereignty" movement rooted in the
global South provide concrete solutions that address at least four of
these goals. In short, fighting the triple crisis will depend not only
on changing the way that we consume, but changing the way that
we produce.

THE CANADIAN AUTOWORKERS: RESPONSES TO NEOLIBERAL RESTRUCTURING AND CAPITALIST CRISIS

Tim Fowler

During the 2008-2009 round of collective bargaining between the Canadian Autoworkers (CAW) and the Big Three auto producers (General Motors, Ford and Chrysler), the Canadian state joined with the auto manufacturers to coerce the CAW to accept concessions and pay for an economic crisis it did not create. Although founded upon principles of 'fighting back,' the CAW has come to internalize the logic of neoliberalism. Such acceptance is both implicit and explicit: the result of a political economic climate hostile to organized labour, and a union that has increasingly come to think of its very survival as tied to the supremacy of capital.

The 2007-2010 crisis has been labelled a great many things: a fiscal crisis, a political one, an economic crisis, a crisis of accumulation, or even one of the capitalist system. The response to this crisis, however, has been interesting: more of the same. While the political-economic crisis at the end of the second world war brought about the Keynesian Welfare State, and the crisis of the KWS laid the groundwork for neoliberalism, the response to this crisis has been more neoliberalism. Through the 20th century the auto sector has "captured the sway of capitalism."[1] The fortunes of those working in the auto sector are linked to the relative success of auto production, and auto production has mirrored trends in capitalist development. The auto sector showed the world the potential of the assembly line and the pressures felt by an increasingly globalized economy. The domestic North American auto sector was hit very hard by the crisis of capitalism: market shares and profits were falling, oil prices were rising, and credit was freezing up.[2] This put intense pressure on the workers in the auto sector.

Domestic auto producers were pressuring workers in the auto sector to cut wages and benefits in order to ensure the long-term profitability of auto production. The economic crisis, then, had the direct effect of putting intense pressure on workers to accept both lower wages and management restructuring of workplaces to increase profitability. This chapter will use the 2008-2009 round of collective bargaining between the Canadian Autoworkers (CAW) and the Big Three auto producers (General Motors (GM), Ford and Chrysler) as a case study of the neoliberal response to the capitalist crisis. The neoliberal project has a number of aspects to it. It is a theory of cultural, economic and political practices and a specific set of policies to achieve these practises. David Harvey provides an encompassing definition of neoliberalism:

> A theory of political economic practises that proposes that human well-being can best be advanced by liberating individual entrepreneurial freedoms and skills within an institutional framework characterized by strong private property rights, free markets and free trade.[3]

The programmatic aspects of neoliberalism are broad and sweeping, and are intended to secure the institutional framework of neoliberalism. Gary Teeple lists sixteen policies that drive neoliberal

1   Greg Albo, Sam Gindin & Leo Panitch, *In and Out of Crisis: The Global Financial Meltdown and Left Alternatives* (Oakland: PM Press, 2010), 75.
2   Ibid.
3   David Harvey, *A Brief History of Neoliberalism* (Oxford: Oxford University Press, 2005), 2.

thought, but the ones of particular importance to this analysis include the "promotion of the primacy of private property rights," "the Market as panacea," and specifically "the circumscription of trade union powers."[4]

Neoliberalism constitutes a full frontal assault on trade unions. Fundamentally, neoliberalism seeks to redefine labour-capital relations to terms more favourable to capital. This redefinition sees legislative measures designed to weaken trade union freedoms, making it easier to decertify unions and more difficult to organize them. Neoliberal trade union legislation also undermines union rights and union security, recognition, and rules governing union financing. Trade unions have had some limited success in protecting their members by moderating the most extreme effects of neoliberalism. Some manufacturing unions, such as the United Steelworkers and the UAW, have given "management more flexibility and control as a trade-off for some job protection and union security."[5] The CAW has had some limited success in staving off the harshest aspects of workplace reorganisation under neoliberalism. While implicitly accepting management reorganization of the workplace, the CAW has bargained in the past to moderate work pace and production standards, training and job design.[6] This suggests that the labour movement retains some degree of agency to resist workplace reorganization under neoliberalism. This agency, however, is to protect union members from the harshest aspects of neoliberalism, *not* to directly challenge the neoliberal ideology.

Whatever the neoliberal project seeks to achieve, the primary goal of neoliberalism is to secure the class position of economic elites and ruling classes. Neoliberalism is class war from above: it is

---

4   Gary Teeple, *Globalization and the Decline of Social Reform* (Aurora: Garamond Press, 2000), Chapter Five. The other policy aspects of neoliberalism are free economic zones, deregulation of the economy, the privatization of public corporations, "popular capitalism" and support for privatization, transformation of the tax structure, reduction of the national debt, downsizing of government, restructuring of local government, dismantling the welfare state, the promotion of charities, circumscription of liberties/human rights, the growth of prison facilities, and restrictions to democracy.

5   Albo, Gindin & Panitch, *In and Out of Crisis,* 93.

6   Ann C. Frost, "Union Involvement in Workplace Decision Making: Implications for Union Democracy," *Journal of Labor Research* 21, no. 2 (Spring 2000): 274.

the continual restructuring of the economy, politics and culture to guarantee the class power of the ruling class. To this end, the state is needed for neoliberalism. The state creates, protects and enforces markets, which fosters capitalist accumulation.[7] This neoliberal state apparatus was laid out bare during the CAW's negotiations with the Big Three during the 2008-2009 round of bargaining. The Canadian state (and to a lesser degree the Ontario state) employed coercive measures to ensure capitalist accumulation for the Big Three while drastically reducing the political capacity of the CAW.

The Canadian Autoworkers

The CAW formed in 1985 when the Canadian division of the United Auto Workers split away to form its own union. The catalyst for this split was the issue of concession bargaining in the 1984 negotiations with the Big Three. The CAW refused to engage in concession bargaining while the UAW was willing to, and the CAW was able to successfully ward off concessions.[8] Since then the CAW has taken a strong line against concessionary bargaining—in 2005 then CAW president Buzz Hargrove railed against concessions: "we must reject an agenda that says we have to go out and sell concessions to our members and tell our members that the times are 'too tough' and that we can't make progress."[9] The CAW anti-concession bargaining stance was broken during the round of collective bargaining in 2008-2009. The CAW gave concessions to The Big Three, giving up a full third of their previously negotiated benefits and wages, "setting back collective bargaining between fifteen and twenty years."[10] The acceptance of concessions did not happen in a political vacuum: the CAW has been changing their politics over the past decade in order to respond to a changing economy, hostile governments and an increasingly neoliberal economy.

---

7   Harvey, *A Brief History of Neoliberalism*, 3.
8   Charlotte A. B. Yates, *From Plant to Politics: The Autoworkers' Union in Postwar Canada* (Philadelphia: Temple University Press, 1993), 211.
9   David Robertson and Bill Murningham, "Union Resistance and Union Renewal in the CAW" in *Paths to Union Renewal: Canadian Experiences*, eds. Pradeep Kumar and Christopher Schenk (Peterborough: Broadview Press, 2006), 175.
10   Rick Laporte, CAW Local 444 President, quoted in Sarah Sacheli & Don Lajoie, "CAW ratifies Chrysler pact; 90% say yes locally," *The Windsor Star*, 27 Apr 2009, A1.

Away from the bargaining table the CAW has situated itself broadly on the Left of the political spectrum. The union has a history of supporting the New Democratic Party (NDP) in English Canada and the Bloc Québécois (BQ) in Quebec. At times, the CAW has criticized the NDP for not being left-wing enough, and has even mused about forming a labour party. Recent developments have seen the CAW distance itself from the NDP in favour of a strategy of strategic voting. The strategic voting strategy is an attempt to elect governments that will be friendly to the union and generally supportive of auto manufacturing in general. The strategy is reformist to the extent that it seeks to promote an electoral strategy that is supportive of the goals of auto manufacturers in an attempt to secure the jobs of CAW members.[11]

The CAW has been slowly moving away from the NDP since the 1980s. The aftermath of the 1988 Free Trade election saw the CAW seriously doubt the NDP as useful allies, and the Ontario Rae government just added fuel to the fire. In 1999, the CAW endorsed strategic voting in the Ontario provincial election, and has endorsed strategic voting in all subsequent Ontario and federal elections. In 2006 the CAW formally withdrew from the NDP.

There has been a dramatic change in the CAW's organizing strategy as the union attempts to increase union density at almost any cost. The best example of this strategy is the Framework of Fairness, best known as "The Magna Deal." In an attempt to organize workers at auto parts manufacturer Magna, The CAW entered into an unprecedented agreement: Magna would grant voluntary recognition to the CAW if Magna workers voted in a majority to join the CAW. In exchange, the CAW agreed to waive the right to strike in Magna plants, instead having all disputes go to binding arbitration. Further, Magna would have a hand in selecting "employee advocates" on the shop floor, doing away with traditional union-only elections by secret ballot of show stewards. The deal was heavily criticized by other sections of the labour movement and some activists within the CAW as a deal that undermined the very principles

---

11 The question of strategic voting has been criticized from both within the CAW and from the broader labour movement. The question of the political implications of strategic voting for the labour movement requires more study.

of democratic trade unionism.[12] The CAW defended the agreement, saying that it would increase membership in the CAW, and increasing union density was the best way to increase CAW strength both at and away from the bargaining table. The Magna Deal is an example of the internalization of neoliberalism by the CAW: the organizing strategy of the Magna Deal accepts the supremacy of capital, and implicitly suggests that union density is the main goal of an organizing drive, *not* the creation of a political entity that can collectively confront the employer in the workplace.

By the coming of the capitalist crisis in 2008 the union was already combating a crisis of its own: the decline of manufacturing jobs in Canada. Plant closures, downsizing and the creation of the "rust belt" have been ongoing in Canada and the United States since 1969.[13] The decline of manufacturing has profoundly affected the CAW: fewer jobs in manufacturing means fewer members for the CAW and a reduction in the union's political capacity. When the CAW was formed, 90% of its members worked in manufacturing; by the start of the 2008 round of bargaining only 45% did. In 1987, 42% of CAW members worked in the auto industry, that number has been reduced to 10% as of 2009.[14] Coupled with a decline in manufacturing jobs the CAW has been faced with a massive restructuring of auto production over the past 15 to 20 years as a result of broader restructuring of industry. This restructuring has seen jobs that were once home in the manufacturing belt of Ontario and the American Northeast move to the American South and to Mexico and across the sea. As John Holmes notes, this restructuring has fragmented the North American labour movement, allowing management to foster competition and extract concessions by forcing unions to compete amongst each other.[15] A reduction in members

12   Geoff Bickerton, "Magna-CAW Framework of Fairness Agreement is an Affront to Union Democracy," *The Bullet*, E-Bulletin no. 67, 24 Oct 2007, http://www.socialistproject.ca/bullet/bullet067.html; Tony Van Alphen, "Critics Fume over Magna Deal," *Toronto Star*, 17 Nov 2007, http://www.thestar.com/Business/article/277259.

13   Steven High, *Industrial Sunset: The Making of North America's Rust Belt, 1969 - 1984* (Toronto: University of Toronto Press, 2003).

14   The Canadian Auto Workers, *Building The Union in Hard Times*, Documentation from the 9th CAW Constitutional Convention, 2009, 9.

15   John Holmes, "Re-scaling Collective Bargaining: Union Responses to Restructuring in the North American Auto Industry," *Geoforum* 35, (2009): 13.

for the CAW seriously curtails the options available to them. The most obvious consequence of a decline in membership is a decline in financial resources. Lower membership numbers also means a major decrease in bargaining power in collective negotiations and a decline in overall political power. The CAW has had a strong commitment to organizing since the mid 1980s, but has had mixed results, especially in the automotive sector.[16]

The 2008-2009 Round of Collective Bargaining and the Capitalist Crisis

CAW-Big Three negotiations began in March of 2008 when the auto manufacturers were facing decreased sales and decreased market share.[17] The result of these negotiations was a conciliatory collective agreement with a cost of living increase in the first year of a three year collective agreement, but wage freezes and reduced vacation pay for the rest of the deal.[18] The CAW accepted concessionary demands in order to ensure the short term future of auto manufacturing in Canada, thus keeping their members employed. The near implosion of the capitalist system in the fall of 2008, however, put further strain on The Big Three, and they pressured the CAW into a second round of negotiations: the CAW agreed to renegotiate the already ratified collective agreements in the hopes of securing the future of the automotive industry. The pressure on the CAW was twofold: auto manufacturers had appealed to both the Ontario and Federal government for loans to allow the companies to remain solvent. The governments made bailout money contingent on restructuring plans that would include cuts to labour costs. The CAW was under pressure from both capital and the state to accept concessions.

The CAW agreed to renegotiation of the collective agreements, and in January 2009 met with GM at the bargaining table. GM was in the process of securing a $3 billion loan from the Canadian and Ontario

16   Charlotte A. B. Yates, "Staying the Decline in Union Membership: Union Organizing in Ontario, 1985 – 1999," *Relations Industrielles / Industrial Relations* 55, no. 4 (2000): 652.

17   Chris Vander Dolen, "U.S. automakers lose ground in Canada; Big Three sales down 6.9 per cent in March," *Edmonton Journal*, 2 Apr 2008, E9.

18   Brett Popplewell, "Clean sweep for historic auto deal; Chrysler workers follow in footsteps of Ford, GM in ratifying three-year deal that freezes wages," *Toronto Star*, 18 May 2008, A3.

governments, and part of the requirements for this loan was the extraction of $150 million in concessions from the CAW.[19] Federal Industry
minister Tony Clement made it very clear that public funds would not be
used to "maintain the standards of living for Canadian autoworkers,"[20]
and the CAW acquiesced under the joint pressure of capital and the state
and signed a concessionary collective agreement on 9 March 2009. The
new four year collective agreement saw wages and cost of living increases
frozen for almost the entire term, a week of vacation pay lost, and the
ending of a $1700 annual bonus. Union negotiators unanimously urged
the membership to ratify this deal, and 87% did.[21] This agreement saw
GM agree to maintain 17% of their North American production in
Canada. CAW leadership maintained that the cuts were necessary to
secure the future of auto manufacturing in Canada.

On the same day that CAW workers accepted the agreement
with GM, Chrysler rejected said agreement for one reason: they felt
they could extract even more concessions from the CAW than GM
had. The stage seemed to be set for this as GM was able to secure
deep cuts from the CAW as the company had full support from the
governments of Ontario and Canada to extract concessions. Chrysler was securing an $8.25 billion loan from these governments, and
again a condition of this loan to Chrysler was the auto manufacturer
cutting labour costs.[22] The CAW made public statements that they
would not give further concessions to Chrysler. In response, Tony
Clement again said that Chrysler could not expect a loan from the
government—thus putting the very future of Chrysler in Canada in
question—unless the CAW made further concessions to Chrysler.
The CAW responded saying that labour costs made up only 7% of
Chrysler's total costs, and blamed Chrysler's failure on poor sales,
poor marketing decisions, and government inaction—excusing
their members of any responsibility for Chrysler's dire economic

19 Nicolas Van Praet, "GM seeks $150M in concessions; CAW struggles with
    demands," *The Windsor Star*, 3 Feb 2009, A1.
20 Nicolas Van Praet, "Chrysler must commit to build in Ontario: CAW; Before
    concessions," *National Post*, 3 Mar 2009, FP2.
21 Tony Van Alphen, "GM workers overwhelmingly accept wage freeze; Union
    says rank-and-file concessions will slash labour costs and help GM qualify
    for aid funds," *Toronto Star*, 12 Mar 2009, B3.
22 Shawn McCarthy & Greg Keenan, "COLLISION COURSE," *The Globe and
    Mail*, 31 Mar 2009, B1.

condition.[23] Chrysler responded in turn by threatening complete closure of Canadian operations if concessions were not made.

On April 21st, 2009 the Canadian government ordered Chrysler and the CAW to return to the bargaining table. The government then went one step further and demanded that the CAW accept all the concessions that Chrysler was demanding, or Chrysler would not receive government bailout money.[24] The CAW was now under unprecedented levels of pressure from the state and from capital at the bargaining table, and eventually gave into the concessionary demands of Chrysler. On April 25, 2009 the CAW agreed to cuts amounting to $19 per hour in wages and benefits.[25]

Before the CAW began negotiations with Ford, GM demanded the union return to the table and give up even more. GM was facing bankruptcy and was demanding more wage concessions from the CAW. Again the CAW publicly declared that the union could not and would not give up more to GM, but again pressure from the government by threatening to withhold loans to GM meant that the CAW returned to the table to give up more. CAW did indeed give in to more concessionary demands from GM, and on May 23, 2009 it resigned a collective agreement with GM that saw total labour cost reductions of $22 an hour.

After the second round of GM negotiations were concluded, Ford pressured the CAW to negotiate concessions. The situation between Ford and the CAW was somewhat different from the situation with the other two manufacturers: Ford had not asked for, and did not want, a loan from either the Ontario or Canadian government. This meant that the Canadian state would not be in a position to actively intervene with the negotiations. In the end of May 2009 Ford announced that it was at a competitive disadvantage to Chrysler and GM and to American auto production, and that in order to continue production in Canada, the CAW would need to cede major concessions to the company.[26]

---

23 Nicolas Van Praet, "Chrysler bankruptcy not in our court: CAW," *The Ottawa Citizen*, 20 Apr 2009, A6.
24 Greg Keenan, Shawn McCarthy & Karen Howlett, "CAW, Chrysler ordered to resume negotiating," *The Globe and Mail*, 21 Apr 2009, B1.
25 Sarah Sacheli & Don Lajoie, "CAW ratifies Chrysler pact; 90% say yes locally," *The Windsor Star*, 27 Apr 2009, A1.
26 Grace Macaluso, "Ford pressures CAW to reopen talks; Eager after Chrysler, GM agreements," *The Windsor Star*, 28 May 2009, A5.

Negotiations between Ford and the CAW began in September 2009, with Ford calling for concessions that would bring their labour costs in line with those of GM and Chrysler. Negotiations between the two broke down at the end of September, as the CAW saw no future commitment to Canadian production from Ford; thus they did not see a reason to negotiate with the producer. At the end of September the two parties walked away from the bargaining table with no deal.[27] At the end of October 2009, Ford echoed its calls for concessions, again threatening to cease all Canadian production as Ford was uncompetitive with rival car manufacturers GM and Chrysler.[28] The CAW, at this point, was willing to give in to concessions in exchange for a commitment from Ford to continue operations in Canada. On November 2, 2009 the CAW and Ford signed an agreement that saw the CAW give concessions to Ford. Labour costs were cut by $5 an hour and wages were then subsequently frozen for the duration of the agreement, further cuts were made to benefits, and there was an increase in employee payments for health care costs.[29] The CAW was able to ensure ongoing production of Ford engines in the Essex engine plant until 2014—but this was the only guarantee of production made by Ford.

November 2009 marked the end of almost 19 months of concessionary bargaining between The Big Three auto producers and the CAW. The CAW had gutted their collective agreements with auto producers, granting massive concessions in wages and benefits, and managed to extract a few token promises to continue production in Canada in the short term. Indeed, the CAW accepted all of the concessions that the Big Three put on the bargaining table. At the same time GM and Chrysler were able to guarantee billions of dollars in loans from the governments of Ontario and Canada—some of which will not come due for fifty years. The CAW has set a dangerous precedence for concessionary bargaining in exchange for minor short term promises. The promises of continued Big Three production in Canada are tenuous, at best, as there are no laws in Canada that prevent plant closure during the tenure of a collective agreement.

---

27   Kristine Owram, "CAW hits an 'impasse' with Ford; Union wants to see commitment before it agrees to concessions," *The Hamilton Spectator,* 24 Sep 2009, A17.

28   Tony Van Alphen, "Ford's stand: Accept cuts or we invest elsewhere; Ford, CAW contract talks resume here as U.S. workers vote," *Toronto Star,* 27 Oct 2009, B6.

29   "Chrysler, Ford; A good week after months of uncertainty," *The Windsor Star,* 7 Nov 2009, A8.

Indeed, GM has already shown it is willing to sign a collective agreement promising continued production and then months later shut down plants, as they did in Oshawa in June 2008.[30]

Conclusions: The CAW's Response to Neoliberal Restructuring

The round of bargaining in 2008-2009 saw a reassertion of the logic of neoliberalism. The Canadian state acted in close consort with the auto producers to restrict trade union power and ensure that the auto producers would be able to continue accumulating wealth. The state and auto manufacturers exerted downward pressure on the CAW, forcing the union to accept concessions as a fix to a crisis that the union did not create. In some ways, the actions of the Canadian state during the negotiations between the CAW and the Big Three acted as a spectre of things to come. Since being returned with a majority mandate, the Conservative government has used the coercive power of the state to legislate the end to legal strikes on multiple occasions. In June of 2011 the Canadian government ended the lockout of postal workers, organized under CUPW, through back-to-work legislation. Also in June of 2011, the Conservative government tabled back-to-work legislation to end the legal strike of workers at Air Canada, coincidentally represented by the CAW. With the threat of back-to-work legislation, the striking workers quickly settled with Air Canada. This was followed in September by the threat of a strike when flight attendants for Air Canada, represented by CUPE, threatened to strike after negotiations broke down. The government indicated that if the CUPE workers were to strike, then back-to-work legislation would immediately be introduced to end the labour dispute; faced with this threat, CUPE settled with Air Canada.

The Canadian government has shown that it will simply not tolerate labour disruptions in the areas that it has jurisdiction over. Besides intervening in free private sector bargaining in 2008-2009, the government has used, or threatened to use, coercive legislation to end the first three labour disputes that occurred during the

---

30   CBC News, "Union Blockades GM Headquarters in Oshawa," http://www.cbc.ca/canada/story/2008/06/04/gm-blockade.html.

Conservatives' term in office as a majority government. The ideological message has been clear: the priority of this government is to maintain capital accumulation, labour disputes will not be tolerated, and workers will bear the brunt of the costs of the economic recovery to a crisis they had no hand in creating.

The CAW became an independent union while fighting back against concessions. The union strongly believed that "fighting back" mattered—that a confrontation by workers to capital and the state was a viable strategy. Indeed, in 1984, fighting back made a major difference to the CAW. During the 2008-2009 round of bargaining the CAW has shown that it is willing to cooperate with capital. Instead of fighting back, the union granted material concession to ensure that the auto producers would remain profitable. The outcome of the concessionary bargaining of 2008-2009 shows that the CAW has internalized neoliberalism: rather than combating neoliberalism, they now seek to exist as best as they can within the neoliberal framework. Perhaps the Ford negotiations are the best example of this: the union granted massive concessions to Ford without any major promises from the auto manufacturer to continue production in the long term. This was done *without* the Canadian state exerting coercive pressure on the union as it had done during the GM and Chrysler round of negotiations. The CAW willingly accepted the logic of neoliberalism. The CAW was born by refusing to succumb to the logic of concessions, arguing that fighting back mattered. The CAW isn't fighting back anymore.

The hollowing out of the collective agreements between the CAW and the Big Three has greatly set back collective bargaining for the union. What's worse, perhaps, than a gutted collective agreement is the precedent that has been set for future collective negotiations. The leadership of the CAW has indicated that it is willing to acquiesce to demands for concessions from capital and the state to ensure ongoing automotive manufacturing in Canada, and the union's membership has endorsed and accepted this strategy. This suggests that the CAW may face an uphill struggle simply to rebuild their collective agreements to a state they were at before the crisis of capitalism: the Big Three can simply cry poverty and demand more concessions. The bargaining power of the CAW has been demonstrably weakened by the concessions it has agreed to during this round of collective negotiations.

This is not to suggest that the CAW has consciously, or willingly, made these transitions. The example of the 2008-2009 bargaining indicates that neoliberalism amounts to is nothing less than full on class war from above. Capital and the Canadian state used the capitalist crisis of 2008-2009 as the impetus to extract unprecedented demands from the CAW. These concessions were supported, by and large, by a population that has grown increasingly individualistic and anti-union. Fighting back would have meant lengthy strikes, largely unsupported by the public, against an employer with the full backing of the state. The union has both implicitly and explicitly accepted neoliberal restructuring. The CAW is struggling to survive in a political and economic climate that is exceptionally hostile to organized labour and that recognizes the supremacy of capital as a policy maker.

Acknowledgements

The author would like to thank the following people for their comments on earlier drafts of this chapter: Jonah Butovsky, Wallace Clement, Larry Savage, and Rosemary Warskett. Any errors are mine and mine alone.

NEOLIBERAL POLITICS, STATE AND PRIVATIZATION IN TURKEY: THE CASE OF TEKEL

Simten Coşar and Aylin Özman

Turkey's articulation into the neoliberal world system, beginning with the 1980 military coup, points to both neoliberal generalities and possible grounds for opposition. In line with the structural adjustment policies of the IMF and the World Bank, privatization of the State Economic Enterprises (SEEs) was crucial to the process of neoliberalization; meanwhile, the sphere of activity of the opposition movements was narrowed and labour struggles were marginalized. This chapter investigates the process of privatization and the grassroots responses to it under the rule of the AKP (Justice and Development Party), closely examining the recent privatization of the state's alcohol and tobacco monopoly (TEKEL), and the 78-day strike of TEKEL workers in downtown Ankara. The study provides an account of the contextual dynamics of the neoliberal era in Turkey, which parallels the dynamics of neoliberalism globally.

In Turkey, a country where military *coups d'état* have been a regular asset of political history until the 2000s,[1] it was the 1980 military coup that marked the introductory phase of

---

1   Turkey hosted three subsequent military interventions into the political system, which resulted in the dissolution of the parliament and the institutionalization of military rule either directly by the military (1960, 1980) or by interim (civilian) governments (1971) appointed by the military. Each military intervention also coincided with the transition within the capitalist system.

neoliberal policies. The interim military regime (1980-1983), the centre-right governments of the Motherland Party (MP) and consecutive centrist governments produced and reproduced the necessary socio-political configurations for neoliberalism to take hold.[2] This configuration is characterized by socio-economic individualism and cultural conservatism; proponents of the new order also prioritized stability as a way out of the economic crisis and political turmoil of the late 1970s, and emphasized the need for de-ideologization. Military rule was justified via political stability and neoliberal policies as the solution to economic instability.

The post-1980 socio-political reconfigurations were also grounded in the prioritization of "centre politics." The workings of centre politics fit well into the neoliberal frame: the category of centre space meant consensus-based policy making, with the exclusion of purported conflict. This reading categorically negates conflict, defining it in terms of any possible opposition to the onslaught of neoliberal prerequisites into the socio-political sphere. Thus the pre-1980 period, especially to the late 1970s, were represented as the times of unresolvable conflict, unresolvable in two senses: first, the late 1970s were characterized with the deadlock in the parliamentary decision making procedure. Second, the period following the mid-1960s witnessed a significant rise in the leftist, and then, the labour movement, to be countered by the rise in the fascist movement. This state of affairs initially increased the Left's hand in the parliamentary decision-making process until roughly the mid-1970s. Yet this progressive development was immediately countered by the hostility against the Left in general, as evidenced by the 1971 military intervention. The hostility was continued through the late 1970s and into the 1980s in the form of either dislocating the Left from the legal decision-making process or direct state suppression (as in the case of the 1980 military coup).

Privatization is best understood as an embedded asset of the neoliberalization process in general, and thus also provides a location in which to seek the whereabouts of the leftist

---

2   For details see Aylin Özman and Simten Coşar, "Reconceptualizing Center politics in Post-1980 Turkey: Transformation or Continuity?" in E. Fuat Keyman, ed., *Globalization, Alternative Modernities, and Democracy Remaking Turkey* (Boulder: Lexington Books, 2007), 202-226.

opposition and labour movement in today's Turkey. In other words, privatization is central for comprehending Turkey's experience with neoliberalism, with a view to the emergence—or lack thereof—of new forms of resistance. Neoliberalism ushered in the dominance of market mechanisms in order to enhance the flow of finance capital. This meant a radical transformation of the ruling economic policies characterized by state-centric economic programs. Blaming state bankruptcy on public expenditures, policy makers pointed to the State Economic Enterprises (SEE), first as objects of reform, and ultimately as burdens to be divested. In this context, privatization has been a central theme on the part of finance capital and its governmental extensions due to the elimination of leftist and labour-based opposition in the post-coup restructuring process.

Centre Space and Neoliberal Politics

The interim military regime in Turkey narrowed the political space. Though military violence touched all the political groups of the previous decade, one of the decisive features of post-1980s legal restructuring was the explicit aim of removing "urban and rural labourers and left wing politics."[3] Examples include legal limitations on trade union and political party linkages, including the banning of mass organizational mobilizations. Such delimitation reflected the dominant preference for the consolidation of a monolithic political structure. Stability also meant pre-empting alternatives that would counter neoliberal policies, which were brought to the fore by the "January 24th decisions," the economic program introduced on January 24, 1980. There was, allegedly, no alternative to neoliberalism. The January 24th decisions ended multiple exchange rates, price regulation, the re-calculation of interest rates, export promotion, incentives to foreign capital, and import liberalization.[4] Persistent emphasis on the necessity for SEE reform accompanied these policies. Decisive in the widespread recognition of the need for reform

---

3   Bülent Tanör, *İki Anayasa 1961-1982* (İstanbul: Beta, 1986), 149.
4   Nazif Ekzen, "1980 Stabilizasyon Paketinin 1958, 1970, 1978 Paketleri ile Karşılaştırmalı Analizi," in İlhan Tekeli et al., eds., *Türkiye'de ve Dünya'da Yaşanan Ekonomik Bunalım* (Ankara: Yurt, 1984), 167-168.

has been the involvement of international financial institutions in the Turkish economy. The January 24th decisions were also accompanied by the imposition of structural adjustment programs under the auspices of the International Monetary Fund (IMF) and Structural Adjustment Loans (SAL) of the World Bank (WB) (June 1980). This opened the door for extensive borrowing from both institutions in the future.[5]

Key policy making buzzwords were "liberalization", "stability", "flexibility", and "efficiency", all under the mantra of "TINA." The new economic doctrine prioritized the flows of finance capital, framed in neoclassical economic terms.[6] The first civilian government formed by the centre-right MP (1983) was instrumental in mainstreaming this neoliberal verbiage. The new vocabulary corresponded with the individualization of justice and the dismissal of social justice concerns and democratic policy making. The individualization of justice in this context has two connotations. First, it means the elimination of the issues by liberal outlook from the sphere of justice on the grounds that they do not correspond to individual rights, i.e., the monopolization of the sphere of justice by the practices based on individual rights in existing liberal legal structures. Second, and related to the first, it also connotes the individualization of rights in general, thus, eliminating the demands for and problems of collective rights from the context of justice.[7] In the case of Turkey, justice has been conceptualized with reference to a combination of classical liberal emphasis on equal opportunities and "voluntary social solidarity, especially the principles of traditional social solidarity and related institutions, natural social solidarity that stems from love and compassion within the family system."[8] This emphasis provided the grounds to strip the state of its social role and restrict

---

5   For a comprehensive evaluation of the relationship between IMF and Turkey see Taner Berksoy, "Türkiye'de İstikrar Arayışları ve IMF," in Cevdet Erdost, ed., *IMF, İstikrar Politikaları ve Türkiye* (Ankara: Savaş Yayınları, 1982), 147-74.
6   Eren Düzgün, "Birikim, Hegemonya ve Yuvarlak Masacılar: Avrupa'dan Bir Kesit," *Toplum ve Bilim*, 112 (2008), 186-188.
7   Thus, here, by the term "individualization of justice" we do not refer to the established liberal legal use, in which the concept is used to denote the legal treatment of criminals on their individual grounds.
8   "Turgut Özal'ın Görüşleri, Özal'a Soruldu, Özal Cevapladı," 1983, http:// www.anap.org.tr/anap/genelbaskanlar/OZAL/yayin/Ozal_gorus.htm.

its sphere of function to establishing the conditions for "export promotion [...] under a regulated foreign exchange system and control on capital laws."[9] This new role also necessitated weakening the bargaining capacity of trade unions by legislative and coercive means. Thus, the introduction of "technocratic centralism" fostered the dislocation of the "political" and the "social" from the policy-making process.[10]

In this frame, privatization has been one of the constant themes of corresponding governments' economic programs, and of the agreements signed with the IMF and WB, which came to a head in 1988.[11] This might be explained in terms of the ambiguity that surrounded the topic of privatization in centre politics given the appeal of populism and neoliberalism.[12] Exemplary are the discursive policies of the main centre political parties, like the True Path Party (TPP), Democratic Left Party (DLP), and the Republican People's Party (RPP).

An example can be found in the TPP's attempt to popularize neoliberal policies in the words of its chairperson: "I pursue 'above politics' policy. [...] I took decisions for my nation. I promised not to engage in politics. [...] I entrusted myself to the people. I work for them. I do not engage in politics."[13] Inherent in this statement are two basic points of neoliberal discursive practices. First, it involves the dislocation of the political from the existing political space, turning the latter into a mere mechanism of administration, and in particular, for administering the society for the good of the finance capital.[14] Actually, this attribute originates from within the Thatcherite UK, which has served as the model for Turkey's initial encounter with neoliberalism in the

---

9   Erinç Yeldan, *Assessing the Privatization Experience in Turkey: Implementation, Politics and Performance Results*, Report Submitted to Economic Policy Institute (Washington, D.C., June 2006).

10 Nilüfer Göle, "Engineers: 'Technocratic Democracy'," in Metin Heper, Ayşe Öncü and Heinz Kreimer, eds., *Turkey and the West* (London and New York: I. B. Tauris, 1993), 213.

11 Yeldan notes that the backstage of the privatization process was started to be set by 1985. *Assessing the Privatization Experience in Turkey.*

12 Kurt Weyland, "Neopopulism and Neoliberalism in Latin America: Unexpected Affinities," *Studies in Comparative International Development* 31, no. 3 (Fall 1996): 3-31.

13 Interview with Tansu Çiller, Derya Sazak, *Milliyet*, 12 August 1994, cited in Kemali Saybaşılı, *DYP-SHP Koalisyonu'nun Üç Yılı* (İstanbul: Bağlam, 1995), 101.

14 Philip G. Cerny, "Embedding Neoliberalism : The Evolution of a Hegemonic Paradigm," *The Journal of International Trade and Diplomacy*, 2, no. 1 (Spring 2008) :1-46.

1980s. Second, are the populist discourses, which appeal to a certain notion of the people not through the concern for social rights but with reference to nationalist/sentimental motives or arbitrary allocations of goods and money or both.[15] Yet the party did not refrain from employing social democratic rhetoric in the early 1990s to counter the MP's neoliberal policies. However, when in power, it immediately shifted to neoliberalism by implementing austerity measures.[16]

The same can also be observed in the DLP's program, which has so far stood as the most differentiated among the centre political parties in its appeal to the "people's sector."[17] Against the rising tide of privatization the DLP has proposed the alternative of autonomization of the SEEs, which meant the transfer of the SEEs' supervision and management to the workers. In this respect, the DLP has argued for the re-nationalization of the SEEs and, eventually, central planning.[18] The private sector is perceived as a natural partner to the state, and is promised incentives so long as it accedes to the targets of the DLD plans. Still, despite the DLP-MP-NAP coalition government (1999-2002), the neoliberal economic agenda stood intact.

Likewise, the centre-left RPP, which claims to represent the social-democratic stance in Turkey, has had a poor record for offering a viable alternative to neoliberal economic programs. The party has presented a socio-cultural, rather than socio-economic opposition. In fact, the CHP explicitly stands as a pro-privatization party by disclaiming an "ideological" approach to "public entrepreneurship and privatization," and reading the latter as a means for handling the country's economic hardships.[19]

The Politics of Privatization

The politics of privatization has been a key feature of centre politics, and the centre space has offered the opportunities for building consent on the piecemeal privatization process. The MP's emphasis on extending capital ownership to the middle class and incorporating

---

15   Weyland, "Neopopulism and Neoliberalism in Latin America."
16   Saybaşılı, *DYP-SHP Koalisyonu'nun Üç Yılı*, 99-114.
17   *Demokratik Sol Parti Programı* (Ankara: n.d., n.p.), 74-75.
18   Ibid., 75-76.
19   "CHP'den Piyasa İncileri," http://haber.sol.org.tr/devlet-ve-siyaset/chpden-piyasa-incileri-haberi-8873 .

them into decision-making processes is the most solid manifestation of this connection. However, workers are still envisaged as the prime beneficiaries of privatization:

> For the first time in Turkish history the right to property will be extended to the people ... The priority ... will be given to the employees of the SEEs themselves ... the workers will have the opportunity to participate in the management of the enterprise. [20]

Of course, the actual state of affairs was different: most SEEs that have been privatized were sold to foreign capital groups.[21] Likewise, though privatization was justified in terms of the losses incurred by the SEEs, the end result turned out to be the privatization of profiting ones, like TELETAŞ (switchboard), ANSAN (fruit juice factory), ÇİTOSAN (cement factories), USAŞ (airport catering), ANADOLU BANK, DENİZ BANK (banking) and SÜMERBANK (textile).[22]

As Yeldan notes, privatization turned out to be the "official state ideology" by the mid-1980s.[23] However, it was only in the 2000s that privatization became the preferred policy agenda. In this respect, the 2001 economic crisis is significant since it offered policy makers the grounds for getting the ultimate consent to the TINA argument. As soon as the crisis hit, privatization was put into over-drive. Decisive in the decision making process was Kemal Derviş, a technocratic figure with roots in the World Bank, who was appointed as the State Minister Responsible for Economic Affairs in 2001.

The structural dynamics of the crisis also meant that the European Union (EU) would begin to play a larger role in Turkey's experiences with neoliberalism. Over the course of European

---

20 *Başbakan Turgut Özal'ın Konuşma Mesaj, Beyanat ve Mülakatları (13 Aralık 1986 - 12 Aralık 1987)* (Ankara: Başbakanlık, 1987), 723-726.

21 This shift regarding the "beneficiaries" of privatization from the "people" to capital groups was rationalized by the state authorities on the basis of the immaturity of the capital market in Turkey. Although at first sight domestic capital groups seemed to be an alternative to the "people," the implementation process ended up with bloc sales to foreign capital groups. Özman, "The Politics of Privatization in Turkey during the 1980s," *Journal of South Asian and Middle Eastern Studies* 23, no. 4 (Summer 2000): 32-33.

22 Yeldan, *Assessing the Privatization Experience in Turkey*, Table 3.

23 Ibid., 11.

integration, expressed in the Lisbon strategy (2000), global financial interests became the decisive factor behind the setting of
common economic policies. It is no secret that accession process at
any level involves the same requisites, contained in the structural
adjustment programs and SALs. This can be observed in the setting of a coherent, legal framework for privatization in 1994 (Law
on Privatization No: 4046), which had been lacking in the 1980s,[24]
partly as a condition for Turkey's membership in the Customs
Union in 1996.

The 2001 economic crisis also introduced a new actor on the
political scene. The Justice and Development Party (JDP) has
overtly displayed its neoliberal leanings both in its pre-election
discourse and in its practices when in power (2002-). The JDP
has portrayed itself as a non- and/or anti-populist party.[25] It has
been argued that the JDP has performed well in its commitment
to the IMF-led neoliberalization,[26] and that it has not preferred
populist means in its relations with the workers who would be
affected by the privatization process. Still, its policies exemplify a populist stance on two interrelated dimensions. The first
dimension can be termed "culturalist" and works through the
emphasis of a Muslim-Turkish identity in the party's approach
to the masses. The second dimension concerns the creation of an
"us versus others" distinction that provides an alternative venue
for the party to appeal to the masses in the implementation of
privatization policies.

The JDP's period in government can be considered a phase of filling
in the blanks in the privatization process. In this respect, the privatization of major industrial establishments, like PETKİM (petrochemicals)

---

24 For an analysis of the legal basis of privatization, see İzak Athias and Berna
Özer, *Türkiye'de Özelleştirmenin Hukuk ve Ekonomisi* (Ankara: TEPAV,
2008).
25 "AKP Genel Başkanı ve Başbakan Recep Tayyip Erdoğan'ın 20 Ocak 2004
Tarihli Genel Kurul Konuşması," 2-3; "AK Parti Genel Başkanı ve Başbakan
Erdoğan'ın Van Mitinginde yaptığı Konuşma," 27 February 2009, http://
www.akparti.org.tr/ak-parti-genel-baskani-ve-basbakan-erdoganin-van-mit-
inginde_5973.html
26 See for example, Ziya Öniş, "The Political Economy of Turkey's Justice
and Development Party," http://papers.ssrn.com/sol3/papers.cfm?abstract_
id=659463; E. Fuat Keyman and Ziya Öniş, "Globalization and Social
Development in European Periphery: Paradoxes of the Turkish Experience,"
Globalizations 4, no. 2 (2007): 211-228.

Erdemir (steel), TÜPRAŞ (refinery), was completed.[27] In this set of privatizations, an alleged "lack of investment" accompanied a discourse of "efficiency."[28] This articulation served in justifying the prevalence of foreign investment in the course of privatization. This is also in line with the exclusion of labour from the economic agenda. The JDP has overtly set the security for the entrepreneur as a precondition for employment and wage security, justifying it on the basis of the workers' and the nation's welfare. This priority setting is reflected in the party's relation to trade unions, as in the case of collective bargaining, and the privatization of certain SEEs—most recently that of TEKEL. The series of privatizations also included universal services such as transportation, telecommunications, electricity distribution, health and education. In this respect, the health sector is exemplary, where one can observe the persistent tendency towards marketization. The program that is devised to restructure the health sector leads to the displacement of the "perception of health services as the rights of the citizens" by the mentality that opts for their "commodification."[29] JDP, unsurprisingly, justifies this transformation on the grounds of efficiency.

The party has also benefited from the pro-EU approach, which it has manipulated to assert its "democratic" and liberal preferences. Though also contentious in terms of the liberal individual rights, the party's performance in terms of democratic preferences is at best dubious. Yet the JDP's democratic credentials shall not be read in terms of the rights' discourse. Rather it pertains to its neoliberal political frame, which is also revealed in its electoral profile. The electoral appeal of the party in three past general elections (2002; 2007; 2011) should be considered in light of the emergence of a "new middle class... which is culturally conservative, politically nationalist and moderately authoritarian, economically liberal or rather, on the side of free enterprise."[30] The JDP, in turn, represents a slightly modified version of the centre political party, which

---

27   Yeldan, *Assessing the Privatization Experience in Turkey.*
28   "İş Kanunu ve İş Güvencesi'ni yeniden düzenleyeceğiz...," Milliyet, 15 March 2003.
29   Bağımsız Sosyal Bilimciler, *2005 Başında Türkiye'nin Ekonomik ve Siyasal Yaşamı Üzerine Değerlendirmeler* (Ankara: TMMOB, March 2005), 44. See also Simten Coşar and Metin Yeğenoğlu, "The Neoliberal Restructuring of Turkey's Social Security System," *Monthly Review* 60, no. 11 (April 2009): 34-47.
30   Ahmet İnsel, "The AKP and Normalizing Democracy in Turkey," *South Atlantic Quarterly*, 102, no. 2/3 (Spring/Summer 2003): 298.

basically appeals to the conservatism of this middle class. It also feeds into the neoliberal mindset of big capital, known with its liberal preferences.

The party's electoral appeal also works through the "us versus others" dimension, noted above. It involves conjunctural inclusion/ exclusion of various groups. The dichotomy connotes an ambiguous claim to represent the masses, variably meaning the nation, the people, the disadvantaged *vis-à-vis* the "non"—of all these categories. The marking line is the consent to the rules of the neoliberal game.

Privatization and Labour: The TEKEL Example

The privatization process in Turkey has not been immune to resistance. The most recent example is observed in the privatization of TEKEL. The resistance by TEKEL workers started in December 2009 and came to a "temporary end" in early March 2010. The end of the 78-day long strike was announced to be temporarily halted since the resistance could not achieve a concrete gain that asked for the abandonment of the Article 4, Provision C of Law on Civil Servants (or 4/C).[31] 4/C was presented as a solution by the government in 2004 to the "inefficiency" of the SEEs. The law basically regulates the policy of decreasing the expenditures of the enterprises by turning the workers into temporary employees, thereby nullifying their social benefits.[32] Considering that at the time of resistance the number of TEKEL workers was approximately 12,000, and that the opposition to the 4/C received widespread social support, the protest hinted at the possibility of substantial labour-based opposition against neoliberalism, which has so far been lacking in Turkey.[33]

---

31 At one point, the workers decided to go on a hunger strike, but the decision was not sustained. By the beginning of March 2010 the Council of State adopted the motion for stay of execution of the regulation on 4/C, which led to the 'temporary' postponement of TEKEL resistance in the capital city.

32 The history of legal arrangement that embraces the 4/C practice dates back to 2004 when the temporary Article 18 was added to the Law on Privatization. The Article brings in the regulation that had already been in force within the scope of the Law on Civil Servants No. 657 to the labour market.

33 For a multi-dimensional account of TEKEL resistance see Gökhan Bulut, ed., *TEKEL Direnişinin Işığında Gelenekselden Yeniye İşçi Sınıfı Hareketi* (Ankara: Nota Bene, 2010), 2nd ed. See also, Gamze Yıkılmaz and Seray Kumlu, eds., *TEKEL Eylemine Kenar Notları* (Ankara: Phoenix, 2011).

The TEKEL case is also important in terms of the attraction and reaction that it has driven. TEKEL's privatization, which started by the IMF-conditioned letter of intent in 1999, resulted in one of the most profitable sales. [34] The process gained momentum, first, by the sale of the alcohol branch of the enterprise in 2004 and, second, by the sale of the tobacco branch in 2008. The whole process ended with the displacement of approximately 12,000 workers, and a drastic decrease in the number of tobacco producers by 60%. [35] The attractiveness of TEKEL for profit-seeking capital is exemplified in the case of the alcohol branch. The consortium (MEY) that won the bid in 2003 in return for $292 million, re-sold it (to Texas Pacific Group) in return of $900 million, profiting approximately $600 million in two years time. [36]

The TEKEL example reveals the interplay between different versions of justification behind privatization. First, it was the emphasis on efficiency that overwhelmed. Then, revenue-raising dominated the grounds for justification. [37] In this respect, underneath the discourse on revenue-raising lies the practice of revenue-sharing among national and foreign capital-owners. [38]

In its last stage, workers were forced into the status of temporary personnel. This meant the surrender of their already gained social rights, including severance pay, membership to trade unions, and overtime payment. The regulation also restricted the right to work to 10 months per year, which would result in a drastic decrease in the wages to a level lower than the legal minimum wage. Workers were also banned from working in other jobs, which many actually require.

Like the earlier privatizations of SEKA and TÜPRAŞ, opposition to TEKEL's privatization kept mounting, at least in early 2010. Decisive in the continuity in this thread was the organizing capacity of the trade unions and confederations, particularly in response

---

34 Yeldan, "TEKEL Worker's Resistance: Re-Awakening of the Proletariat in Turkey," January 2010, http://www.sendika.org/english/yazi.php?yazi_no=29021.
35 The decrease in the number of TEKEL workers from 31,000 in 2001 to 12,000 in 2009 signifies the magnitude of the liquidation of labour. (Ibid.)
36 Yeldan, "TEKEL Worker's Resistance."
37 Yeldan, *Assessing the Privatization Experience in Turkey.*
38 Ibid.

to 4/C.[39] One of the most symbolic manifestations of this cooperation was the joint decision for a one-day general strike on February
4th and May 26th, 2010.[40] Thus, despite the divergences among the
confederations regarding the resolution of the conflict, the TEKEL
case has opened up an opportunity for lasting cooperation.

However, when the reception of workers' resistance is considered
one cannot come up with a decisive prospect. The official reception of the workers' resistance in the public sector displays a certain
level of continuity through earlier decades. The current government
has adopted the conventional position of "intimidating the workers
through the use of security forces ... assuming a despising attitude
toward the workers ... agitating the people against the strikers... [and]
turning deaf ears to the workers' demands."[41] The differences lie in
the contingencies of neoliberalism. The JDP government's position is
marked with what can be termed post-privatization syndrome. In this
respect, the resort to the "us versus others" dichotomy is explanatory:
"These people just stay in the tobacco depots. The cost of approximately 10 thousand persons for us is 40 trillion TL. Whose money
are we spending? People's money."[42] Moreover, what highlights the
JDP's difference is that this dichotomy is fed by culturalist priorities.
Accordingly, it is certain that the majority of the TEKEL workers, who
had voted for the JDP in the 2007 general election, did not do so for
the party's privatization program.[43] They did so, it is argued, because
the party managed to appeal to the masses, through an authoritarian
leader, its discourse of "getting things done," and its advocacy of identity politics, which prioritized Muslim-Turkish state of being.

The opposition, too, manipulates the labour-capital conflict with an emphasis on cultural dimensions. To begin with,

---

39 Certainly there are exceptions like HAK-İŞ (Confederation of Justice
    Seekers' Trade Unions), a pro-government confederation.
40 The process was not without pains, though. The decision to go on a one-
    day general strike could not find widespread trade union support, but it was
    limited by the attempts of the trade union (Tek Gıda-İş) to which the TEKEL
    workers were registered. For an elaboration see, Yalçın Bürkey, "Tekel
    Direnişi: Ne Eskinin Basit Devamı, Ne Yeninin Kendisi, " in Bulut, 22-24.
41 Kurthan Fişek, Türkiye'de Devlet-İşçi İlişkileri Açısından Devlete Karşı
    Grevlerin Kritik Tahlili (Ankara: AÜ SBFY, 1969), 175-176.
42 "Tekel işçisine yetim hakkı resti çekti," Hürriyet, 28 December 2009, http://
    www.hurriyet.com.tr/ekonomi/13322837.asp.
43 Atilla Özsever, "TEKEL işçisi: 5 Vakit Komünistim," Cumhuriyet, 28
    January 2010.

nationalists have been giving support to the workers' resistance along their opposition to the increasing activity of *foreign* capital in Turkey and criticizing privatization as a policy instrument for "selling the country." A different vein of culturalist discourse can also be noted for the "social democratic front." In this respect, the RPP's manipulation of the state of affairs is striking. Despite the party's infamous indifference to neoliberalization, it has been making good use of the conjuncture, by merging its laicist opposition against the JDP governments with the latest resistance wave.

Conclusion

By late 2011, when the Wall Street Occupation had been ongoing for several months, and as masses in Barcelona, Berlin, Madrid, Paris, Ottawa, Toronto and other cities around the world organized in protest against the increasingly-cruel neoliberal practices, the date was finally set for occupation in Turkey. This delay in both the calls for and the date of Turkish anti-neoliberal protests (scheduled for October) is all the more interesting since it has been only a year and a half since the TEKEL resistance had been staged and achieved recognition, making it possible to refer to the movement either within the context of "new social movements,"[44] or as signifying the roots for the emergence of the new labour movement in Turkey in neoliberal times. The movement comes after a long period of silence, characterized by incremental and thus ineffective—in respect of gaining public recognition and support, and affecting the policy making process—and unsustainable resistance. In fact, the TEKEL resistance can be considered as the initial signal of the organization of resentments toward neoliberal practices in Turkey into mass protests in general. This state of affairs should be considered with a view to the societal contradictions embedded in the framing of neoliberal policies. As far as the TEKEL example is concerned these contradictions can be read through the brushing aside of identity conflicts—if tentatively. In other words, TEKEL resistance provided the grounds for solidarity among different identity groups through a claim for

---

44   Yavuz Yıldırım, "TEKEL Direnişi Bir Toplumsal Hareket Miydi?," *Ankara Üniversitesi, SBF GETA Tartışma Metinleri* 111 (September 2010): 1-19.

social rights.[45] On the other hand, the brushing of identity issues aside was tentative since the very contradictions within the labour movement could not be resolved in such a short time. To put it differently, the resistance had its own historical contradictions since it inevitably arose out of the trade union movement that had long been divided in itself. What is promising in this picture is that despite the old divisions, the TEKEL case proved to offer the grounds for responding to neoliberal policies through new means of organization. Yet it has also met with the increasingly authoritarian discourse and practice by the JDP government against any further opposition, which, we argue, have been effective in the silencing of the possible extensions of the resistance.

All in all, TEKEL's privatization process signifies the latest instance of Turkey's experience with neoliberal policies. The privatization process in the country witnessed periodic ups and downs depending on the electoral concerns of the governments, as well as on the synthetic and thus, patchy character of Turkey's neoliberal path. Apart from the repression of Leftist opposition in the restructuring process of the 1980s, this patchy evolution also affected the style and intensity of the resistance to privatization. Briefly, grassroots resistance turned out to be relatively sporadic, gaining visibility in different steps of the privatization of particular SEEs. Moreover, the power of the trade unions to sustain cooperation proved to be significantly limited due to both the curtailment of their capacity and their rather concessional stance *vis-à-vis* the neoliberal programs. Thus, the workers' resistance did not lead to substantial change in the course of the privatization process. Instead, its repercussions have been effective in "convincing" the workers to halt the opposition through policies that would re-locate them in different jobs. Yet the fact that the Council of State also brought the 4/C to the Constitutional Court for annulment (March 2010) on the grounds that the regulation violates the equal right to social security hints the possibility for a breach in the neoliberal structure.

---

45   For an elaboration of the shaping of the resistance on the demands for rights see Elif Hacısalihoğlu, Göksu Uğurlu and Gamze Yücesan-Özdemir, "21. Yüzyılda Sosyal Hak Mücadelesi: TEKEL Direnişi, " Paper Submitted at II. Ulusal Sosyal Haklar Sempozyumu, Pamukkale Üniversitesi, Denizli 4-6 November 2010, http://www.sosyalhaklar.net/2010/bildiri/hacisalioglu.pdf.

It can be argued that the TEKEL resistance marks the edge where the three synthetic attributes of the post-1980 Turkish politics seem to dissolve and remould simultaneously. First, the centrist alliance among the government(s) and the electorate seems to be loosening. Second, the consent to the JDP governments is increasingly questioned. Third, the wide social support to the resistance signals the possibility of the replacement of the patchy style of opposition by a new form of organization that might enable political and social actors with different agendas to connect their opposition in a systematic program for action.

EMPIRE IN THE PHILIPPINES: A WAR AGAINST THE PEOPLE

Priscillia Lefebvre

During the neoliberalizing decade of the 2000s, the labour and human rights activist community in the Philippines experienced a massive increase in cases of torture, enforced disappearances, and extrajudicial killings. This chapter critically examines the neoliberal agenda pushed by the Arroyo government and its relationship to people's struggles against privatization and exploitation. Foreign capital, and the states that safeguard it (such as the United States and Canada), are understood to play a significant role in the repression of the labour movement—a brutal legacy of imperialism and resistance.

In Defence of the Ruling Class: Attacking Human Rights through State Violence

From January 2001 to October 2009, 1118 extrajudicial killings took place in the Philippines along with 204 enforced disappearances, 1026 people tortured, 1946 illegal arrests, and 255 political prisoners jailed under trumped up charges.[1] The height of the killings, in 2006, saw a total of 220 killings—an average of twice a week. This meant every other day grassroots organizations were receiving word that yet another comrade had been brutally murdered; these were people they knew, with whom they had worked and struggled. It was at this time that the Filipino activist community, including the families of victims and parliamentarian allies,

---

1   Karapatan, *Oplan Bantay Laya: Blueprint for Terror and Impunity*, (Quezon City, Philippines: Karapatan, 2009).

began to scream out against the blatant disregard for human and labour rights at the hands of their government and initiated an ongoing call for international solidarity. This call prompted UN investigations both in 2006 and 2007, the results of which indicated that the Armed Forces of the Philippines (AFP) is either indirectly, but more often directly, implicated in these deaths and other human rights violations.[2] The peak of the killings in 2006 also marked the end of Phase 1 of a counter-insurgency campaign waged by the government of former president Gloria Macapagal-Arroyo (GMA)—Oplan Bantay Laya (OBL), a national policy that has been compared to legislated state terrorism.[3] GMA, as Commander in Chief of the AFP was not only well aware of, but as part of her position, directed the actions taken by her military. The 2010 election year marked the end of Phase 2 of the OBL, which also represented a deadline for GMA and her administration to reach their military targets, a large part of which included "dismantling the political structure of the communist terrorist group."[4] Sadly, both the OBL and the killing of political activists continue under newly elected president Benigno 'Noynoy' Aquino III.

From Arroyo to Aquino—Oplan Bantay Laya

During her term of office, Gloria Macapagal-Arroyo (GMA) managed to accumulate a substantial amount of unexplained wealth. Educated in the US, she is worth a declared US$188 million, although said to actually be worth much more due to the ownership of properties in the US and money laundered through business in Hong Kong.[5] During her state of the nation address she announced her intent to "neutralize (read: physically eliminate) the social support system of the armed rebel movement" in the Philippines. The armed rebel movement to which she was

---

2   UN Special Rapporteur Philip Alston, Press Statement, 22 Feb. 2007.
3   Benjie Oliveros, "Oplan Batay Laya as Arroyo's Inhumane War," *Bulatlat*, 6, no. 20 (2006).
4   Karapatan. *Karapatan Monitor*, Jan-March, (2009), 1-4.
5   Malou Mangahas, "Can President explain her wealth?" *Philippine Center for Investigative Journalism*, 8 Oct. 2009, http://www.abs-cbnnews.com/nation/08/10/09/can-president-arroyo-explain-her-wealth (accessed 15 Oct. 2011).

referring is the New People's Army (NPA) that has taken up armed resistance in the countryside. However, according to the trail of bodies that surfaced following that statement, the "social support system" refers to activists and critics of the anti-people politics of the then GMA government. This continues to include legitimate social progressive organizations run by unarmed civilians – labour organizers, union leaders, teachers, lawyers, human rights activists, women's groups, peasant groups, indigenous groups, journalists, and the list goes on. There is no distinction made between armed combatants and unarmed civilians; to be vocal in your resistance is to be at risk of being targeted and charged with the accusation of being a member of the NPA or of an organization that is a communist front for the NPA.[6]

With OBL the GMA regime effectively legally sanctioned the Cold War mentality of persecuting "Communists" as enemies of the state. An ugly precedent set forth by GMA was the targeting and killing of family members of activists. Most shocking is that noone was spared—children, youth, and whole families have been among the dead.[7] This continues to occur in an atmosphere of impunity as not a single conviction has been made in relation to any of these atrocities. In fact, the notorious General Jovito Palparan, also known as 'the Butcher' because wherever he goes the killings intensify according to the Order of Battle, which is essentially a military hit list, was elected as congressman under GMA.[8]

In addition to physical state violence is the "legal offensive" strategy to repress political opponents and social progressive organizations, which, according to OBL, can be categorized as enemies of the state. The Inter-Agency Legal Action Group (IALAG), now abolished, was constructed by the GMA government in order to investigate, track, and prosecute legal cases falling under OBL, which are classified as matters of national

---

6   Benjie Oliveros, "Oplan Batay Laya as Arroyo's Inhumane War," *Bulatlat,* 6, no. 20 (2006).

7   *Permanent Peoples' Tribunal Repression & Resistance: The Filipino People vs Gloria Macapagal-Arroyo, George W. Bush, et. al.* (Quezon City, Philippines: IBON Books, 2007).

8   Leila Salaverria, "Palparan guilty of murder in privilege speech," *Philippine Daily Inquirer,* 29 Sept. 2009, http://newsinfo.inquirer.net/inquirerheadlines/ nation/view/20090924-226631/Palparan-guilty-of-murder-in-privilege-speech (accessed 15 Oct. 2011).

security. However, what the IALAG seems to actually special-
ize in actually is the prosecution of national and regional union
and human rights leaders under trumped up charges. The most
common charges appear to be possession of drugs and/or weap-
ons, murder, kidnapping, arson, and libel. It is not unusual
for organizers to be arrested by police, searched and jailed for
months on end without due process. Also, charges can be filed
against a single individual or a group of up to 100 people.[9] A
recent example of this was the mass arrest, on February 6, 2010,
of 43 health workers (the Morong 43) who have been accused of
having ties to the NPA as medics and explosives trainees and
who were held in custody illegally for ten months, one of whom
gave birth to a baby boy while in prison.[10]

Despite the call for a peaceful and democratic transition
between administrations, in the first 16 days after Benigno
"Noynoy" Aquino took office as president on June 30, 2010, six
activists, including a union leader, human rights organizers and
progressive journalists, were summarily killed. Two of them,
farmers Julio Etang and Borromeo Cabilis, were murdered in
Mobo, Masbate, on the very first day of Aquino's term.[11] The
recent deaths have put to rest any hope that Aquino would, in
any real sense, end the brutal persecution of activists despite his
hollow promise to hold those responsible for human rights violations in the Philippines accountable.[12] Instead, it would seem,
Aquino chooses to hide behind his military forces by stating that
the killings occurred, not because of state policy such as OBL, but

---

9   Ronald V. Olea, "Dismantling of IALAG, Arroyo's Shadowy Agency, 'Just for
    Show'," *Bulatlat.com,* (2009), 1-4.
10 Gill Boehringer, "Blighted: Philippine jurisprudence and State Repression –
    The Morong 43," *Bulatlat.com,* http://www.chdphilippines.org/Blighted%20
    -%20Philippine%20jurisprudence%20and%20State%20Repression%20
    _%20The%20Morong%2043.htm (accessed 15 Oct. 2011). The Morong 43
    have since been released. For further information and trajectory of the case
    see http://freethehealthworkers.blogspot.com.
11 Jerrie M. Abella, "Six killings in two weeks as groups seek UN action on RP
    human rights," *GMANews.TV,* 2010, http://www.gmanews.tv/story/193884/
    nation/six-killings-in-two-weeks-as-groups-seek-un-action-on-rp-human-
    rights (accessed 15 Oct. 2011).
12 Benigno S. Aquino III, *State of the Nation Address,* 26 July 2010,
    http://2010presidentiables.wordpress.com/2010/07/27/noynoy-aquino-
    2010-sona-speech-transcript-official-english-translation/ (official English
    translation accessed 15Oct. 2011).

due to personal rivalries among warring clans. This is in blatant disregard of the evidence gathered by local human rights organizations, such as Karapatan,[13] as well as Amnesty International,[14] Human Rights Watch,[15] and UN Special Rapporteur Philip Alston, documenting clear ways in which the OBL policy is used to target unarmed community activists within its counter-insurgency platform.[16] As long as Aquino refuses to acknowledge the systemic nature of the killing occurring under his presidency, and those before him, there remains little chance the violence will stop. Another reason to turn a blind eye to the AFP's oppressive actions is the enormous funding the military receives from the US.[17] As the remainder of this chapter will explore, the well-being and economic freedom of the Filipino people are routinely sacrificed for the benefit of the country's ruling class as well as their colonial counterparts.

US and Canadian Imperialism in the Philippines

Even though the US granted the Philippines independence on paper after a bloody colonial war and intense US military 'pacification' operations in the country,[18] the colonial relationship between the US and the Philippines is still going strong through economic control of agriculture, export-oriented industries,

---

13 KARAPATAN, founded in 1995 by its member organizations, is self-described as "an alliance of individuals, groups and organizations working for the promotion and protection of human rights in the Philippines. Its founders and members have been at the forefront of the human rights struggle in the Philippines since the time of Marcos' martial law regime. For more information see http://www.karapatan.org

14 Amnesty International, "Make Human Rights A Priority: Amnesty International's Agenda for the May 2010 Elections," http://www.amnesty.org.ph/news.php?item=news&id=134 (accessed 15 Oct. 2011).

15 Human Rights Watch, *World Report: The Philippines*, http://www.hrw.org/world-report/2009/philippines (accessed 15 Oct. 2011).

16 UN Special Rapporteur Philip Alston, Press Statement, 22 Feb. 2007.

17 BAYAN News Release, "Bayan to Aquino: Problem is AFP's counter-insurgency policy," 13 July 2010, http://www.bayan.ph/index.php?start_from=&ucat=1&subaction=showfull&id=1278983294&archive=1280638882& (accessed 15 Oct. 2011).

18 John M. Gates, "The Pacification of the Philippines, 1898-1902," in *The American Military in the Far East: Proceedings of the 9th Military History Symposium, U.S. Air Force Academy,* ed. Joe E. Dixon, (Washington D.C.: US Government Printing Office, 1982), 79-91 & 261-264.

and the imposition of foreign debt.[19] The Millennium Challenge Corporation, developed under George W. Bush and currently chaired by Secretary of State Hilary Clinton, is used by the US to push neoliberal open-market economic policy in exchange for foreign aid for major 'development' projects. The latest string attached to the US$434 million grant is the possibility of a bilateral free-trade agreement between the US and Philippines.[20] The military presence of US troops in the Philippines is also still very evident through initiatives such as the Visiting Forces Agreement (VFA) ratified in 1999. The VFA is especially problematic since there are no restrictions as to the duration of the agreement itself, the length of time US troops can spend in the Philippines or the kinds of operations carried out while there; although, one of the objectives of the US military assistance program is to enact "more punitive measures on the counterterrorism front."[21]

The GMA government supports the war on terror, as well as the invasion of and military presence in Iraq and Afghanistan by the US and Canada.[22] In addition to the implementation of OBL, in July 2007 the GMA government passed the Anti-Terrorism Law (ATL), also known as the Human Security Act.[23] This law closely resembles the US Patriot Act and was enthusiastically supported

19   Bayan's publication "US Imperialist Globalization and Its Elite Partners in the Philippines Trade, Inequality and State Terrorism" provides a useful introduction to US imperialism in the Philippines. Bayan, established in 1985, is self-described as "a multisectoral formation struggling for national and social liberation against imperialism, feudalism and bureaucrat capitalism." The article can be found at http://www.bayan.ph/site/2005/11/us-imperialist-globalization-and-its-elite-partners-in-the-philippines-trade-inequality-and-state-terrorism/

20   Marya Salamat, "Progressive Groups Say $434 Million Compact Grant to Benefit US, Not the Philippines," Bulatlat.com, 25 Sept. 2010, http://bulatlat.com/main/2010/09/25/progressive-groups-say-434-million-compact-grant-to-benefit-us-not-the-philippines/ (accessed 15 Oct. 2011).

21   Renato M. Reyes, Jr., "Permanent presence and combat involvement of US troops undermine Philippine sovereignty," submitted to the Legislative Oversight Committee on the VFA on behalf of BAYAN Secretary General, 25 Sept. 2008. For more information see http://www.bayan.ph/vfa.htm

22   Nymia Pimentel Simbulan, "The Philippine Human Rights Situation: Threats & Challenges," *Philippine Human Rights Information Center*, http://www.asienhaus.de/public/archiv/simbulan-hrsituation-complete.pdf (accessed 15 Oct. 2011).

23   RA 9372: Human Security Act of 2007, Congress of the Philippines, Metro Manila, http://www.congress.gov.ph/download/ra_13/RA09372.pdf (accessed 15 Oct. 2011).

by the Bush administration, which meant it was also a high priority for GMA. This law is what makes the arrest and indefinite detention of activists and organizers without due process, labelled as "suspected terrorists," permissible under the guise of national security.[24] After the ATL was passed, the Bush administration increased military aid to the Philippines, his major non-NATO ally, to the tune of 1600% in 2008 when compared to 2001. As a result, no other country in the East Asia-Pacific region receives more military funding than the Philippines, ranking it the 3rd country in the world in terms of receiving additional funding specifically for the training and education of its military.[25] It is perhaps then no coincidence that the GMA government has been most aggressive in the repression of resistance groups in the Southern Philippines island of Mindanao, where the US has expressed the most economic interest due to the presence of oil and natural gas.[26] The Obama administration continues to provide the Philippines with its sizeable foreign aid.[27]

The US has increased its military presence in the Philippines through joint military exercise training programs such as the US Joint Special Operations Task Force – Philippines (JSOTF-P).[28] Filipino human rights organizations are concerned by evidence indicating that US troops are involved in more than training exercises such as the one for assisting the AFP in combat operations under the guise of counterterrorism efforts against indigenous groups in the region struggling for self-determination.[29] Canada also has RCMP located in the Philippines through the Canadian Military Training and Assistance

---

24 Human Rights Watch, "Philippines: New Terrorism Law Puts Rights at Risk," 15 July 2007, http://www.hrw.org/news/2007/07/15/philippines-new-terrorism-law-puts-rights-risk (accessed 15 Oct. 2011).

25 Karapatan, *Oplan Bantay Laya: Blueprint for Terror and Impunity,* (Quezon City, Philippines: Karapatan, 2009).

26 Mindanao Peoples' Peace Agenda, *Towards a Mindanao Peoples' Peace Agenda,* (Philippines: Initiatives for International Dialogue, 2010).

27 Thomas Lum, "The Republic of the Philippines and U.S. Interests (CRS report for Congress)," US: Congressional Research Service, 3 Jan. 2011, http://opencrs.com/document/RL33233/2011-01-03/ (accessed 15 Oct. 2011).

28 Official website of the JSOTF-P can be found at http://jsotf-p.blogspot.com/

29 Herbert Docena, "Unconventional Warfare: Are US Special Forces engaged in an 'offensive war' in the Philippines?" *Focus on the Philippines Special Reports* 1 (2007), 1-40.

Program (MTAP) and the Police Training and Assistance Program (PTAP).[30]

Neoliberal policy put forth by the GMA government has also cleared the path for multi-national corporations to extract wealth from the country. The Philippines is hugely rich in minerals and fertile land, which has attracted huge mining and agro-industrial projects by foreign companies, including from Canada.[31] The GMA government's pandering to such foreign capital interests has driven the country into tremendous foreign debt (US$54 billion in 2006).[32] Onerous taxes are also pushed: for every ten Philippine pesos collected, six go to the foreign debt repayment of American and Japanese commercial banks, as well as international lending institutions such as the World Bank.[33] This has resulted in massive cuts to social spending particularly in health and education. Public-private partnerships between multi-national corporations and universities, for example, have been pushed by the GMA government as a solution, as well as total privatization measures targeting the National Power Corporation, the National Food Authority, as well as municipal water districts.[34] The US based investment firm, Water Bank, has special interests in the privatization of water services in the Philippines with the goal of permits in place to bottle and export. Foreign big business such as Nestle, Coca-cola, and Pepsi-cola work in tandem with the local San Miguel Corporation and have already secured permission to bottle and sell spring and mineral water. This is, in large part, due to national policy brought about by the World Bank and international organizations such as the World Water

---

30   The Stop the Killings Network–Canada & Canadian Advocacy Group on the Philippines, *Extrajudicial Killings in the Philippines and Canada-Philippine Relations,* submitted to the Standing Committee on Foreign Affairs and International Development, 15 Apr. 2008, http://www.kairoscanada.org/fileadmin/fe/files/PDF/HRTrade/SubmissionsEtc/Submission_Philippines_ForeignAffairs_April08.pdf (accessed 15 Oct. 2011).
31   Gerardo Gobrin and Almira Andin, *Development Conflict: the Philippine Experience* (London, UK: Minority Rights International, 2003).
32   Alecks P. Pabico, "Gloria's inglorious record: Biggest debtor, least popular," *Philippine Centre for Investigative Journalism Report – Til debt do us part?,* Aug-Sept 2008.
33   Edberto M. Villegas, *The Philippine Fiscal Crisis and the Neo-Colonial State,* (2004), http://www.yonip.com/main/articles/fiscalcrisis.html (accessed 15 Oct. 2011).
34   Ricco A. M. Santos, "Arroyo Gov't Unleashes APEC-Driven Third Privatization Wave," *Bulatlat.com,* 13, no. 35 (2003), http://www.bulatlat.com/news/3-35/3-35-apec.html (accessed 15 Oct. 2011).

Forum, held every two years and promoting corporate control and liberalization of water resources, through the Integrated Water Resource Management (IWRM) initiative. The IWRM pushes the country to consider a system of tradable water rights where water rights would be sold freely at negotiated prices to anyone for any purpose. According to a Family Income and Expenditures Survey, conducted in 2000 in the National Capital Region of Metro Manila, the lack of access to public water services have resulted in Filipino families being forced to spend up to 50% of their household income to purchase bottled water.[35]

For its part, Canada is the biggest importer of Filipino foreign labour through the Live-In Caregiver Program. There are approximately 400,000 Filipinos living in Canada, 45% of whom are temporary workers.[36] The migration of about 3000 Overseas Foreign Workers (OFWs) out of the Philippines every day, 80% of whom are women, amounts to about 1,000,000 annually. OFWs are arguably what keep the Philippines afloat economically. The influx of foreign capital into the country in the form of remittances alone from OFWs reaches about US$14-15 billion, which is about 15% of the national GDP. This number was set to increase by 6-8% in 2010. As such, this practice of shipping people as export labour out of the country is highly encouraged and fiercely protected by the government. Even though the bulk of this money does not go directly to the government, but to the families of OFWs, it inflates the GDP and improves credit ratings, which enables the government to borrow more money.[37]

Considering Canada's dependence on Filipino foreign labour, as well as Canadian mining activity occurring in the Philippines, it is perhaps not surprising, although not any less disturbing, that Canada does not appear to have done much to stop the corrupt

---

35 Water for the People Network, *Water for the People: People's Water Resource Management Strategies,* (Quezon City, Philippines: IBON International, 2009).

36 Aubrey S. C. Makilan, "Canada Not All 'Rosy' for Filipino Migrants," *Bulatlat.com,* 6, no. 44 (2006), http://bulatlat.com/news/6-44/6-44-canada.htm (accessed 15 Oct. 2011).

37 Migrante activist (name omitted), interview with author, January 2010 at the Salam Mosque Compound, Philippines. For more information about Canada's Live-In Caregiver Program see 'Scrap the Live-in Caregiver Program: Submission to the Parliamentary Standing Committee on Citizenship and Immigration' by National Alliance of Philippine Women in Canada at www.philreporter.com.

practices of the GMA government or the killing of Filipino activists. In fact, the Canadian government has maintained a weak stance on the subject in the interest of diplomacy. Nor does Canada readily recognize people who flee the Philippines as political refugees.[38] Also, there is additional Canadian involvement in the Philippines through Economic Development Canada (EDC), which has provided roughly CAN$120 million in loans to fund Canadian companies in the Philippines, as well as involvement in the Counter Terrorism Capacity Building (CBRN) of the Philippines government.[39] Stop the Killings in the Philippines (STKP), a nationwide coalition of organizations in Canada including NGOs and solidarity groups, has demanded that the Harper government recognize the human rights situation and state violence occurring in the Philippines and pressure the Aquino government to end the persecution of political activists and their families, but, as of the time of this writing, to little avail. The Canadian government continues its lucrative trade relations with the Philippines to the tune of approximately CAN$1.5 billion dollars yearly.[40]

While foreign markets profit, funding to essential social services for Filipinos is slashed in the national budget as debt repayment takes priority with an increase from 19.98% in 2009 to 21.75% in 2010. Health and education, on the other hand, were cut from 1.19% and 6.90% to 1.0% and 6.85% respectively, while government spending for housing was eliminated completely.[41] On the recommendation of the World Bank, the Filipino government has been enforcing a limited- or zero-growth doctrine on

---

38 Tom Sandborn, "Philippines Bloody for Unionists, But Invest There Says Ottawa: Canada's government is too quiet on abuses say human rights advocates," *TheTyee.ca*, 25 Nov. 2009, http://thetyee.ca/News/2009/11/25/ PhilippinesBloody/ (accessed 15 Oct. 2011).

39 The Stop the Killings Network – Canada & Canadian Advocacy Group on the Philippines, *Extrajudicial Killings in the Philippines and Canada-Philippine Relations*, submitted to the Standing Committee on Foreign Affairs and International Development, 15 Apr. 2008, http://www.kairoscanada.org/ fileadmin/fe/files/PDF/HRTrade/SubmissionsEtc/Submission_Philippines_ ForeignAffairs_April08.pdf (accessed 15 Oct. 2011).

40 Stop the Killings Coalition of Canada, "Letter of concern to Canadian PM on latest wave of political killings in Philippines," submitted to the Prime Minister of Canada, 16 July 2010, http://cap-cpc.blogspot.com/2010/07/ letter-of-concern-to-canadian-pm-on.html (accessed 15 Oct. 2011).

41 Gabriela, presentation for Worker-to-Worker Solidarity Exchange delegates (Canadian Union of Public Employees), Jan. 2010, Quezon City, Philippines.

spending for public education since 1997. This lack of funding has resulted in a historically unprecedented decline in school enrolment for Filipino children with a 78% increase of youth without access to education between 2002 and 2006. Of course, the vast majority of these children are consistently among the poor. Teachers' salaries have also undergone a six year wage freeze while the cost of living continues to rise. Contrary to government expenditure, one aspect of the educational system in the Philippines that has not changed has been its pandering to US colonialism with an emphasis on English, under Executive Order 210, as the first language of instruction and vocational training geared toward an export labour force.[42]

Women are disproportionately affected by extreme poverty with many turning to overseas domestic work. Others are subsumed in sex trade and trafficking, largely through the mail-order bride industry, exposing them to physical and sexual violence. In fact, over the past ten years, 60-70% of Filipinos who have left to work and marry abroad are women. The Philippines, compared to 35 Asian countries, is second only to India for having the longest list of online postings of potential brides. Furthermore, according to the US Immigration and Naturalization Services, 70% of mail order bride listings are Filipina with roughly 200,000 women listed. A shocking number of women are also forced into sex work in order to feed their families and provide for their basic needs.[43] The International Labour Organization's 1996 study stated over 500,000 women were engaged in sex work. This is not to mention the increasing occurrence of "prosti-tuition" in which students' only option is to become sex workers in order to gain access to post-secondary education.[44] Women also experience sexual harassment in the workplace with bosses who enforce

---

42   Alliance of Concerned Teachers (ACT), presentation for Worker-to-Worker Solidarity Exchange delegates (Canadian Union of Public Employees), Dec. 2009, Quezon City, Philippines. For more information regarding EO 210 see http://www.up.edu.ph/upforum.php?i=105&archive=yes&yr=2.

43   Gabriela, presentation for Worker-to-Worker Solidarity Exchange delegates (Canadian Union of Public Employees), Jan. 2010, Quezon City, Philippines. For more information about cuts to social services in 2010 see 'Alternative Budget: Protecting the People in Times of Crisis' at http://www.socialwatch-philippines.org/abi.htm

44   Gabriella Quimson, "Gender Based Corruption in the Philippines," presentation for TASA 2001 Conference, University of Sydney, 13-15 Dec. 2001.

a "lay down or lay-off" policy. Those who struggle against this oppression face additional violence. Gabriela, an organization in the Philippines consisting of over 150,000 women across the country,[45] reports that in 2008 alone 107 women were victims of extra-judicial killings, 271 were illegally detained by the state, and 31 disappeared altogether for being political resistors. Many of these women experience torture and sexual molestation during their abduction. Gabriela also works with solidarity organizations in the US, Japan, Belgium, Korea, and Australia.[46]

Labour Rights are Human Rights: Union Busting in the Philippines

The Philippines is second only to Columbia for being the most dangerous place in the world for union activists.[47] In an effort to protect its own, as well as foreign, ruling class interests the GMA government has implemented anti-people/anti-labour legislation, which is viciously enforced through paramilitary forces, corporate private armies, and the government's use of the AFP and Philippines National Police (PNP). September 2005 marked the revival of a "no permit/no rally" law, originally enacted in 1985 by Marcos, and coupled it with what is called the Calibrated Pre-emptive Response (CPR).[48] This official response protocol permits the violent dispersal of peaceful protests, including picket lines, which is a clear violation of the legislated right to associate.[49] In these dispersals the use of water cannons, smoke bombs, physical attacks with night sticks and police shields is common. Another

---

45 Official website for Gabriela can be found at http://members.tripod. com/~gabriela_p/home.html

46 Gabriela, presentation for Worker-to-Worker Solidarity Exchange delegates (Canadian Union of Public Employees), Jan. 2010, Quezon City, Philippines.

47 Canadian Labour Congress, *The International Department Report to the CLC Executive Council*, (2008), http://copesepb.ca/librairies/sfv/telecharger. php?fichier=639 (accessed 15 Oct. 2011).

48 Philippine Centre for Investigative Journalism Blog, "CPR, 'no permit, no rally' policies unconstitutional — FLAG," 17 Oct. 2005, http://www.pcij. org/blog/2005/10/17/cpr-no-permit-no-rally-policies-questioned-before-the-supreme-court (accessed 15 Oct. 2011).

49 The LawPhil Project, *Philippine law and jurisprudence databank*, Batas Pambansa Blg. 880, http://www.lawphil.net/statutes/bataspam/bp1985/ bp_880_1985.html (accessed 15 Oct. 2011).

interesting and frightening piece of legislation is what is called the "Assumption of Jurisdiction," which is similar to a back to work order; however, the difference is that it is violently enforced by the AFP and PNP.[50]

Union organizers employed by the Dole Plantation in General Santos have complained to the Department of Labour that the management have hired the military to conduct seminars for workers in order to demonize the union. However, they have yet to receive a response. Seventeen employees have been fired—including the union vice-president, treasurer, one of the board of directors, and the secretary. Dole also pays workers to file against the union and they have been suspended for passing out the union newsletter. seventy percent to 80% of the 22, 000 workers are contractual, with no benefits, no tenure, and make only 245 PHP a day. They work on a quota system and many must bring in their children to labour alongside them in order to make their quotas—tantamount to child labour. Many workers experience health issues because of the harsh chemicals used in growing the pineapples without protective gear (which is only distributed when the inspectors are there). Endosulphan in particular, one of the more toxic pesticides in existence has actually been banned in the Philippines (and 54 other countries) yet Dole continues to use it. The privatised land used to grow pineapples can be referred to as "green deserts" in which 90% of the product goes to export, leaving nothing for the surrounding community.[51]

Under the guise of the global economic crisis, multi-national companies with manufacturing operations based in the Philippines have put brutal cost–cutting measures into force including massive layoffs and violent union busting tactics. Workers within the Export Processing Zones (EPZs) of Cavite also face extreme violence in their organizing efforts against atrocious working

---

50 Marya Salamat, "Why Workers Abhor AJ, Which Makes Arroyo Worst Violator of Labor Rights," *Bulatlat.com*. 23 Nov. 2009, http://bulatlat.com/main/2009/11/23/why-workers-abhor-aj-which-makes-arroyo-regime-worst-violator-of-labor-rights/ (accessed 15 Oct. 2011).
51 Dole Philippines union activist (name omitted), interview with author, Jan. 2010, General Santos, Philippines.

conditions.[52] EPZs are guarded by the private security of mul-
tinational corporations, who adopt a strict "no union/no strike"
policy, from countries such as China, Korea, and the US. They are
filled with mostly subcontractors that work for big brand names
such as Honda, DKNY, and Bridgestone-Japan; and suppliers for
Ralph Lauren, Walmart, American Eagle, and the GAP, to name a
few. Shifts are a minimum of 16 hours, six days a week and can be
as long as 24 hours with overtime and many of these workers are
not making minimum wage or even half. Those who even attempt
to form a union are met with beatings on site, some have been
abducted, hog-tied, blindfolded, and thrown out of vans; others
have experienced attempts on their life and some have actually
been shot and killed for demanding job security, the end of contract labour and the outsourcing of jobs, access to healthcare
benefits, and a living wage.[53]

On Bloody Ground: Land Reform and the Aquino Legacy

The Aquino family's political history is a long one marred by peasant struggle and an empty promise for genuine land reform in the
Philippines and "give the land to the tiller" handed out by current
president Aquino's mother, Corazon Aquino, who was also president from 1986 to 1992.[54] Her Comprehensive Agrarian Reform
Policy, never actualized, sparked the Mendiola Massacre in which
13 farmer protesters were shot dead by the military on January
22, 1987.[55] The Hacienda Luisita Massacre of November 16, 2004

52 Workers' Assistance Centre Inc., Press Statement, *ILO: Cavite Workers seek justice to anti-labor NUNS policy*, 24 Sept. 2009, http://www.wacphilippines.com/news-and-stories/ilo-cavite-workers-seek-justice-to-anti-labor-nuns-policy (accessed 15 Oct. 2011). For more information on working conditions in EPZs see 'Behind Brand Names: Working conditions and labour rights' in export processing zones at http://www.icftu.org/www/PDF/EPZreportE.pdf
53 EPZ workers and union activists (names omitted), interview with author, Jan. 2010, Cavite, Philippines.
54 James Putzel, *A Captive Land: The Politics of Agrarian Reform in the Philippines*, (Ney York, NY: Monthly Review Press, 1992).
55 Jerry Esguerra, "The Mendiola Massacre of 1987: Past atrocities shape present-day Filipino reality," *LiberationNews.org*, 9 Jan. 2009, http://www.pslweb.org/liberationnews/news/09-01-25-the-mendiola-massacre-1987.html (accessed 15 Oct. 2011).

is a monument for land reform struggle in the Philippines. The Hacienda is a sugar cane plantation spanning about 15 000 acres and owned by the Cojuangco family, to whom Noynoy Aquino is related, and who bought the huge piece of land from the government in the 1950s.[56] The workers there went on strike demanding better work hours and a living wage. The landless farmers were peaceful in their protest; however, they refused to move from their picket line. On the third day of the strike, when the usual intimidation tactics and violent actions failed at dispersing the crowd of workers, the PNP opened fire killing seven people and injuring 32 from gunshot. Far more insidious is that, not only were seven workers shot on the front lines of the strike, seven more were assassinated in the months that followed the incident.[57] These were clearly strategic killings in that those who were targeted were key labour organizers or supporters at the Hacienda, where workers continue to live and labour. Noynoy Aquino still owns roughly 1% of the Hacienda. On November 17, 2004, the Philippine Daily Reporter has Aquino, a senator at the time, actually defending the dispersal that took place at the Hacienda by saying, "It was an illegal strike. No strike vote was called." The unwillingness to enforce genuine land reform remains one of the biggest tells of current President Aquino's intention, or lack thereof, to seek justice for the Filipino people.[58]

The Struggle for Freedom in a Culture of Impunity

At the time of writing, the Ampatuan Massacre was the most recent mass killing in the Philippines to receive international attention. On the morning of November 23, 2009 in Maguindanao Province, located in Southern Mindanao, 57 unarmed civilians were brutally gunned down by 100 men consisting of members of the Civilian Armed Forces Geographical Unit and the Civilian Volunteers Organization, these

---

56   Walden Bello et al., *The anti-development state: the political economy of permanent crisis in the Philippines*, (London, UK: Zed Books Ltd, 2005).

57   Bobby Tuazon, "The Hacienda Luisita Massacre, Landlordism and State Terrorism," *Bulatlat.com*, 4, no. 42 2004, http://bulatlat.com/news/4-42/4-42-massacre.html (accessed 15 Oct. 2011).

58   Stephanie Dychui, "Hacienda Luisita's Past Haunts Noynoy's Future," *GMANews.TV*, 2010, http://www.gmanews.tv/story/181877/hacienda-luisi-tas-past-haunts-noynoys-future (accessed 15 Oct. 2011).

groups having obvious links to both the Philippine Army (PA) and PNP. These gunmen were apparently led by the son of the head of the Ampatuan clan.[59] Included in the victims were over 30 journalists along with two female public interest lawyers, and relatives of the Vice-mayor Esmael "Toto" Mangudadatu. The group was traveling to register their candidacy in the upcoming May 2010 elections, which would have allowed the Vice-mayor to run as an opposition candidate against the Ampatuan clan member in power at the time. None of the 100 gunmen involved in this mass murder has been arrested.[60]

Karapatan, a human rights organization in the Philippines, has called the Ampatuan Massacre "carnage waiting to happen" due to the nature of OBL and the formation of paramilitary groups, which are part of its counter-insurgency strategy and act as support units of the PA and PNP.[61] There are also very important links to be drawn between the Ampatuans and GMA. The Ampatuans, a ruling family in the Philippines, were alleged to have provided GMA with the fraudulent votes needed to steal the elections in 2004 and 2007.[62] This incident is indicative not only of dangers that face many electoral candidates who dare run against a ruling party, but also, and this reaches far beyond election time, of the lengths those in power will go to in order to retain absolute authority.

The struggles against privatization and labour exploitation, and the move toward genuine land reform and social change in the Philippines, are ones of subsistence and survival. The violence that organizers are met with touches the Filipino activist community and their loved ones in very tangible, tragic, and immediate ways. Due to the urgency and danger of the situation, resistance at the local level has become

---

59 International Federation of Journalists, "Massacre in the Philippines: International Solidarity Mission Rapid Assessment," *Report of the International Federation of Journalists-led Mission to the Philippines*, 5-11 Dec. 2009, to investigate the November 23 2009 Ampatuan Town Massacre,Maguindanao,Mindanao, Philippines, http://asiapacific.ifj.org/assets/docs/203/037/15d11cb-013d725.pdf (accessed 15 Oct. 2011).

60 Emily Rauhala, "A Year After Massacre, the Philippines Still Waits for Justice," *Time World*, 2010, http://www.time.com/time/world/article/0,8599,2032802,00.html (accessed 15 Oct. 2011).

61 Karapatan, *Oplan Bantay Laya: Blueprint for Terror and Impunity*, (Quezon City, Philippines: Karapatan, 2009).

62 Christian V. Esguerra and Marinel R. Cruz, "Susan Roces: Let those with details finally come out," *Philippine Daily Inquirer*, 2011, http://newsinfo.inquirer.net/26193/susan-roces-let-those-with-details-finally-come-out (accessed 15 Oct. 2011).

highly coordinated. Bringing together the resistance efforts of several social organizations and activists is not without conflict; however, the basis of unity is simple: an engagement in the struggle for freedom from oppression and for genuine democracy, which emphasizes the mass movement of the people as anti-imperialist and anti-fascist, and a broad united front both on the ground and in the electoral arena.[63] Human and labour rights organizations in the Philippines support each other and their communities by providing strike support, mobilizing and coordinating organizations in calls for action in order to pool efforts for demonstrations, protests, and relief work; as well as by supporting progressive candidates in local and national elections.[64]

International solidarity has been emphasized in order to garner international pressure on the Filipino government to stop state violence and call attention to the OBL and the breakdown of the democratic process in the Philippines. In May 2010, at the request of numerous human and labour rights organizations, a delegation of 86 people including union organizers, community activists, progressive politicians, and journalists from 14 countries including Canada, US, UK, Germany, France, Taiwan, Australia, and New Zealand, participated in the People's International Observers Mission (PIOM) of the 2010 national elections.[65] Organized in part by concerned groups and individuals in the Philippines, including Pagbabago, People's Movement for Change, it was the hope of the PIOM that an international presence and media coverage would contribute to a more peaceful and democratic election overall and help protect progressive candidates from military harassment and assassination.[66]

The possibility of a failed election worried many due to the introduction of an automated ballot system at the national level and given the proliferation of electoral fraud in past elections, including GMA's assumption of presidency in 2004. The

---

63 Baging Alyansang Maka Bayan (Bayan), *What is Bayan?*, http://www.bayan. ph/site/about/ (accessed 15 Oct. 2011).

64 O. C. Valdecanas, R. R. Tuazon, and D. R. Barcelona, *How social mobilization works: the Philippine experience*, (Quezon City, Philippines: University of the Philippines, College of Mass Communication, 1997).

65 People's International Observers Mission 2010, *Breaking News and Official Statements,* http://piom2010.wordpress.com/ (accessed 15 Oct. 2011).

66 The Philippine Reporter, "Canada to send 22 observers to RP's May 10 elections," Press Statement, 16 April 2010, http://www.philippinereporter. com/2010/04/16/canada-to-send-22-observers-to-rp%E2%80%99s-may-10-elections/ (accessed 15 Oct. 2011).

automated ballot system was riddled with malfunctioning machines, ballot tampering and fraud, and deemed a disastrous failure by the PIOM delegation due to the underlying violence, vote-buying and voter intimidation that took place. However, the People's Mission itself was successful in that no progressive par- tylist candidate was among those injured or killed, even though they did face intense campaigns of negative propaganda on behalf of the PNP and AFP. There was no official announcement of a general failure of elections and no martial law was called.[67] The showing of international solidarity to the struggle in the Phil- ippines by labour and human rights activists will hopefully be strong enough to one day stop the killing and persecution of activists and bring those accountable for human rights violations to justice.

The 2010 May presidential elections in the Philippines signi- fied the end of a nine-year fascist regime by the GMA government; however, within the first 100 days of his presidency, Noynoy Aquino has already failed to meet the challenge of ending human rights violations in the Philippines and serving the needs of marginal- ized groups and the urban poor.[68] It is clear that the violence and struggle endured by the Filipino people is far from over.

---

67   Aleli D. Ayroso, Bernadette Libres, and Annie dela Fuente, eds., *Fast, Fair, Fraud-free! Report of the People's International Observers' Mission on the 2010 First Automated Philippines National Election,* (Manila, Philippines: People's International Observers' Mission 2010 and Pagbabago, People's Movement for Change, 2010).

68   Amnesty International, "Briefing: Philippines: Human Rights Report Card for Aquino's First 100 Days," 2010, http://www.amnesty.org/en/ library/asset/ASA35/006/2010/en/55268fb1-f402-4a1a-9301-d08429398382/ asa350062010en.pdf (accessed 15 Oct. 2011).

THE SOUTH AFRICAN CONSTITUTION AS A SOURCE OF CONFLICT: MOVEMENT AND COUNTER MOVEMENT

Elizabeth Cobbett

The African National Congress came into government in 1994 inspired by a vision to improve the life of the majority. Yet local governments are finding it difficult to provide basic services as South Africa re-enters the global economy and gives the private sector a dominant role in development. In the absence of effective services such as water, electricity, and housing, violent protests have ensued. While the new South African constitution guarantees certain freedoms, the poor are becoming increasingly excluded and marginalized. South Africa provides a case study as to how the reduction of the role of the state and the increased role given to international investors leads to decentralization, privatization, financialization, and—ultimately—social unrest.

The African National Congress (ANC) came into power in 1994, inspired by a vision of improving the life of the majority. In its first general electoral manifesto, it declared that "for years, our economy ran for the benefit of the minority, with opportunities and facilities limited to a few. While all parties speak of improving the quality of life, only a government that represents the majority can be trusted to do this."[1] This promise was repeated

---

1   African National Congress, "1994 National Election Manifesto," http://www. anc.org.za/show.php?include=docs/manifesto/1994/manifesto.html, para. 22.

in subsequent electoral campaigns. Yet thousands descend on the streets every year in violent protest against the lack of basic service provision of water, electricity, toilets, and housing in poor communities.[2] "Water, electricity, unemployment: nothing has gotten better," commented Lifu Nlapo, a leader of the protests in a township 50 miles east of Johannesburg, in the *New York Times*; he added, "and when we are ignored, what else is there to do but take to the streets."[3]

In 2009, a parliamentary committee studied these violent protests and concluded that governance grievances were at the root of the problems.[4] In response, the Local Government Turnaround Strategy was adopted, a policy that aims to attack all gaps: "be they institutional weaknesses, service delivery deficiencies or lack of technical capabilities, within each municipality."[5] But this verdict of malgovernance did not resonate widely, even within the tri-partite alliance that constitutes government. For a tri-partite member, the Congress of South African Trade Unions (Cosatu), these waves of community service-delivery protests are related to economic structural problems and to the obvious fact that the patience of the poor is running thin. The roots of the crisis are in the privatisation of basic services and the enactment of conservative fiscal and monetary policies centred on appeasing the interests of financial markets.[6] For academics, malgovernance may be part of the problem, as it accompanies neoliberalism and downsizing, but responsibility of the protests must be placed in the refusal of central government to transfer adequate funding

2   Johan Burger, "The Reasons behind Service Delivery Protests in South Africa," 2009, http://www.polity.org.za/article/the-reasons-behind-service-delivery-protests-in-south-africa-2009-08-05.
3   Barry Bearak, "South Africa's Poor Renew a Tradition of Protest," *New York Times*, September 06, 2009, sec. Africa, para. 3.
4   Ad Hoc Committee on Coordinated Service Delivery, "Report on Coordinated Oversight on Service Delivery," Parliament of the Republic of South Africa, 2010, http://www.pmg.org.za/programmes/comreports.
5   BuaNews, "Government Turnaround Strategy (LGTAS) Kicks off," 2010, United Nations Development Program South Africa Website. http://www.undp.org.za/democratic-governance-news/270-government-turn-around-strategy-lgtas-kicks-off, para. 11.
6   Zwelinzima Vavi, "Speech to the National Congress of the South African Municipal Workers Union by COSATU General Secretary, Zwelinzima Vavi," South African Municipal Workers Union Website, http://www.samwu.org.za/index.php?option=com_content&task=view&id=535&Itemid=1, para. 9.

for services required by poor people.[7] The massive movement of local militant action is seen by other academics as a rebellion of the poor, resulting in local insurrections where residents take control of their townships.[8]

In this article, I make the surprising argument that these protests are occurring because of the constitution and *not* in spite of it. There is widespread belief that these protests and service delivery problems are occurring *despite* pledges to protect socio-economic rights embodied in the 1996 constitution.[9] I maintain, however, that the institutional arrangements made in favour of capital markets and at the expense of the poor are set out in the supreme law of the country. While human rights are lodged in the constitution, the law's commanding design is to favour the expansion of capital and respect human rights via the market and private enterprise. What is unfolding in South Africa speaks directly to the impasse set out by Karl Polanyi in *The Great Transformation*.[10]

Firstly, the South African government, the ANC, has left the welfare of society so clearly in the hands of the market and the private role of capital and, secondly, the revolt by the population to this rule of privatisation, capitalization and commodification of material life is visible and unambiguous. The 1996 constitution plays the foremost and determining role in disembedding post-apartheid society as it facilitates the creation of new sites for capital accumulation. It is enabling capital to move into spaces, financial opportunities, which were previously closed to it. This is the first movement of Polanyi's "double movement" and is explained in the first section of the paper through an examination of the constitution. The constitution is the framework on which subsequent laws, which reduce the role of the state and increase that of capital markets, are built. Capital pries

---

7　Bond Exchange of South Africa and Johannesburg Stock Exchange, "BESA and JSE Circular to Shareholders," 2010, Johannesburg Stock Exchange Website, http://www.jse.co.za/Documents-and-Presentations/BESA-Annual-reports.aspx, para. 4.

8　Peter Alexander, "Rebellion of the Poor: South Africa's Service Delivery Protests: A Preliminary Analysis," *Review of African Political Economy* 37, no. 123 (2010): 37.

9　War on Want, "Anti-privatisation in South Africa," 2010, http://www.waron-want.org/overseas-work/informal-economy/anti-privatisation-in-south-africa (emphasis mine).

10　Karl Polanyi, *The Great Transformation* (Boston: Beacon Press, 2001).

open areas of society, of material life, and transforms them into elements of the market economy. Critically, this is legally mandated by the state. I focus on the bond market and its role right where the poor live and are governed, the local government. The second, and counter movement, is apparent in the energy and revolt voiced by people as they try to live in a society where the market has been given precedence over their basic survival needs. The point being made, and highlighted in the conclusion, is that township protests will not go away because the underlying problem is constitutional and national rather than processual and local.

'Movement': The 1996 Constitution of South Africa

The South African state is proud of its 1996 constitution and advertises it as one of the most progressive and highly acclaimed internationally.[11] But the shocking revelation that South Africa is now a more unequal society than it was at the end of Apartheid, obviously in spite of the constitution, needs to be explained.[12] A new reading of the constitution, apart from its Bill of Rights, reveals a vision of society shaped by private and capital interests. The interests and wellbeing of South African society are, in actual fact, subjugated to the process of capital accumulation that has been underway in earnest for the last fifteen years. While South Africa has had a state that has promoted the interests of capital for well over a century, the transformation under way is shocking because it stands in the face of pledges of improvement for the masses that brought the ANC to power. The state has further disembedded the market from society. This condition calls to mind the process spelled out by Polanyi in *The Great Transformation* where the interests of society were subordinated to those of the self-regulating market (SRM).[13]

11   Republic of South Africa, "Constitution of the South African Republic," 1996, http://www.info.gov.za/documents/constitution/index.htm.
12   P. Craven, "COSATU Condemns World-Record Inequality," 2009, http://www.cosatu.org.za/show.php?include=docs/pr/2009/pr1001d.html&ID=2458&cat=COSATU%20Today.
13   Polanyi, *The Great Transformation*.

As a rule, economic life was historically absorbed, or embedded, and enmeshed in social relations and institutions.[14] The economy was part of human social relationships and was manifest in three historic forms: reciprocity, redistribution, and exchange. This association between the society and the economy underwent an historic transformation in nineteenth century Britain when agricultural societies were forced to adapt to the industrial economies and civilizations of the Industrial Revolution. Societies with economies became societies ordered by the market economy, the SRM. This market system was the outcome of state policy developed within the liberal ideology of free trade, a competitive labour market, and the gold standard.[15] The SRM is governed by market prices—nothing but market prices. The mechanism of price-setting by the market economy was applied to monitor the continual supply of labour, land and money for industrial production.[16] Land and labour, people and nature were transformed into factors of production that were regulated—commodified—through a market price determined by the mechanism of supply and demand.

This singular historical departure represented a complete reversal of affairs from where formerly the economic order had been a function of the social to a new set of relationships where society became subordinated to the market economy's requests. The separation of the social and political from the economic in the form of the SRM was sanctioned by the state even as the workings of these markets threatened to destroy society. For Polanyi, all this action was possible through continuous and centrally organised action of the state.[17] Markets absolutely require the legal sanction and framework offered by the state in order to operate. This is the relevant point for South Africa. The institutional change of importance was the adoption of the constitution that effectively legislates a reinforced role for capital markets in the development of the country.

Chapter One, the Founding Provisions, states that human dignity, the achievement of equality and the advancement of human rights and freedoms defines the Law.[18] Chapter Two specifies that the Bill

---

14 Ibid., 71.
15 Ibid., 141-145.
16 Ibid., 45-78.
17 Ibid., 146.
18 Republic of South Africa, "Constitution of the Republic of South Africa, Public Law 108," 1996, http://www.info.gov.za/documents/constitution/1996/a108-96.pdf.

of Rights is "the corner stone of the democracy." Section 27(1) claims that: Everyone has the right to have access to: (a) health care services, including reproductive health care; (b) sufficient food and water; and (c) social security, including, if they are unable to support themselves and their dependants, appropriate social assistance. Section 27(2) sets the responsibility with the state to take reasonable legislative and other measures to achieve the progressive realization of each of these rights. According to this vision it would seem that the interests of the poor have been defended. But a close study of other sections of the constitution reveals that the interests of capitalists underpin this rights-based vision of South African society. The first complication to meeting the Bill of Rights is the decentralization of the state.

Decentralization

Decentralization of the state apparatus brought an end to the ideology of centralized welfare state development and promoted the emergence of subnational spheres of government responsible for basic service delivery. The decentralized state goes against the wishes of social movements who focused on a strong central post-apartheid state as the means of undoing the political, social, and economic fragmentation wrought by apartheid.[19] A strong central state could be accountable to all its citizens wherever they found themselves and in whatever situation they found themselves. But the responsibility of responding to the basic needs of the community and of promoting the social and economic development of its citizens was, in effect, relocated to municipalities: Section 152(1) of the constitution.

Decentralization of government is presented as a tool of development, a lever that can expand and improve basic service delivery as lower spheres of government respond more directly to people's priorities.[20] The argument is that there is likely to be a closer match between the preferences of local populations and the services rendered if the decisions are made locally.[21] The downward shift in responsibility of services and local

---

19 Martin Wittenberg, "Decentralization in South Africa," in *Decentralization and Local Governance in Developing Countries*, ed. Pranab Bardhan and Dilip Mookherjee (Cambridge, MA: MIT Press, 2006), 329-355.
20 World Bank, *World Development Report 2004: Making Services Work for Poor People* (Washington: Oxford Univ. Press, 2003).
21 Wittenberg, "Decentralization in South Africa."

government budgets has the theoretical advantage of making consumers aware of costs and therefore more responsible in their utilization of services, thus increasing efficiency of human and material resources.[22]

Theoretically, this is not in and of itself problematic. Practically, however, it poses an enormous setback for the poor in contemporary South Africa. The core of the problem is that only 10% of the budgeted income needed by municipalities comes from the central state's *National Revenue Fund*.[23] In other words, the shift in responsibility for service delivery from central state to the local sphere has not been accompanied by the transfer of sufficient funds to achieve the desired goal of ironing out the deeply rooted inequalities inherited from the apartheid regime. Municipalities are faced with a situation where the demand for their services effectively outstrips their supply; this situation is particularly acute in the areas of housing, clean water, roads, and electricity.

Chapter 13, Section 229 specifies that a municipality may impose rates on property and surcharges on fees for services provided by or on behalf of the municipality.[24] Of the three different income sources available to municipalities—own-source revenues, national government grants and borrowing—it is the latter, debt capital raised through borrowing or bonds, that is gaining in importance as the other two sources fail to meet expanding budgetary needs. The problem is that decentralization with the cost of servicing the needs of community through own-source revenues is a policy void of sense when people do not have the money to pay for basic services. This is not surprising considering that half of the population, 25 million people, survive on 8% of national income.[25]

---

22   Mila Freire and John E. Petersen, *Subnational Capital Markets in Developing Countries: From Theory to Practice* (Washington and New York: World Bank and Oxford University Press, 2004).

23   Greg Ruiters, "Public Services: Transformation or Stasis" in *Beyond the Market: The Future of Public Services*, Daniel Chavez (ed.) (Amsterdam: Transnational Institute, 2006), 127-135.

24   David A. McDonald and Greg Ruiters offer an excellent overview on the process of privatisation of public services in South Africa. See McDonald and Ruiters, "Rethinking Privatization: Towards a Critical Theoretical Perspective" in *Public Services Yearbook 2005/06* (Amsterdam: TransNational Institute, 2006), 8-23.

25   Gordhan, Pravin, "Budget Speech 2010," in Republic of South Africa [online database], 3, http://www.treasury.gov.za/documents/national%20budget/2010/speech/speech2010.pdf.

But the constitution makes clear that "[a] municipality must strive, within its financial and administrative capacity, to achieve the objects set out in subsection (1)," Section 152(2). And strive they do. Research points out that most municipalities show signs of chronic fiscal stress due to a reduction in transfers from the national government and an inability or unwillingness to collect money from residents.[26] The second complication to meeting the Bill of Rights, therefore, is the lack of necessary funds by munici-palities. One way for municipalities to move out of this dilemma is through funds raised on the capital markets.

The Management of Public Services by Capitalists

A solution for this financial impasse is set out in Chapter 13, Section 230A of the constitution, which states that a municipality can raise loans for capital or current expenditure and bind itself and a future council to secure loans or investments. By pledging future revenue streams against long-term debt, municipalities are able to offer new security provisions for investors who take these pledges as guarantees underpinning their investments. Thus, as the central state disengages from its responsibility of ensuring adequate public services for all, it creates new spaces and opportunities for capitalists. Municipality capacity will be met through the large and liquid financial sector of the economy, eager to lend to national government and municipalities.[27] It is here, at the local level of gov-ernment, that opportunities have been opened up for new capital accumulation. Monetization of the municipal debt is put forward as the appropriate response to difficulties through the provision of private funds for infrastructure programmes and budgetary deficits. For the government, subnational municipal debts have the desired effect of deepening capital markets as they aggregate

26   SabinetLaw, "FFC Recommends Dedicated Courts to Deal with Municipal Debt," http://www.sabinetlaw.co.za/provincial-local-and-traditional-government/ articles/ffc-recommends-dedicated-courts-deal-municipal.

27   Matthew Glaser and Roland White, "South Africa," in *Subnational Capital Markets in Developing Countries: from Theory to Practice*, ed. Mila Freire and John E. Petersen (Washington: World Bank and Oxford University Press, 2004), 313-336.

investment capital from multiple sources within the country.[28] To all intents and purposes, the ANC has tied its rhetoric of socio-economic welfare to the organizational logic of private markets.

There are 284 municipalities in South Africa, each requiring funds from capital markets. In accordance with provisions made in Section 46 (3) of the *Local Government: Municipal Finance Management Act*, the two largest metropolitan cities of South Africa, Johannesburg and Cape Town, have both issued their own bonds on the capital markets.[29] As these bonds are listed on the Johannesburg Stock Exchange (JSE), creditworthiness becomes the overriding goal guiding municipal councils' actions. The head of investor relations at the City of Johannesburg put it this way: "As the City, we need to constantly satisfy our investors, meaning that throughout the year we need to make sure that we take care of them, the way they are taking care of us."[30] Conditions of reduced risk and good returns on investment are fundamental to building investor interest and confidence. These variables are interpreted by Moody's, Standard & Poor's, and Fitch—among the largest international credit rating agencies—as they rate municipal bonds. Rating agencies essentially give value to debt by making judgements about the risk and the opportunities involved in various investment opportunities. Moody's positive debt rating of the City of Cape Town "reflects the city's buoyant budgetary performance and its comfortable liquidity position."[31] But favourable ratings are difficult for most municipalities to obtain. Moody's notes that even for Cape Town there is risk of fiscal pressure as demands for service delivery swell.[32] This will lead to a significant increase in debt levels in the near term, creating cause for concern for investors as the city becomes less financially sound.

The logic of finance draws investment to municipalities that already have money and are considered to be less risky than poorer, smaller

---

28 Republic of South Africa, "Policy Framework for Municipal Borrowing and Financial Emergencies," 2000, 18. http://www.info.gov.za/view/Download FileAction?id=70340.

29 Republic of South Africa, "Local Government: Municipal Finance Management Act," 2003, http://www.info.gov.za/acts/2003/a56-03/a56-03a.pdf.

30 Mosilo Mothepu, "Doing a Good Job of Selling the City," 2006, City of Johannesburg Website, http://www.joburgnews.co.za/2006/jan/jan17_sellcity.stm.

31 Moody's Investor Services, "Credit Opinion: City of Cape Town, 18 Feb. 2010" in Moody's [online database], http://www.capetown.gov.za/en/Treasury/ Documents/City_of_Cape_Town_Credit%20Opinion_18-Feb-2010.pdf.

32 Ibid., 1.

municipalities. Rating and financing of municipal debts depends on
the local levels of performance—higher tax collection rates, privatisation of basic services such as water and electricity through cost
recovery—as well as the risks seen to be involved.[33] In 2008, Moody's
Investor Services launched its *Municipalities Services* and assigned
first-time ratings to 10 municipalities in South Africa.[34] If a municipality fulfills its constitutional mandate beyond its financial means, it
is rated down as it is seen as a financial risk. The paradox, therefore, is
that a municipality becomes a good investment destination when its
finances are "healthy," i.e., when it least needs the capital investment
to answer the pressing needs of the population considered to be a risk:

> The ratings assigned to the abovementioned [10] munici-
> palities acknowledge the sound institutional framework
> and legislation that governs the municipal sector in South
> Africa. However most of the challenges facing the munici-
> palities are common to all. Infrastructure backlogs exist
> in the townships and maintenance of existing assets is
> inadequate and increases the spending pressures.[35]

Moody's statement poignantly points to the political economic
problem: insufficient financial means for backlogs and growing
demands. For the government, this political problem will be met
through the financialization of municipal debts. This has vast
political implications as power is transferred to investors and the
state stands back and lets capital govern. The number of public
institutions under analysis is increasing.

But for former governor of the South African Reserve Bank, Tito
Mboweni, capital markets of adequate depth play an essential role in
development as funds are mobilized to finance longer-term government
projects.[36] Mboweni goes on to remark that "in 2005, a total net amount

33   Cost recovery refers to the practice of charging consumers the full, or nearly
      full, cost of service provision.
34   Financial Markets Directory, "Moody's Release on South African
      Municipalities," 2008, http://www.fmd.co.za/data/M00121/W01402.htm.
35   Ibid., para. 7.
36   T. T. Mboweni, "Deepening Capital Markets: The Case of South Africa," 1,
      South African Reserve Bank Website, http://www.reservebank.co.za/internet/
      Publication.nsf/LADV/590E9E23E07AC8B34225721F003B90DE/$File/IMF-
      capital+markets-7+nov06a.pdf.

of R23.8 billion was raised through the primary issuance of bonds on the Bond Exchange of South Africa (BESA), and R82.2 billion of share capital was raised by companies listed on the JSE. Combined, this equals almost 7% of the GDP."[37] The South African bond market was formalized in the form of the Bond Exchange of South Africa (BESA), established in 1996, the same year that the constitution was adopted. Figure 1 demonstrates that over 70% of the BESA's business is conducted through central and municipal government debt.

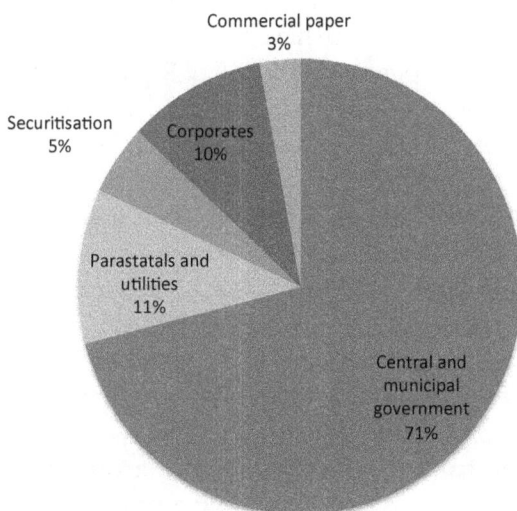

Source: Bond Exchange of South Africa. 2010. "Market performance." http://www.jse.co.za/Documents-and-Statistics/BESA-Annual-reports.aspx.

Figure 1. BESA's market performance, 2004[38]

If, as illustrated in Figure 1, 70% of bonds issued on BESA are public institutions, this represents a value of R16 billion loaned to central and municipal government by private investors. It is clear that expanding local government debt will only continue to offer increasing opportunities for investors.

The state-capital relationship, articulated through municipal debt as additional sites of capital accumulation, strips citizens of the rights

37 Ibid., 3.
38 Bond Exchange of South Africa, "Market Performance," 2010, http://www.jse.co.za/Documents-and-Statistics/BESA-Annual-reports.aspx.

pledged in the constitution because the means to their ends passes through private capital markets. In this way, the constitution does not undo apartheid's legacy of social and economic fragmentation. Rather, it facilitates the creation of new pockets of exclusion as municipalities act in response to the specific logic of capital investment: low risk and good returns. Service delivery protests are a sore in the side for the national government who argues that it cannot allow itself "to get drawn into a succession of (local) responses it has neither the capacity nor the fiscal resources to sustain."[39] The capacity is reduced because these sections of governance have been transferred to the market. The third complication to meeting the Bill of Rights, therefore, is the financialization of public debt through capital markets that employ the market logic of low risk, creditworthiness and good returns on profit.

'Counter Movement': The Rebellion of the Poor

Society would have been annihilated if it were not for the protective countermoves of the affected population to defend society.[40] Polanyi recognises that resistance by members of society to market logic occurs of its own accord, through the agency of the oppressed as they rise up against the insufferable impacts of the SRM. Society protects itself from the market forces in a variety of ways—revolt, protest, violent opposition—creating a movement of resistance to the initial movement of the extension and commodification of the SRM. From a Polanyian perspective this is fundamental. The disembedding of the economy is socially unsustainable.

Failure of the ANC government to pursue an agenda of redistribution and economic justice create the present crisis of delivery of basic services to all members of society. These protests have soared over the last years, according to Municipal IQ, which produces a Municipal Hotspots Monitor that records and analyzes service delivery protests.[41]

---

39   Republic of South Africa, "Policy Framework for Municipal Borrowing and Financial Emergencies."

40   Polanyi, *The Great Transformation*, 79.

41   Municipal IQ, "2010 A Record Year for Service Protests, but Tallying Up Only Slightly More Than 2009." Press release in Municipal IQ [online database]. http://www.municipaliq.co.za/index.php?site_page=press.php.

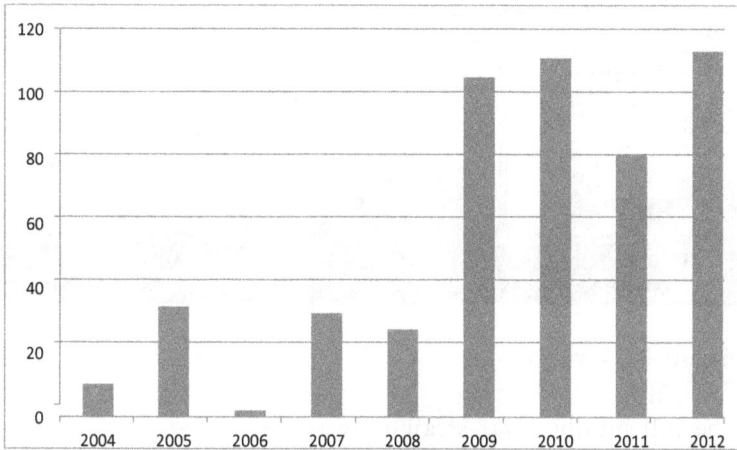

Source: Municipal IQ. 2012. "2012: a record high in service delivery protests (already)."
Available from 'Press Releases' at http://www.municipaliq.co.za/

Figure 2: Major service delivery protests, by year (2004 – 2010)

Another report uses a more expansive definition to include all instances of unrest where protestors took to the streets and cited grievances against general living conditions.[42] According to Jain, the country saw an average of 8.73 protests per month in 2007, 104 for the year, 9.83 protests per month in 2008, 117 for the year, and in 2009, the average number rose to 19.18 a month, 230 for the year. The first half of 2010 saw an average of 16.33 protests per month across the country.[43] This level of protests reflects that people are exasperated, desperate and see no issue for their grievances. The following cartoon refers to hotline number, 17737, launched in 2009 by President Jacob Zuma to allow citizens to get through to the President's office with questions or gripes about government service delivery.[44]

---

42 Hirsh Jain, *Community Protests in South Africa: Trends, Analysis and Explanations* (Cape Town: Community Law Centre, Local Government Working Paper Series No. 1, 2010). http://www.ldphs.org.za/publications/publica-tions-by-theme/local-government-in-south-africa/community-protests/Final%20 Report%20-%20Community%20Protests%20in%20South%20Africa.pdf.
43 Ibid., 3-4.
44 Wonkie, "Viva South Africa" in Wonkie.com [online database], 2010, http:// www.wonkie.com/2010/03/09/service-delivery-south-africa/.

Figure 3: "Viva South Africa"

The toll number was straight away inundated with calls; over 6,000 calls were made in the first three hours of operation, 10,500 calls by 2pm that same afternoon.[45] Zuma told the call centre operators: "You may receive calls from very angry people, who would have been provoked by your colleagues from other departments [housing, local government]."[46] The President went on to urge the staff "to work together to eradicate the stigma that makes people think anything from the government is bad or is of inferior quality."[47] The people are not "thinking" about the government; they are living it and are enraged. Lindela Figlan, a member of Abahlali baseMjondolo (Shack Dwellers) Movement, put it this way:

> (We) tell the government that we need this, we need what you told us, because they said in the constitution that the people shall share, the people shall have equal rights. But the only thing we notice now, (is that) we are not having equal rights. Some of the people are too poor, some of the people are too rich. We don't really need that division.[48]

---

45 Gill Gifford and Beauregard Tromp, "Hello, President Zuma Speaking…," in *Independent Online*, 2009, http://www.iol.co.za/news/politics/hello-president-zuma-speaking-1.458549.

46 South Africa Info, "17737: Your Hotline to the President," 2009, http://www.southafrica.info/services/government/preshotline-020909.htm

47 Ibid., para. 13.

48 Xin W. Ngiam, "Taking Poverty Seriously: What the Poor are Saying and Why It Matters," 2006, para. 16. Abahlali baseMjondolo [Shack Dwellers' Movement], http://abahlali.org/node/27.

Ngiam points out that "the contract has been broken—and this more than anything elevates the movement above mere 'spontaneous outbursts' of passion, and places it on the solid grounds of moral and political contention in the democratic state":

> We are suffering with poverty, water cut-offs [,] travel in packed trains and buses, furthermore, we live in shacks, and we were promised better life all by Mandela. Ask you yourself where is that better life now? History is telling us that if we want to be free from these social ills we must go to the streets and fight the states.[49]

The issue is not about "service delivery," a term that does much to obscure what is happening on the ground, but about the need for *public* services to answer basic living needs.[50] But this is precisely the point of confrontation; basic services have been privatised, commercialized and their value set by the market. In other words, they have been commodified. "The commodification of everything is still underway in South Africa" and South Africans are fighting for "decommodification" of goods and services needed for daily survival.[51] For South Africans, the brutal privatisation and financialization of public goods and services is a catalyst for their counter movement. This extension of the market economy based on the rapacious commodification of public resources and services is being sponsored and endorsed by the state.[52] Bond lists this fight as demands for anti-retroviral medicines to fight AIDS, for a minimum amount of free water and electricity for each individual every day, and for prohibitions on service disconnections and evictions.[53] The popular response is: "We cannot be expected to live like this. Under these conditions it is right to rebel. It is moral to rebel. It is necessary, as a matter of survival, to rebel."[54]

---

49 Ibid., para. 35.
50 Steven Friedman, "People are Demanding Public Service, not Service Delivery," *Business Day*, 2009, http://www.businessday.co.za/articles/Content.aspx?id=77115.
51 Patrick Bond, "Globalisation/Commodification or Deglobalisation/ Decommodification in Urban South Africa," *Policy Studies* 26, no. 3/4 (2005): 352.
52 Ibid., and David A. McDonald, *World City Syndrome* (New York: Routledge, 2008).
53 Bond, "Globalisation/Commodification or Deglobalisation/Decommodification," 435.
54 Unemployed People's Movement, Grahamstown, "The Rebellion of the Poor Comes to Grahamstown," in Pambazuka, http://www.pambazuka.org/en/category/socialmovements/70859, para. 4.

Conclusion

Polanyi notes that "the market has been the outcome of a conscious and often violent intervention on the part of government that imposed the market organization on society..."[55] How true this is of South Africa. The protestors are confronting a political economic structure where capital accumulation is privileged by the state at the expense of the poor. These sites of accumulation occur exactly where the rights and needs of the poor are supposed to be met—at the level of local governance and basic service delivery. Decentralization of the state apparatus, inadequate transfer of funds from National government, cost recovery through the commodification of the necessities of daily life, privatisation of public services and dwindling revenues are answered through financialization of municipal debt. The ANC government promotes social development through capital markets. The consequences are that financial investors, lending to these subnational government bodies, require the municipalities to be run like private corporations, low risk and high profit.

The constitution thus embodies an important tension where the rights of the poor, legislated in the Bill of Rights, are embedded in a legal framework that actually relies on the capital market to provide the funds for water, electricity, housing and infrastructure. Society has been embedded in the economy and its market. In other words, the common good has been subjected to the financial logic of investment and capital accumulation and this relationship between the state, society and capital finds its *raison d'être* in the supreme law of the country, the 1996 constitution. Protests are not about malgovernance, although there are almost certainly grounds for grievances relating to nepotism and corruption; rather they are about deliberate, structural governance choices that have handed over governance to private capital markets. In other words, the protests will not go away because the underlying problem is constitutional and national rather than processual and local.

---

55   Polanyi, *The Great Transformation*, 258.

PART III

ORGANIZED ANARCHISM IN THE ANTI-CAPITALIST STRUGGLE

Kyle Wark, David Brons and Greg Macdougall

Anarchist ideals and principles are widespread in anti-capitalist movements today. This chapter discusses the principles that set the basic groundwork for an alternative anarchist system as a struggle against all forms of domination, coercion, and control. The means of ending all oppressions must themselves be based on the principles of freedom, equality, and solidarity; yet, in order to restructure society in a non-authoritarian, non-hierarchical manner, a high level of formal organization is necessary. The experiences of past and current anarchist organizations have much to teach about how to self-organize, work with allies to address current issues and structural problems, and play an important role in anti-capitalist movements in the future.

Capitalism has proven itself to be completely inadequate to meet basic human needs. At the dawn of the twenty-first century, the world is deeply divided into have and have-nots. Extreme inequalities have been intensifying since the 1970s. While a minority of the world's population lives in opulence, the masses struggle in poverty.[1] The latest crisis that has plagued the global economy for the past few years has exacerbated these inequalities even further.

The solution to this crisis must be a revolutionary solution. The problem is not that the current manifestation of capitalism is defective or corrupt, but rather the entire system is flawed. The trouble is

---

1   Micheal Schmidt and Lucien van der Walt, *Black Flame: The Revolutionary Class Politics of Anarchism and Syndicalism* (Oakland: AK Press, 2009), 10-11.

not the administration of the system, but rather the system itself.[2] As such it is necessary to put an end to capitalism altogether. Reformism is destined to fail because reforms fail to address the exploitative basis of capitalism. Reformists

> [b]elieve in good faith that it is possible to eliminate the existing social evils by recognizing and respecting, in practice if not in theory, the basic political and economic institutions which are the cause of, as well as the prop that supports these evils.[3]

The point here is not to advocate for some type of ideological purity. Reforms can make huge differences in the day-to-day life of people. Reformism is a type of harm reduction, and while harm reduction undeniably saves lives, the root problems need to be addressed in a manner that goes beyond mere reforms.

However, while a revolutionary solution is necessary, it is far from inevitable. The current economic crisis is the worst the world has seen since the Great Depression. It is important to bear in mind that for much of the world the Great Depression did not lead to socialism or even social democracy, but rather to fascism in much of Western Europe and the consolidation of Stalinism in the Soviet Union.[4]

Although there is popular dissatisfaction with the current system, anarchist alternatives do not currently have popular support. The current crisis may open up opportunities to attack capitalism from the Left, but it also presents dangers for the rise of the most reactionary elements in capitalist society. If anti-capitalists fail to provide a viable and coherent solution to this current crisis of capitalism, the door will be left wide open for reactionary opportunists to exploit public anger and suffering. The growth and influence of the Tea Party Movement in the United States is evidence of how anti-capitalists have failed to present convincing solutions to the masses.

---

2   Alexander Berkman, *What is Anarchism?* (Oakland: AK Press, 2003), 73.
3   Errico Malatesta, "Majorities and Minorities and Other Essays" in *Malatesta Life and Ideas*, ed. Vern Richards (London: Freedom Press, 1965).
4   Northeastern Federation of Anarcho-Communists, "Nature of the Period: Backgrounds and Perspectives," 2010, http://libcom.org/library/nature-period-background-perspectives-nefac.

While careful critique and analysis of the current system remain essential, the more difficult task that anti-capitalists are faced with is developing an alternative to capitalism. As was pointed out during a recent talk hosted by the Workers Solidarity Movement in Ireland: "It's not enough to fight capitalism, you need to know what to replace it with, and you have to make that alternative the most popular one around and that would be the most important task for revolutionaries today."[5]

When anarchists set out to find alternatives, it is essential to have a clear idea of the principles that any possible alternative would be based upon. The three main principles that social anarchists wish to base any society on are liberty, equality, and solidarity.[6] Anarchists have a broader definition of liberty than liberals. Liberals use the word to mean lack of legal restraint while anarchists use the term to mean the capacity to actually do something (freedom to). For example, even though poor people are not legally restrained from eating good food, they still are not truly free to eat good food. Similarly, anarchists use the term equality to include real economic equality, not just the formal "equality before the law" of liberals. For this reason anarchists are often called "libertarian socialists." Anarchists see no conflict between liberty and equality; instead they are regarded as mutually reinforcing. Liberty without equality leads to those with more exploiting those with less. Similarly equality without liberty is a contradiction—it is the tyranny of a minority coercing the majority to be "equal." Solidarity in anarchist terms refers to acts of mutual aid rooted in the consciousness that one's freedom and equality are bound up with the freedom and equality of others. Mass solidarity opens the possibility for the creation of a new society.

These three principles set the basic groundwork for the basis of an alternative anarchist system. There is a lot of room to maneuver within the parameters of these principles, but it is essential that they serve as a guide for an alternative anarchist society. It is also important to recognize that these three principles must be taken together as a package: they cannot stand on their own. Each one of these principles is at best hollow and meaningless unless it is accompanied by the other two.

---

5   Workers Solidarity Movement, "Will we see a Revolution in our Time?," 2010, http://www.anarkismo.net/article/16500.
6   Peter Kropotkin, *The Conquest of Bread* (Oakland: AK Press, 2007), 156.

These three guiding principles help to define anarchism in slightly more concrete terms. At the beginning of *Anarcho-Syndicalism: Theory and Practice*, Rudolph Rocker defines anarchism as:

> [a] definite intellectual current of social thought, whose adherents advocate the abolition of economic monopolies and of all political and social coercive institutions within society. In place of the capitalist economic order, Anarchists would have a free association of all productive forces based upon cooperative labour, which would have for its sole purpose the satisfying of the necessary requirements of every member of society. In place of the present national states with their lifeless machinery of political and bureaucratic institutions, Anarchists desire a federation of free communities which shall be bound to one another by their common economic and social interests and arrange their affairs by mutual agreement and free contract.[7]

The key insight provided by this definition is the recognition that freedom must exist on economic, political and social levels. Just as the principles of liberty, equality, and solidarity cannot be separated from each other, the application of said principles must take place on all societal levels—political, economic, social, conceptual, etc. (levels that are not entirely "separate" from each other). The struggle against capitalism is indispensable but it is not the only struggle that needs to take place. Anarchists insist that emancipatory struggle is class-based but recognize that there is no place for reductionism:

> The broad anarchist tradition stresses class, but this should not be mistaken for a crude workerism [...] The stress on class also does not mean a narrow focus on economic issues. What characterizes the broad anarchist tradition is not economism but a concern with struggling against the many injustices of the present.[8]

---

7   Rudolph Rocker, *Anarcho-Syndicalism: Theory and Practice* (Oakland: AK Press, 2004), 1.
8   Schmidt and van der Walt, *Black Flame*, 7.

Coherent anarchism is one that opposes the state, capitalism, patriarchy, white supremacy, colonialism, heteronormativity, etc. while not privileging one struggle (for example, class) over another and realizing that all hierarchies are connected. In order to be consistent with anarchist principles, all forms of hierarchy must be opposed. A victory against one form of oppression is at best an incomplete victory. Hierarchies and oppressions cannot be dealt with implicitly or at a later date; they must be confronted directly the minute that they are recognized, and this organizing must be done prefiguratively: the means of ending all oppressions must themselves be based on the principles of freedom, equality, and solidarity.

The concept of intersectionality is useful here: it is counter-productive to rank the importance of various social struggles. There are no "primary" and "secondary" struggles.[9] Social struggles cannot easily be separated, nor should they be: they must be fought collectively. For example, the struggle against capitalism must by its very nature be a working class movement. However, the needs and priorities of all segments of the working class must be addressed and that includes women, people of colour, queers, the disabled, etc. Therefore, the working-class movement must also be a movement that fights other forms of domination and hierarchy in addition to opposing capitalism. A good example of how class struggle can integrate other struggles is the 1981 strike by the Canadian Union of Postal Workers in which they won maternity leave benefits.[10]

Anarchism provides a theoretical framework to seek out and oppose all forms of hierarchy and oppression. For example, during the Mexican Revolution the liberal revolutionaries, such as Madero held racist and paternalistic views towards the indigenous population. They viewed native peoples as an inferior and backwards "race" that ought to have no say in the operations of a "democratic" government. This racist view of the indigenous population was indistinguishable from the views held by those in the Porifirato dictatorship. On the other hand, anarchists inspired by Ricardo

---

9   Deric Shannon and J Rogue, "Refusing to Wait: Anarchism and Intersectionality," 2010, http://www.anarkismo.net/article/14923.

10   Martha Friendly, "Walking The Picket Line For New Mothers," June 2011, http://rabble. ca/blogs/bloggers/child-care-canada-now/2011/06/walking-picket-line-new-mothers.

Flores Magon fought alongside indigenous peoples for their rights and viewed indigenous civilizations as viable alternative models to the state capitalist system.[11]

This difference in attitude does not exist because Flores Magon and the other anarchists were personally more enlightened than their less radical counterparts, but rather because their ideologies were different. If an ideology allows for one form of hierarchy, it is much easier to accept a series of other oppressions. Although it cannot be claimed that anarchists always succeed at identifying and addressing all types of hierarchies—and although we must concede that oppressions might exist that have not yet been identified—nevertheless, anarchism is a struggle against all forms of domination, coercion and control. And while any form of racism, sexism, ableism, etc. could be assimilated into a capitalist or statist worldview, none of them could ever be assimilated into an anarchist worldview, provided that one consistently upholds anarchist principles.

One of the major debates within anarchism is over how (or even *whether*) anarchists "ought" to be organized. This debate between anarchists who advocate for formal organization (organizationalists) and those who prefer looser networks of association (anti-organizationalists) tends to be characterized by advocates of the latter tendency as a generational divide. David Graeber speaks of the "new anarchists" who are organized in loosely based "affinity" groups.[12] While Andrej characterizes the divide as one between

> [t]wo co-existing generations within anarchism: people whose political formation took place in the 60s and 70s (which is actually a reincarnation of the second and third generations), and younger people who are much more informed, among other elements, by indigenous, feminist, ecological and culture-criticism thinking. The former exists as various Anarchist Federations, the IWW (Industrial Workers of the World), IWA (International Workers Association), NEFAC (Northeastern Federation of Anarcho-Communists) and the like. The

11   Benjamín Maldonado Alvarado, *La Utopía Magonista* (Oaxaca: Colegio de Investigadores en Educación de Oaxaca S.C., 2004), 59-66.
12   David Graeber, "The New Anarchists," *New Left Review* 13 (2002).

latter's incarnation is most prominent in the networks
of the new social movement.[13]

Characterizing this debate as a generational one is a misrepresenta-
tion. Following Grubacic's formula, there are a significant number
of activists involved in anarchist organization whose political formation must have taken place decades before they were even born.
Also incorrect is the implication that organizationalists are class
reductionists that ignore indigenous, feminist, ecological, and cultural struggle.

The debate between organizationalists and anti-organizationalists is not at all new. It has been ongoing in the anarchist community
for at least a century. On the heels of the failure of anarchists to prevent the consolidation of the Bolshevik dictatorship following the
Russian Revolution, a group of exiled Russian and Ukranian anarchists called the Dielo Trouda (Workers' Cause) wrote of "this disease
of disorganization [that has] introduced itself into the organism of
the anarchist movement and has shaken it for dozens of years."[14]

It can be tempting for anarchists to reject most forms of organization. After all, the types of organizations that most people are
used to dealing with are hardly non-hierarchical groups that adhere
to anarchist principles. Mainstream political parties, many unions
and NGOs tend to have power placed at the top. It is understandable that anarchists would be skeptical of organization. However,
the problem with most organizations is *how* they are organized,
not *that* they are organized.

The enemy is not organization, but hierarchy. As Malatesta
writes, "[o]rganization, far from creating authority, is the only cure
for it and the only means whereby each one of us will get used to
taking an active and conscious part in the collective work and cease
being passive instruments in the hands of leaders."[15] As long as
organizations are based on anarchist principles, they are not only
effective, but essential tools in combating hierarchy and oppression.

---

13   Andrej Grubacic, "Towards Another Anarchism. WSF: Challenging
     Empires," 2003, http://www.choike.org/documentos/wsf_s107_grubacic.pdf.

14   Truda Dielo, "The Organizational Platform of the General Union of
     Anarchists (draft)," 1926, http://www.struggle.ws/pdfs/leaflets/platform/plat-
     formA4.pdf.

15   Malatesta, "Anarchy and Organization," 1897, http://www.spunk.org/texts/
     writers/malatest/sp001864.html.

Lack of formal organization can tend to create structures that are contrary to anarchist principles. Just because these structures are informal does not mean that they do not exist. Jo Freeman, writing about the difficulties facing the way the feminist movement was organized, demonstrates this point in her essay, "The Tyranny of Structurelessness."[16] Those activists who are best connected and most privileged tend to become part of an informal elite who wields significant power over others, often without even being conscious of it:

> As long as the women's liberation movement stays dedicated to a form of organization which stresses small, inactive discussion groups among friends, the worst problems of unstructuredness will not be felt. But this style of organization has its limits; it is politically inefficacious, exclusive and discriminatory against those women who are not or cannot be tied into the friendship networks. Those who do not fit into what already exists because of class, race, occupation, parental or marital status, or personality will inevitably be discouraged from trying to participate. Those who do not fit in will develop vested interests in maintaining things as they are.[17]

She also points out the political ineffectiveness of small, unstructured groups who are often able only to accomplish small-scale tasks:

> Purely educational work is no longer such an overwhelming need. The movement must go on to other tasks. It now needs to establish its priorities, articulate its goals and pursue its objectives in a co-ordinated way. To do this it must be organized locally, regionally and nationally.[18]

If these organizations do not exist, people will tend to turn to other organizations because "at least they are doing something." This was evident during the Russian Revolution when large numbers of anarchists joined the Bolsheviks, not for ideological reasons, but

---

16   Jo Freeman, "The Tyranny of Structurelessness," http://struggle.ws/pdfs/tyranny.pdf.
17   Ibid.
18   Ibid.

because the Bolsheviks were actually organized and accomplishing something. This process is unfortunately visible today, as masses of people angry with the system are turning toward right-wing movements in order to express that anger. Anarchists need to create coherent organizations that can attract mass popular support and help folks connect the dots.

As described by Tom Wetzel, social anarchists participate in two major types of organizations: the first are mass organizations of oppressed people dealing with specific social struggles; the second are specifically anarchist political organizations.[19]

When anarchists refer to "mass" organizations, they don't necessarily refer to organizations with large memberships. The key characteristic is that such organizations are mainly composed of poor and working class people engaged in direct struggle to improve their lives. Such organizations have an open membership. People join to support the aims as well as to win concrete improvements in their lives. Mass organizations require a certain level of tactical agreement but not necessarily deep theoretical agreement.

Social anarchists view mass social movements as the engine that drives social change. Self-managed, directly democratic social-movement organizations are understood by many anarchists as the potential nucleus of a post-capitalist social order. This is what the IWW preamble means when it refers to "building the new society in the shell of the old."

An excellent example of a mass organization that has a high level of anarchist involvement is the Ontario Coalition Against Poverty (OCAP). Clarke provides an overview of the twenty years that the organization has operated.[20] Formed in 1990, OCAP organizes poor people mainly in the city of Toronto. They have made extensive use of direct-action methods to win numerous small victories, such as preventing evictions. Among their larger victories is having embarrassed the city into converting two vacant buildings, which OCAP had occupied, into social housing. They also have managed to make use of a little known Special Diet provision in

---

19   Tom Wetzell, "Anarchism, Class Struggle and Political Organization," 2009, http://www.zcommunications.org/anarchism-class-struggle-and-political-organization-by-tom-wetzel.

20   John Clarke, "OCAP Marks its First Twenty Years," *The Bullet: Socialist Project E-Bulletin* 432 (2010), http://www.socialistproject.ca/bullet/432.php.

provincial legislation to get millions of dollars of extra money into the pockets of people living on social assistance.

Labour Unions are other examples of mass organizations. Anarchists are quite critical of the bureaucratic and undemocratic nature of many unions. Despite this, anarchists in unionized workplaces are very active in rank and file struggles. Anarchist labour activist Rachel Stafford describes a campaign in which rank-and-file members of her Canadian Union of Postal Workers local successfully resisted the compulsory overtime being demanded of workers by Canada Post.[21] The campaign utilized methods advocated by anarchists such as direct action by the rank and file instead of the more bureaucratic grievance process. This struggle illustrates that it is still possible to win victories at a time when many union leaders seem content to negotiate away the gains they made in the past.

Mass organizations of the type advocated by anarchists will need to play an important role in the context of the current economic crisis and the attempt by governments and corporations to roll back wages, pensions and social programs. Only by large numbers of people becoming engaged directly in struggle in a coordinated manner will it be possible to fight back against these attacks on the working class.

In addition to being involved in mass organizations, many anarchists are also active in specifically anarchist political organizations. Such political organizations are not an end in themselves. They have value in providing concrete support to social struggles and spreading anarchist ideas and methods. To do this, such organizations bring together people who are already engaged in social movement work such as the labour movement, indigenous solidarity, women's struggles, queer struggles, housing, anti-poverty struggles, etc. An anarchist political organization represents an opportunity to pool collective experience in order to develop short and long term strategy that will guide work across these struggles. And it also allows pooling of skills and resources in order to put this strategy in practice.

Political organizations are a necessary part of building a strong and effective anarchist movement. People will be attracted to anarchism not only because anarchist ideas make sense, but also because

---

21   Rachel Stafford, "Postal Worker Solidarity Defeats Compulsory Overtime," Recomposition Blog, 2 May 2011, http://recompositionblog.wordpress.com/2011/05/02/postal-worker-solidarity-defeats-compulsory-overtime/.

anarchist methods produce results. This can only be accomplished by being effective organizers, and helping to win concrete victories. And in turn, this can best be accomplished only by being strategic and working together over the long term.

The political organization needs to be a strong voice for anarchism. It must be able to provide a credible anarchist analysis of all the key issues facing people today. It must be able to offer concrete alternatives both short-term and long-term. And it must be able to get these ideas in the hands of ordinary people.

In order for a political organization to be coherent and to maintain anarchist principles, the Dielo Trouda suggested that it contain four basic elements: theoretical unity, tactical unity, collective responsibility, and federalism.[22] This is not a magic formula for how an organization *must* operate, but the Dielo Trouda suggested that these four elements are basic general guidelines for the operation of an effective anarchist organization.

Theoretical unity means that there should be general agreement on what the goals and principles of the organization are in order to avoid paralyzing infighting as much as possible. This means that the anarchist principles of liberty, equality and solidarity need to be agreed upon by all members. Related to theoretical unity is tactical unity. There should be general agreement over what methods the organization will adopt in order to reach its goals. The organization should not be working in contradictory directions, but rather in a common direction. There is a lot of room for disagreement on details, but the guiding principles and tactics should be agreed upon. An organization is generally formed around common principles and it makes sense to exclude individuals and ideas that are antithetical towards those goals. There is no contradiction between this and liberty. Individuals are obviously free to form their own groups or work in no groups at all if they so desire, while working with the organization in areas where interests and principles do converge.

There is a tendency towards individualism among some anarchists. While individual rights are essential, they cannot exist outside of a collective. Because of that, collective responsibility is necessary. Any revolution must be collective in nature and the

---

22 Dielo Truda, "The Organizational Platform of the General Union of Anarchists (draft)," 1926, http://www.struggle.ws/pdfs/leaflets/platform/platformA4.pdf.

same holds true for any revolutionary organization. This collective responsibility goes in both directions—individuals are responsible to the collective, but the collective is also responsible to individuals. This might best be summed up by the Three Musketeers' motto, "all for one and one for all."

While centralism places the power of the organization in the hands of a few in a top-down structure, federalism is organized from the bottom up, which should allow all individuals to share collective power. There can be a lot of flexibility in the specific details of how an organization operates, but federalism provides a structure for meaningful democratic decision-making. Any member in a position of added responsibility, such as a delegate, must be answerable to the group as a whole and never the other way around. These positions should also be temporary and recallable in order to prevent the formation of any centralized authoritarian structure.

Capitalism must be opposed wholesale. Reforms may be helpful in softening up some of its harsher aspects, but the exploitative nature of the system cannot be done away with through reform. Not all forms of oppression can be placed at the feet of capitalism and so therefore a project for true liberation must include the struggle to end all oppressions and hierarchies—and as such, a revolution against capitalism is a necessary but insufficient condition for liberation. Anarchists recognize the need to identify and oppose oppression wherever it may exist. Identifying as an anarchist is not important, but identifying, agreeing with and acting upon anarchist principles is essential. Any free society must be based on the principles of liberty, equality and solidarity.

In order to arrive at such a society, anarchists and those struggling for anarchist principles need to be organized. The structures of the organization need to reflect anarchist principles; they also need to be formal and clear, or else the door will be open for the creation of informal elites.

Anarchist political organizations have a long and often overlooked history. An important historical example is the Iberian Anarchist Federation (FAI) in Spain during the 1930s. The FAI brought together anarchist militants active in the National Worker's Confederation (CNT), an anarcho-syndicalist labour union. The FAI was formed to combat the influence of Marxist political parties and reformists within the CNT.[23] The CNT and FAI put anarchist ideas about self-management and direct democracy into practice during the Spanish Revolution and Civil War. Tragically, the Spanish anarchists and their allies were defeated by the fascists. However, anarchism remains a significant influence within the labour movements of many countries, including Spain.

An excellent contemporary example of an anarchist political organization is the Workers Solidarity Movement (WSM) in Ireland. The organization was formed in 1984 and initially was focused in Dublin. Until 2002 the group had about a dozen members. As outlined in a 2009 article in the WSM publication Red and Black Revolution, the organization's formal directly democratic structure and cohesive politics allowed it to grow rapidly during the resurgence of anarchism in the anti-globalization movement to its present membership of over 70 members.[24] While this is still a relatively small number, the organization's history illustrates the continuing viability of anarchist organizing models.

In addition to the WSM, there are many anarchist political organizations around the world, including Common Cause in Ontario, Canada, that are following in the traditions of mass organized anarchism developed during past periods of revolutionary struggle. Along with mass struggle organizations, these anarchist organizations provide the seeds of hope for the development of a society based on liberty, equality, and solidarity.

---

23   Vadim Damier, *Anarcho-Syndicalism in the 20th Century* (Edmonton: Black Cat Press, 2009).
24   Workers Solidarity Movement, "Practical Anarchist Organising–the WSM as a case study, Red and Black Revolution," 2009, http://www.wsm.ie/c/ practical-anarchist-organising-wsm-case-study.

ECOFEMINISM IN THE INDIAN HIMALAYAS: AN ALTERNATIVE TO TECHNOCRATIC AND MARKET SOLUTIONS

Anupam Pandey

> Our search for alternatives to capital need not be limited to the capitalist vision of modernity, but can rather be rooted in traditional knowledges. This chapter draws upon research into concrete practices adopted by the women of the Garhwal region of the Himalayas that challenge market fundamentalism and the putative supremacy of technocratic solutions to social problems. Ecofeminism is crucial to these practices, which highlight the role of women's indigenous knowledges in constructing alternatives.

This article highlights the critical role of ecofeminism in keeping the "Third World" alive through subsistence practices at a time when it has been failed by the technocracy (in terms of provision of even basic infrastructure and social security or welfare) and deeply exploited by the market as a result of the increasingly penetrating forces of global capital. The last two decades, globally, are characterized by two distinct yet intertwined trends, i.e. the rise of the technocracy and the free-market economy. The most commonly used definition of a technocracy is the increasing role of technicians, engineers and so-called experts in running the government. While most governments in the North embraced technocracy led market reforms, the same trajectory has been followed in the South as is visible in various parts such as Latin America, Eastern Europe, South-East Asia, South Asia, China, etc. There exists a natural affinity between technocracy and capitalism for the simple reason that both have unbounded confidence in increasing productivity through greater efficiency and scientific and rational means.[1] What this translates into, essentially, is the rolling back of the welfare state and cutting down of subsidies while championing the cause of the neoliberal economic reforms. In more ways than one, it becomes obvious that the technocracy and market are antithetical to democracy in general, and discriminate against class, race and women, in particular.[2] This democratic deficit is as much a product of the very effects that it helps to create, namely, the expert/non-expert divide, a more non-representative government and a more inegalitarian world in terms of class.[3] In our specific context, it becomes clear that poor women of the South are the worst affected by the technocracy-market nexus because as the bottom-most rung of society, they have clearly been left out of, or rather, penalized by the economic reforms. India is a classic example of the technocracy and market supporting and promoting each other which is ever more manifest since the government of India opted for market "reforms" and Structural Adjustment Programs, two decades ago. Under such circumstances, poor women's needs and interests are hardly represented by the technocrats or the market, and their own indigenous and historical knowledges have been systematically marginalized as "unscientific" and "irrational." This technocratic approach uses a reductionist variety of science that has caused systematic epistemic violence by categorizing women as "non-knowers."[4] Thus, while they have actually been adversely impacted by technocratic and market solutions, they have also been forced to abdicate their traditional methods and practices regarding farming, forestry and water conservation, which has jeopardized their own survival and that of their environment and way of life.

In this chapter, I draw upon my field research to show how women have strived to reverse this trend and provide certain concrete examples of eco-friendly alternatives to technocratic as well as market solutions adopted by the women of the Garhwal region in the Himalayas of India. These women agents are impoverished, largely illiterate, subsistence farmers, in charge of female-headed households. Here, I highlight the role of women's indigenous knowledges

---

1   Miguel Angel Centeno, "The New Leviathan: The Dynamics and Limits of Technocracy," *Theory and Society* 22 (1993): 307-325.
2   Beverly H. Burris, "Technocracy and Gender in the Workplace," *Social Problems* 36, no. 2 (1989): 165-180.
3   See Burris, "Technocracy and Gender in the Workplace"; Centeno, "The New Leviathan"; and Jürgen Habermas, *Toward A Rational Society* (Boston: Beacon Press, 1970).
4   Vandana Shiva, *Staying Alive* (New Delhi: Zed Books, 1988).

and eco-friendly practices, based on a symbiotic relationship with nature, that ensure the survival of these women agents and their families. In the face of most adverse circumstances, an ecofeminist ideology and life-style have proven to be the only means to combat the extreme hunger, grueling poverty, ecological degradation and threat to biodiversity, all of which are exacerbated by the growing impact of capitalist forces which are manifest in the government's introduction of High Yielding Varieties (HYV) of seeds in keeping with the Green Revolution in the 1970s and the introduction of agri-business MNCs after the introduction of SAP in 1991. While these knowledges were always a part of the traditional Garhwali way of life, they were increasingly being lost with the invasion of capitalist forces and high-end, alien technology being imposed on the people. However, they have now been given a new lease of life in order to combat the very same capitalist forces that signaled their demise and serve to make technology much more relevant and appropriate to the given context.

This paper begins by elucidating just what is ecofeminism and what it means in the context of the Third World. The second part builds a brief history of the traditional economy of the region which provides a backdrop to the ecofeminism prevalent in the region, and the final part is devoted to citing certain concrete ecofeminist interventions that demonstrate the fundamental thesis that it is possible to imagine and implement alternatives to the existing capitalist and technocratic order and resist it.

Ecofeminism in the "Third World"

Ecofeminism contends that andro-centric ideologies are responsible for environmental degradation as well as the oppression of women and that, under specific circumstances, it is possible to posit an alliance between nature and women. Ecofeminists believe that there exists a symbiotic and mutually nurturing relationship between nature and women that is non-exploitative, non-hierarchical and harmonious. It contends that women's relationship with nature is shaped by the gendered division of labor and regards the given material circumstances of women agents and their labor as the crucial factors in determining their emotional, physical and practical world and worldview. Thus, poor, most-often illiterate, subsistence farming peasants are often

practicing ecofeminists in their orientation as well as way of life due
to their specific material circumstances of grinding poverty, consequent dependence on nature and above all, the fact that a very large
number of them are responsible for their female-headed households.
Under such conditions, a materialist ecofeminist existence is the key to
ensuring survival for themselves and their dependents.[5]

History and Background

This research was conducted in the Central Himalayan region of
Tehri Garhwal where certain villages were selected for observation
and study. One of the key factors for choosing Tehri Garhwal was the
simple fact that it is the land of "*Chipko.*"[6] The state of Uttaranchal,
especially Garhwal is characterized by an agricultural economy where
subsistence agriculture employs more than 80% of its population and
women are the subsistence farmers.[7] Subsistence farming and associated activities to supplement the family income are a matter of material
necessity and survival. Women's inherited indigenous knowledges
with respect to the flora and fauna of the region, passed down over

---

5   For details on Materialist ecofeminism, see Mary Mellor, "Myths and Realities:
     A Reply to Cecile Jackson," *New Left Review* 217 (1996): 132-137; Mellor,
     Feminism and Ecology (New York: NYU Press, 1997); Val Plumwood, *Feminism
     and the Mastery of Nature* (London: Routledge, 1993); Plumwood, "Integrating
     Ethical Frameworks for Animals, Humans and Nature: A Critical Feminist Eco-
     Socialist Analysis," *Ethics and the Environment* 5, no. 2 (2000): 285-322; Ariel
     Salleh, *Ecofeminism As Politics: Nature, Marx and the Postmodern* (London:
     Zed Books, 1997); Karen Warren, "A Philosophical Perspective on Ecofeminist
     Spiritualities" in *Ecofeminism and the Sacred*, ed. C.J. Adams (Bloomington:
     Indiana U. Press, 1993): 119-132; Warren, *Ecological Feminism* (London:
     Routledge, 1994); Anupam Pandey, "Greening Garhwal Through Stakeholder
     Engagement: The Critical Role of Ecofeminism, Community and the State in
     Sustainable Development," *Sustainable Development* 18, no. 1 (2010): 12-19.
6   The 'Chipko' movement is regarded as the icon of ecofeminist movements
     all over the world. See Ramachandra Guha, *The Unquiet Woods: Ecological
     Change and Peasant Resistance in the Garhwal Himalayas* (Delhi: OUP,
     1991). In 1972, stiff resistance was put up by the illiterate, peasant women
     of Garhwal against axe-wielding contractors who wanted to cut down trees
     in the forests for the sake of profit. The women adopted a Gandhian form
     of protest and clung to the trees, challenging the axe-wielders to chop them
     down along with the trees if they dared. This led to the government having
     to ban tree felling beyond an altitude of 10,000 meters.
7   R.K. Maikhuri, U. Rana, R.L. Semwal and K.S. Rao, "Agriculture
     in Uttarakhand: Issues and Management Prospects for Economic
     Development," in *Uttarakhand: Statehood and Dimensions of Development*,
     ed. M.C Sati and S.P Sati (New Delhi: Indus Publications, 2000), 151-172.

centuries through generations, have proven indispensable to the survival of the community and are now being used to resist the intrusion and exploitation of capitalist forces that are increasingly eroding the traditional self-sufficiency of these societies. In this article, I cite four key examples of ecofeminist interventions to show the courage and impact of turning our backs on an increasingly powerful capitalist economy as well as super-imposed technocratic solutions.

The Traditional System of Mountain Farming in Garhwal

The traditional system of mountain farming in Garhwal is "closed," self-sufficient and self-reliant. It comprises forests, croplands, livestock and households as the four components in organic linkages with each other.[8] The traditional Garhwali cropping system comprises four elements which include a kitchen garden, where seasonal vegetables and some fruits are grown for home consumption, irrigated land cropping system where rice and wheat are the main crops, unirrigated cropping system dominated by millets and pulses and summer cropping system where pseudo-cereals, such as amaranthus and buckwheat or beans such as kidney beans are grown.[9] However, such a multi-cropping pattern that is the basis of nutritional security and soil fertility is now rapidly being phased out by a growing culture of mono-crop plantation for the market. Today, the farmers of these hills are heavily dependent on grains and aid from the plains, to the extent that withdrawal of this support could lead to a famine situation.[10]

---

8   Vir Singh and M.L. Sharma (ed.), *Mountain Ecosystems: A Scenario Of Unsustainability* (New Delhi: Indus Publishing Company, 1998), 33.

9   The Himalayas and Garhwal, in particular, are home to an incredible biodiversity and genetic pool. The total number of food-providing plants in Henwal valley of Garhwal is as large as 127. (See Vir Singh, "Traditional Biodiversity Management Strategies in the Mountains: Farmers' Experimentation in Garhwal Himalaya," in *Mountain Ecosystems*, 36-41.) This includes wild fruits, buds, flowers, seeds, spices, condiments, pulses, lentils, oilseeds, grains, etc. Singh quotes yet another study to show 177 food providing species within the Garhwal region. Genetic diversity in this area knows no bounds as is demonstrated by the fact that a single village in the Henwal valley of Tehri Garhwal cultivates as many as 126 varieties of rice, all of them being indigenous.

10 Vijay Jardari and Ashish Kothari, *Conserving Biodiversity: The Case of Tehri Garhwal and the Implications for National Policy* (Ottawa: International Development Research Centre, 1997), http://www.idrc.ca/books/focus/833/jardhari.html.

The introduction of HYV seeds by the Government of India a few decades ago due to the emphasis on the Green Revolution meant the end of a self-sufficient traditional system of agriculture. Earlier, the farmer spent nothing on seeds or fertilizers, but the introduction of the HYV seeds has meant that the cropping pattern has changed to monoculture and cash crops. This has cultivated a dependence on the market for seeds that need high quantities of fertilizers. The introduction of SAP in 1991 has meant the entry of agri-business MNCs such as Cargill, Monsanto, Ciba-Giegy and McGain, which has further increased the vulnerability of the small farmer by gaining control over India's seed sector.[11] It also means further commercialization of agriculture because it would mean exporting agricultural products and contesting MNCs for IPRs. Not only does this mean that the farmer loses her rights over the knowledge base and germplasm that she has acquired over generations but also that she has no incentive to make any further innovations to the existing base because she has lost ownership rights.

Return to Roots—Organic Farming

Under the leadership of some social workers and activists, such as Vijay Jardhari and Vandana Shiva, the women of Garhwal have resorted to organic farming in order to rejuvenate an ancient practice of farming which is increasingly being lost to younger generations due to the break-down of the traditional system of a closed and self-sufficient economy in the mountains. With the support of an NGO, called *Mahila Samakhya* (meaning Women's Congregation), 50 villages in Tehri Garhwal took up organic farming in order to reverse the trend of using ever-increasing volumes of fertilizers in their farming methods since it was proving to be unaffordable.[12] The women farmers of these 50 villages have resorted

11   Ashish Kothari, *Conserving India's Agro-biodiversity: Prospects and Policy Implications* (London: International Institute of Environment and Development, 1997).

12   This project is called SAWERA (Sustainable Agriculture and Women's Empowerment through Rural Approach) and is supported by UNDP, which in turn relies on *Mahila Samakhya* for facilitating the project at the grassroots level. The word SAWERA itself means "dawn" in Hindi. The main aims of this project, which started in 2000, are to: provide food security and self-sufficiency; protect biodiversity; find alternative and better means of food grain production and distribution; and help the woman farmer find her identity as a farmer and the "main worker" in the field. Unpublished Mahila Samakhya Document: "Organic Farming" (Tehri Garhwal: Mahila Samakhya Office, n.d.-typewritten) and unpublished Mahila Samakhya Document: "SAWERA, Sustainable Agriculture and Women's Empowerment Through Rural Approach" (Tehri Garhwal: Mahila Samakhya Office, n.d.-typewritten).

to preparing special organic manure that has insecticide and pesticide properties. Since the introduction of organic farming, the women report a highly increased fertility in soil and better produce, as well as the use of far less manure and greater moisture retention in the field. They are pleased that waste matter is being disposed off in a highly constructive and productive manner.[13]

Conservation of Biodiversity

Simultaneously, the women have been involved in a "Save The Seeds" campaign where they are trying to cut down their reliance on the market for seeds and instead want to reuse their own seeds, which they save from each year's produce.

The traditional method of farming in the Garhwal region has highly evolved techniques of maintenance of soil fertility and biodiversity through special fallowing practices and crop rotations, pest and weed management, genetic resource management, etc. For instance, the practice of *barahnaja*, which literally means "twelve foodgrains," involves cropping 12 grains together in each plot of land. This helps to maintain soil nutrition, water levels and alkalinity and such a multi-cropping pattern means food and nutritional security amongst the Garhwalis. It also meant the conservation and growth of biodiversity. The farmers used to exchange seeds with each other and never relied on the market. All of these practices are now being revived in order to get over the dependence on the market.

Thus, a campaign was launched in order to recover the lost biodiversity of the region. At the time the *Beej Bachao* or "Save the Seeds" campaign began, the Hemvalghati region of Tehri Garhwal had only two to three indigenous rice varieties left in cultivation, and most of the *barahnaja* fields had been converted to new soybean. The "Save the Seeds" workers traveled extensively through Tehri Garhwal and Uttarkashi districts, and found several remote areas where agronomy had not replaced traditional farming. Here, indigenous crop diversity survived. The workers collected these crops and began growing them on an experimental basis in the Hemvalghati region. Today, some 126 varieties of rice, 8 of wheat, 40 of finger millet, 6 of barnyard millet,

---

13   Mahila Samakhya Document: "Organic Farming" and Mahila Samakhya Document: "SAWERA."

110 of kidney beans, 7 of horsegram, 8 of traditional soybean, and 10 of
French beans, are being grown. No chemical inputs are being provided.
The characteristics of each—growth, resistance, special properties, and
so on—are being carefully observed. Varieties with desirable properties,
like high productivity and resistance, are being propagated amongst
other farmers. Seeds are given to these farmers in return for an equivalent amount of their seeds. Practices like *barahnaja* are being revived
and encouraged in place of the new cash crop of soybean.[14]

Maiti and Forest Conservation

The forests of the Himalayas have been subject to intense exploitation and hence denudation, due to the profit generated by the
natural bounty of timber, which has been ruthlessly pursued by
what is commonly referred to as the "bureaucrat-contractor-
politician nexus" in India. Between the years of 1972 and 1982,
exploitation of the forests of the province of Uttarakhand (where
Garhwal is situated) reached its peak when 8.56% of the forest
area was reduced.[15] However, since then, there seems to have been
somewhat of a turnaround in the situation. The forests are being
rejuvenated through revival of the traditional eco-forestry practices and ecofeminist activism taken on by Garhwali women. One
such key intervention by the women is a movement of tree plantation and forest conservation called "Maiti."

Maiti is a recent innovation in an ancient tradition of tree plantation by women in the state of Uttaranchal and particularly in the
region of Garhwal. It has become a movement spanning 5000-6000
villages in the province itself and is now spreading across many other
provinces within India.[16] The word "Maiti" is derived from the word
"mait" which means 'mother's home' in Garhwali. This is in reference to the fact that women regard the mountains as their mother's
home—a place of refuge from the harshness of their lives in the joint
family patriarchal set-up and a source of fodder and fuel.

14   Kothari, *Conserving India's Agro-biodiversity.*
15   G.S. Mehta, *Development of Uttarakhand* (New Delhi: APH Publishing
     Corporation, 1999), 48.
16   Anupam Pandey, unpublished interview with Kalyan Singh Rawat,
     Originator of *Maiti* Movement, Dehradun, Interviewee's residence, June
     11th, 2004—tape recording.

Essentially, Maiti is, in its present form, a movement where young unmarried girls of each village have taken over the responsibility of planting trees that provide shade, fruit, fodder and fuel for the village and after their marriage, it is the responsibility of the parents and the entire village to nurture the tree and regard it as not only a memory of their daughter, but look after it as their daughter herself. What this has meant in real terms is massive afforestation in Garhwal because if every year, even five girls of each village are married, it ensures the plantation and protection of five trees. Maiti is regarded as a continuation of a tradition of women-agents planting trees which is an integral part of Garhwali folklore and Hindu mythology.

Maiti is more than a movement to plant trees; it is a tribute to relationships—relationships between humans, i.e., the bond between mother and daughter. Simultaneously, it is a recognition of the profound and unique bond between women and nature. The ability to be able to see a beloved daughter in a tree is symbolic of the interconnectedness between humans and nature. The critical point being made here is that relationships need not be contractual and exploitative, which is what capitalism has reduced them to. It is not necessary to view nature as a "resource" that finds its value only in terms of its "use" to capitalism and its ability to generate profits. A Garhwali woman's identity cannot be separated from her land and nature. It is a testament to the fact that the "material" and the "spiritual/ ideational" are two sides of the same coin and need not be seen as polar opposites as is the case with capitalism.

Rebuilding and Conserving Traditional Water Sources

There is now an increasing attempt to resuscitate traditional methods of water conservation that were popular with the mountain people over centuries—simple technologies that had withstood the test of time but now been forgotten due to an increasing reliance on the government's promise to deliver water through pipelines. However, such dependence on the government's developmental efforts and technocracy has been met with disappointment, because the state, as in most developing countries, is plagued by corruption and red tape, unable to deliver even the most fundamental of necessities. Therefore, civil society has no recourse but to increasingly rely on its own self and organize its own means, in order to ensure its survival. It is in this context that Garhwali women's attempts to rejuvenate their traditional water sources have to be understood. With the help of NGOs and activists such forgotten technologies and indigenous knowledges have been revived by the women folk and new and old sources of water are being created and conserved.

A committee for the discovery, cleaning and operationalization of the sources of water emanating from the River Bhagirathi (a tributary of the river Ganges) and rainwater harvesting was created through a workshop that involved 50 villages. The committee has as its leaders two women who help in coordinating water conservation related activities across the network of villages. In many villages, such as Mishrangaon, Semalth and Sunkhet women have revived the dysfunctional water bodies called *Chahals* (ponds) and created new ones. The *Mahila Sangh* (Women's Association) has been striving to involve the men and the youth of the community in this process and to try to increase this awareness of and responsibility towards the environment.[17]

Conclusion

That technology propels capitalism and vice-versa was theorized rather clearly by Marx, and its stark manifestation is visible in the nexus that exists between technocratic states and capitalism. However, the point I have attempted to make through these examples is the fact that technology need not be monopolized by the state or capital. There are ancient and indigenous knowledges and technologies that need to be revived in order to generate solutions that curtail our reliance on the state and capitalism/neoliberal order (which is offered as the panacea to all evils). In other words, traditional/ historical/ pre-capitalist knowledges can be perfectly scientific and are capable of being deployed in the present context as alternatives. The case studies I have used are localized in implementation but global in practical context, as well as philosophically relevant, evident because they are an immediate response to the SAP and a globalized economy and the entry of MNCs in India. The need to look for alternatives to the technocratic and capitalist

17   Mahila Samakhya Document: "Organic Farming" and Mahila Samakhya Document: "SAWERA."

framework where the trinity of state, science and capitalism has come together in the form of globalization (economic and cultural) is a universal one because the latter has largely translated into the globalization of greed, poverty and exploitation for most of the world. Under such circumstances, I have espoused the cause of ecofeminism in the "Third World" to resist such injustice.

ONTARIO'S SPECIAL DIET CUTBACK—AUSTERITY AND RESISTANCE

John Clarke

The Ontario Coalition Against Poverty (OCAP) has spent nearly two decades mobilizing communities under attack to resist the ongoing intensification of poverty in Ontario. This chapter focuses on the implications of the unfolding crisis for poor communities, as poor people are made to foot the bill for the costs of stabilizing capitalism and bailing out its key institutions. For people on social assistance in Ontario, this has been seen most sharply in the Liberal government's attack on Special Diet benefits. Understanding OCAP's ongoing fight to restore these benefits helps to lay the foundations for effective methods of building a common front of resistance in ways that offer the prospect of winning.

In the summer of 2010, the Government of Canada established an armed camp in the City of Toronto for a meeting of the G20. From behind a billion dollar veil of massive security, and with the Harper government on the right wing of the gathering, they drew up plans for an international drive to impose massive austerity measures on poor and working people throughout the world. Community opposition to this vile gathering was confronted by a security operation that was unprecedented in its scale and brutality. The largest mass arrests in the history of Canada took place, civil liberties were effectively suspended for thousands and those deemed to have played any organizing role in the challenge to the G20 have faced serious criminal charges along with months of pre trial detention or massively restrictive bail conditions.

The background to Toronto's dress rehearsal for a police state is not hard to discern. After some three decades of neoliberal attacks on public services and living standards, a crisis of the capitalist system broke in 2008 and, without pausing to blush, the same governments that had preached fiscal restraint suddenly found countless billions of dollars to bail out financial institutions and prop up failing corporations. Now, their clear intention is to impose the bill for the cost of restoring a shaky stability on us. As events in Greece, France and a range of other countries show, the decade ahead will be marked by ruthless austerity initiatives, on the one hand, and by social mobilization and resistance on the other.

Poor people in Ontario who live on social assistance are already dealing with one of the early manifestations of this austerity agenda. It takes the form of the McGuinty Government's attack on a program known as the Special Diet. Before looking at this, it is necessary to realize the appalling reduction in living standards for people on assistance that has taken place since the mid 1990s. In 1995, the Harris Government slashed welfare rates by 21.6%. The Tories gave no increases whatever in the years that followed this cut and those provided by the Liberals since they took power in 2003 have not even kept up with inflation. As a result, people on social assistance in this Province have incomes that have lost a huge amount of spending power. A single person on Ontario Works would need his or her $585 a month income increased by 54%, to $904, in order to return to the situation that existed in 1994.[1] No one could credibly deny that the income provided by social assistance is far short of what would be needed for recipients to maintain their housing and eat an adequate and nutritious diet.

The Ontario Coalition Against Poverty (OCAP) is a poor people's organization that has spent nearly two decades mobilizing communities under attack to resist the ongoing intensification of poverty that has been central to the neoliberal agenda. Faced with the McGuinty Liberals' clear intention to perpetuate and deepen the impact of the Mike Harris welfare cuts, OCAP was determined to create an effective resistance to this process. In 2005, we began to seek ways to win full entitlement. We looked at the various benefits that exist within the

---

1   John Stapleton, "The Recession's Repeat Performance," *The Mark,* 2010, http://www.themarknews.com/articles/2574-the-recession-s-repeat-performance.

system but that are frequently withheld from those who need them. The one that immediately struck us as having the greatest possibilities was the Special Diet. This was a little known benefit that would provide people on assistance up to $250 more a month if a medical provider filled in and signed an application form. We asked ourselves what would happen if we promoted knowledge of this benefit widely and found sympathetic medical providers to help people obtain it. Obviously, the system would respond by denying applications on a huge scale, but we had a lot of experience in using collective action to force welfare and disability offices to respect the rights of poor people. If we applied that experience in this situation, we could overcome attempts to hold back Special Diet income.

It should be acknowledged that the decision to make a concerted effort to access the Special Diet, while it may have been the best option open to us, was also a reflection of our relative weakness. In truth, if the political left were more powerful and better orientated, we would have been in a position to press for united working class action on sub poverty social assistance rates. A powerful joint campaign by the Labour Movement and low income communities to raise the rates would have been possible rather than a limited effort to increase access to a particular benefit. However, our long term perspective is still very much to work for a common front with employed workers. Indeed, as we demanded access to the Special Diet, we continued to put forward the proposition that this campaign should not be necessary. Decent and adequate income was the real issue and the Government should raise social assistance rates to at least the level they stood at before the Harris cutbacks.

We began to organize hunger clinics with the support of progressive medical providers. In 2005, at least 8,000 people came through our clinics in Toronto and allies in other cities organized to make the Special Diet available. The impact was enormous. Knowledge of the benefit spread rapidly and access to it was obtained on a very large scale. Moreover, from the standpoint of building resistance in poor communities, the struggle for the dietary allowance proved to be of enormous importance. Precisely because people had to fight for the Special Diet, it became a rallying point. In Toronto, many communities played a part in this struggle, but always it was women from the Somali Community at the forefront. They made up a large part and, often, the great majority of those who marched into welfare offices, invaded City Hall and occupied the Minister of Community and Social Services' office.

This leading role by the Somali Community can be partly explained by subjective and chance factors. OCAP simply happened to have developed working relationships with several key Somali activists. However, there were perhaps a few factors at work that made the Somali Community relatively receptive to participation in the Special Diet Campaign. Firstly, the experiences people had had in their home country were significant. Somalia has been pushed in the direction of social and political breakdown. Banding together to survive in conditions of social dislocation was within the life experience of many in the Community. Once living in Toronto, moreover, Somalis have been subjected to extreme and exceptional forms of racism and abandonment. Poverty rates among Somalis are high, and the Community faces discrimination based on race and religion, and by virtue of there being a large proportion of its families headed by single mothers. Perhaps most significantly of all, precisely because the layers of privilege are so thin in the Somali population, the network of gatekeeper social agencies is quite weak and mechanisms to control and channel dissatisfaction are lacking. For these reasons, it can be said that Somali people in Toronto were among the most likely to join and lead the Special Diet Campaign.

The Province reacted to increased access to the Special Diet by changing the application forms in November of 2005. From this point on, a medical provider could no longer simply state that certain dietary items were required but had to find that specific medical conditions existed. While this measure caused numbers of people to lose the benefit and suffer considerably, overall access to the Special Diet continued to increase. This year, the Provincial Auditor found that the program had gone from paying out $6 million to one that provided $200 million to people in need and was being accessed by one social assistance recipient in five.

By the end of 2009, it was becoming clear that a major attack was being prepared. Dr. Roland Wong, a Toronto community physician who had played a vital role in assisting poor people to obtain the Special Diet, was accused by the College of Physicians and Surgeons of incompetent medical diagnoses. This apparently is the label they would try to put on an effort to ensure adequate nutrition for low income patients.

Roland Wong and a small grouping of other medical providers (particularly those organized in Health Providers Against Poverty) were central to the fight to win the Special Diet and they deserve nothing but the greatest respect in that regard. However, it is necessary to point out that they were the exceptions. Most medical providers took on very conservative attitudes to the effort to get the forms filled in. Despite the overwhelming medical evidence that exists around the links between poverty and ill health, the great bulk of medical providers opposed the Campaign or stood aside as it was undertaken. Much greater access to the Special Diet would have been possible if this conservatism had not been present on such a rampant basis.

Having targeted the most important medical ally, the Province sent memos to all social assistance offices advising staff that they should consider themselves able to reject forms where they disagreed with the medical diagnoses made by the providers who filled them in. This incredible measure represented a total violation of the basic notions of administrative fairness. For years, we had been fighting and defeating efforts by local offices to take upon themselves the power of medical decision making. Now, these very abuses had been sanctioned at the top and suddenly became considerably harder to defeat. We dealt with cases where people had gone to doctors who they had been seeing for years, had blood tests performed and submitted forms. Their local welfare office would simply say, "We don't accept the findings of this doctor. Find another one." Mass delegations to the offices and even an occupation of the head office of Social Services by hundreds of people affected, were met with police mobilization. The so-called progressive politicians on Toronto City Council stood aside and allowed this abuse to unfold. Access to the Special Diet was finally being seriously reduced.

Then, in the April 2010 Provincial Budget, the Government made the final attack by announcing that the Special Diet was to be eliminated. With access for new applicants massively restricted, those presently on the program continue to receive benefits for the present but the intention is to formally replace it with a much more restricted and limited system that will be run by the Ministry of Health. This may assist in some measure a minority of recipients with massive health issues, but as a means of challenging the growing poverty of those on assistance, the Liberals are moving to destroy the dietary allowance.

It is a matter of historical record that the McGuinty regime, with its hollow promises of poverty reduction, has become the third Ontario Government in history to actually cut income to poor people. They share this distinction with the governments of Mitchell Hepburn[2] and Mike Harris. It is true that this cut comes at a time when governments are out to bring down deficits at our expense but a $200 million program is not large enough to justify such serious efforts as they have put into attacking the Special Diet. The larger issue for the Liberals is that the Special Diet was impeding progress towards a low wage economy. Better paying jobs in the industrial sector have been lost on a massive scale. One in six workers in Ontario now works at or close to the minimum wage. The lowest possible level of social assistance income is needed if people are to be driven into such jobs. The Special Diet had actually created a situation where people were paying their rent and feeding their families. It was reducing the level of desperation and readiness to accept super exploitation. As such, it has been targeted for elimination.

The impact of the Special Diet cut on hundreds of thousands of poor people is going to be enormous. There will be an increase in homelessness, people's health will be undermined and lives will be shortened. However, as severe as this cut is, if the Liberals are able to put it into effect without massive opposition, there is every reason to imagine that worse measures will be implemented in the period ahead. Many US states have eliminated social assistance payments for single people. Time limits on the receipt of assistance are a possibility. Cuts in the base amount paid out to people are an option as governments work to pay for the crisis of capitalism by attacking the basic needs of the poor. If we are to resist the unfolding attack, we must ask ourselves how we can fight back in a way that offers the prospect of winning.

Income support systems have emerged as a reluctant concession. They are always as inadequate as possible and meet people's needs only to the degree that the threat of social dislocation and unrest compels such provision. In a period such are the present one, when governments are working to make income support less adequate, a vital question is the degree to which the poor respond

2   James Struthers, *No Fault of Their Own: Unemployment and the Canadian Welfare State 1914-1941* (Toronto: Univ. of Toronto Press, 1994), 168.

with precisely social unrest. Taking the anger and desperation created by this cut and turning it into a disruptive opposition that can create political crisis for the Liberals is the task facing those who want to defeat it and win a concession around rate levels.

Prior to the formal announcement of the cut, OCAP mobilized supporters to disrupt a fundraising dinner of the Ontario Liberals in Toronto. The night of the announcement, we invaded a town-hall television show featuring the Finance Minister. We organized a large rally and march to the Ministry of Community and Social Services in Toronto in April 2010. Actions at various MPPs' offices have been held. More rallies and actions are unfolding and these include mass case actions to compel welfare offices to accept new applications for the Special Diet. We intend to raise the level of resistance to a point where the members of the Liberal Caucus face ongoing challenge and disruption as they go about their rounds of political activity. People are acting, in an immediate sense, to defend their right to dietary benefit. This fight, however, presents those who engage in it with the necessity of fighting for social assistance rates that provide for health and dignity. Moreover, because we are challenging a particular element of a much broader austerity drive, we are sure that we are contributing to laying the foundations of a common front of resistance.

The struggle around a healthy diet and decent income for the poor is beginning to link up with broader questions of resistance to austerity and the attack on working class living standards. The Canadian Auto Workers (CAW) recently decided to offer support to the fight around the Special Diet and it has been prompted to do this largely because the of increasing numbers of its own laid off members who are being forced to turn to welfare. The Canadian Union of Public Employees Ontario Division has decided to offer material assistance to the campaign based on a recognition that cuts to social assistance are a major part of the assault on public services.

The elimination of the Special Diet by the Liberals is an indication of the political agenda of the years ahead. Workers and poor communities are going to face unheard-of attacks and will need to respond with a social mobilization that is powerful enough to generate political crisis for those in power. As the G20 leaders gather in Toronto, their deliberations remind us that they are preparing their solutions to the crisis of their system. The urgent need is to fight for our solutions and create a movement capable of defeating the misery and poverty that neoliberal policies impose.

THE GREATER TORONTO WORKERS' ASSEMBLY: LESSONS, PROSPECTS, CHALLENGES

Stephanie Ross

> Despite the perpetuation of the crisis, the Left has thus far been unable to effectively shape the North American political and economic landscape via its existing organizations. This chapter explores the political potential of, and the challenges facing, the newly formed Greater Toronto Workers' Assembly (GTWA). The GTWA recognizes the need to create broad forms of solidarity in the context of an organizational form that allows for shared strategizing, collective decision-making, and common action. As a non-sectarian organization that aims to bring together organized labour and community groups, it offers hope for a Left that can go beyond fighting austerity toward a more transformative class-based politics.

In 2010, we were confronted with the near-complete failure of the Canadian left (social democratic, socialist or otherwise) to intervene effectively in the most serious crisis in capitalism in several generations. Heroic and localized resistances to the economic crisis emerged, but remained defensive, sporadic, and limited in their political ambition. The political and organizational capacities these struggles may have built for the next round of movement upsurge—which seems to have emerged in the form of the Occupy movement—remain unclear. Indeed, the failure of spontaneous resistance to achieve any victories for working class people has deepened cynicism about collective action, lowered expectations, and fostered a turn to right-wing populism, particularly in the US.

While the left has been in a state of perpetual self-examination since the early 1990s, it is now more crucial than ever to engage in not only a serious rethinking of the left's structures, politics and strategies, but also a process that will create new organizations that could generate new solidarities, capacities and interventions. Given the wave of global social movement activity that emerged between 1999 and 2003 around questions of global economic and social justice, and the emergence in 2011 of a movement explicitly challenging the maldistribution of wealth and power in class terms, it is important to assess what political agencies now exist and what potential they have to win even the most modest reforms, let alone build the basis for alternatives to capitalist economic and social relations.

I will argue that the Greater Toronto Workers' Assembly (GWTA), formed in October 2009, represents an important development on the left that recognizes the need to create broader forms of solidarity, but in the context of a *new organizational form* that allows for shared strategizing, decision-making and common action. In that sense, the GTWA is both inspired by developments in left/global justice politics of the last decade, and seeks to overcome the impasse of those politics and to create the kinds of agencies and capacities that those movements did *not* develop. However, the Assembly faces major challenges in becoming the kind of entity that is needed, as conflicts over political strategy and priorities, the relationship between class and other forms of oppression, the habits of sectarianism, and the ways to build and preserve a left democratic culture are yet to be worked out. It remains to be seen whether these issues can be worked out so as to allow the Assembly to intervene effectively as a new social force on the Toronto left.

Taking Stock: The Political Terrain of the Toronto Left

The Greater Toronto Workers' Assembly did not emerge out of thin air. Its emergence must instead be understood against the backdrop of Toronto's particularly dense social movement sector in which many activists have long, intertwined histories of collaboration and conflict in multiple and overlapping organizations and campaigns. The Assembly also emerged in the context of previous attempts at left reinvigoration in Toronto, Canada and internationally over the past fifteen years. Those attempts revealed both the desire for a more radical kind of politics, as well as the major obstacles to be faced in its creation. Activists' involvement in both longstanding left institutions and more recent social movement experiments has shaped their political analysis, strategic thinking and assumptions about democracy, and they carry positive, negative, and conflicting lessons about these issues into new organizations like the GTWA. It is worth exploring a few key areas of recent left activism and their influence on the GTWA's formation and evolution.

One such moment of left regroupment in Toronto was Rebuilding The Left (RTL) in 2000-2001. RTL attempted to do something similar to the GTWA, in the context of a waning struggle against the Harris Government's 'Common Sense Revolution' and the withdrawal of the organized labour movement from extra-parliamentary struggle, as indicated by the end of the Ontario Days of Action in 1998. The failure of both social democratic and socialist parties to effectively block, let alone reverse, neoliberalism led to a call to "rebuild the left" via "a structured movement against capitalism", creating an organization that was "more than a movement, less than a party".[1] Over 750 activists from both labour and social movements attended the RTL conference in October 2000. A series of monthly meetings ensued, bringing together around 70-100 people to discuss common and divergent political and organizational traditions and explore how various sections of the left could work together, including the creation of "a new organizational vehicle".[2] According to Albo, There was broad agreement that the left had to invent new approaches to democratic decision-making, in contrast to the centralisms of both Leninist and social democratic parties. The RTL thus generated several working groups: an Activist Network, an Organizational Working Group, and an Educational-Cultural Working Group, each operating on a fairly decentralized basis but with a Co-ordinating Committee linking them together and setting the agenda for monthly meetings.[3]

---

1   Sam Gindin, "Rebuilding the Left: Towards a Structured Anti-Capitalist Movement," *Studies in Political Economy* 64 (2001): 91-97.
2   Greg Albo, "Toronto: Moving Slowly, But Moving," *Canadian Dimension* 35, no. 2 (2001): 10.
3   Albo, "Toronto," 11.

However, tensions amongst participants were immediately apparent at the conference and RTL collapsed within a year, with many different interpretations of this failure. One clear problem was a collective inability to work through the relationship between the politics of class and other identity-based oppressions, and between intellectual and experiential knowledge, the latter criticized as a form of "activistism", in which analysis is seen as a barrier to action.[4] Questions of representation and the real challenge of creating a multi-racial movement resulted in a kind of paralysis, and socialists who maintained a commitment to working-class politics found it difficult to fight for that position without being accused of insensitivities to other identities and oppressions. RTL was never able to move beyond meetings to create a new organizational form that some sought, participants retreated to smaller organizations or groups of like-minded people—chief among them the Socialist Project (SP), which traces its own origin directly to the RTL's collapse—and the difficult work of sorting out these issues was left undone.

The Global Justice and Social Forum movements constitute another important backdrop to the Workers' Assembly. While these movements have many origins, we can date their most contemporary forms' starting point to the December 1999 protests against the World Trade Organization in Seattle. A broad, progressive coalition, using creative forms of civil disobedience and decentralized democratic processes, succeeded in impeding the WTO's work and generated an enormous amount of energy, creativity and cross-movement collaboration as this protest model spread globally in a wave of demonstrations against international organizations.[5] Anti-globalization / global justice activists soon moved to create their own 'alternative space' to discuss the nature of the 'other world' that protesters claimed was possible, in opposition to the neoliberal vision of globalization discussed by economic and political elites at the annual World Economic Forum in Davos, Switzerland. Since

4   Liza Featherstone, Doug Henwood and Christian Parenti, "Beyond Activistism: Why we need deeper thinking in our protests," *Utne Reader*, November/December 2004, http://www.utne.com/2004-11-01/beyond-activism.aspx.
5   Naomi Klein, "Farewell to 'The End of History': Organization and Vision in Anti-Corporate Movements," in *Socialist Register 2002: A World of Contradictions*, eds. Leo Panitch and Colin Leys (London: Merlin, 2002), 1-14.

2001, the annual World Social Forum's explicit anti-statist, non-party orientation, decentralized and inclusive organizational form, and emphasis on exchange and dialogue (rather than decision-making) has attracted thousands of civil society activists from around the world and inspired hundreds of national and regional forums, including the Toronto Social Forum in 2003.[6]

However, these aspects of the global justice movement have increasingly drawn criticism from activists themselves. Protests against global organizations have tended to create temporary, ephemeral organizations designed to intervene in particular events and don't necessarily build long-term working relationships or political projects.[7] 'Summit-hopping'[8] and physical engagements with security forces have taken on the character of spectacle, and the broader educative impact of such forms of protest is debatable given the capacity of the powerful to frame such activity in negative ways. Social forums may create regular and useful spaces for networking and information sharing, but the explicit injunction against making formal decisions to take common action has inhibited the forging of consensus around strategies and the development of more sustained forms of collective intervention.[9] In particular, the emphasis on 'changing the world without taking power' has left the state, with all its material, ideological and coercive power, in the hands of neoliberals (Ross 2009).[10] As many global justice activists concluded that these political strategies have been exhausted, some returned to the local sphere to build alternative, non-market institutions like workers' centres and cooperatives as well as engage in forms of organizing, like No One Is Illegal and the Ontario

---

6   Janet Conway, "Social Forums, Social Movements and Social Change: A Response to Peter Marcuse on the Subject of the World Social Forum," *International Journal of Urban and Regional Research* 29, no. 2 (2005): 425-428.

7   Stephanie Ross, "Is This What Democracy Looks Like? The Politics of the Anti-Globalization Movement in North America," in *Socialist Register 2003: Fighting Identities: Race, Religion and Ethno-Nationalism*, eds. Leo Panitch and Colin Leys (London: Merlin, 2003).

8   AK Thompson, "Bringing the War Home," in *Black Bloc, White Riot: Anti-globalization and the Genealogy of Dissent* (Oakland: AK Press, 2010).

9   Peter Marcuse, "Are Social Forums the Future of Social Movements?" *International Journal of Urban and Regional Research* 29, no. 2 (2005): 417-424.

10   Stephanie Ross, "The Strategic Implications of Anti-Statism in the Global Justice Movement," *Labour, Capital and Society* 41, no. 1 (2008).

Coalition Against Poverty, that highlight and resist the negative local effects of global economic and political processes. That said, such local, issue-based organizing has also been subject to dynamics of fragmentation and working in silos.

Elements of Toronto's union movement have also recognized the need to (re)create greater unity while increasing their capacity to intervene in broader economic and political struggles. Inspired by the ideals of social unionism (as well as the legacy of many of their leaders' socialist histories), the Toronto and York Region Labour Council in particular has placed greater emphasis on activism and coalition politics, with some impressive results. Their 2003 "Million Reasons" campaign, calling for major policy changes that would ensure a living wage for the million Toronto workers earning under $30,000/year, was based on a broad coalition with community-based organizations and effectively forced the provincial Liberal Government to begin phased increases to the minimum wage (which had remained unchanged since 1995).[11] In 2008, their Good Jobs for All summit drew over 1000 people, as did their May 2009 city-wide stewards' meeting, called to discuss responses to the economic crisis and accelerating unemployment. Their November 2009 Good Green Jobs for All conference attracted over 500 people from both labour and environmental organizations which have not worked much together. However, despite its activist orientation and numerical success, the Labour Council remains limited by the less radical politics of many of its affiliates. Important elements of their programme remain traditional and top-down in form, with stewards as the 'troops' getting signatures on petitions and turned on and off in a "faucet" model of mobilization.[12] Their policy solutions have remained within the neoliberal (or at best Keynesian) framework and include cooperation with private capital. The Labour Council's support for Mayor David Miller exposed some difficult contradictions and weaknesses within the Toronto labour movement as the City of Toronto went head to head with their own municipal workers' unions to extract concessions, leading to two

---

11   Toronto and York Region Labour Council, "A Million Reasons to Take Action," http://www.amillionreasons.ca/.
12   Sheila Wilmot, "What's Next for the Ontario Minimum Wage Campaign?" *Relay: A Socialist Project Review* 17 (2007): 14-15.

bitter and divisive strikes in 2002 and 2009.[13] As yet, they have not mobilized the potential base in sustained ways and it is unclear whether they can cement this participation into coherent action across affiliates.

Building for the Assembly

The Assembly thus emerged in the aftermath of these experiments, as people hoped to retain their positive and energizing innovations while overcoming their important limitations. More immediately, the impetus for the Assembly came after a number of Toronto Socialist Project members attended the 2008 *Labor Notes* Conference in Detroit. At a meeting of Canadian labour activists there, a consensus emerged that we lacked, in part, an permanent, cross-organizational space that could bring together labour/left/working-class activists in a more than sporadic way (either around specific campaigns, union conventions or protests). We wanted and needed an ongoing political space to critically analyze the strengths and weaknesses of our collective practices, to bring together left activists to engage with each other more regularly, and to develop the capacity to intervene in struggles and labour organizations in a new, coherent and effective way, pushing them to become more militant, progressive and democratic. A number of us left that meeting committed to convening a *Labor Notes*-type 'conference' the following year, but with a more explicit political focus than has been typical of *Labor Notes*, which has tended to focus on struggles for rank-and-file democracy in US unions rather than the political-ideological orientation of the labour movement. In some sense, we were returning to the place where the RTL initiative had left off, posing the same needs albeit in a markedly different political moment.

Less than six months later, the global financial crisis significantly altered the terrain of the project. SP Labour Committee members concluded that a 'conference' to bring together already leftist activists wasn't ambitious enough. Instead, the question of a new organization of the left should be posed more urgently and directly. Issued by the Socialist Project, the call for the first

---

13   Julia Barnett and Carlo Fanelli, "Lessons Learned: Assessing the 2009 City of Toronto Strike," *The Bullet* 298 (January 19, 2010), http://www.socialist-project.ca/bullet/298.php.

Assembly was six months in the making, as the authors wished to capture the urgency of the moment and the way the left's current political formation was an obstacle, while remaining plural and respecting the differing commitments of the call's potential audience. The initial aim of the Assembly was to "bring together activists in the broad working class movement, including unions and community-based organizations, to explore the experiences and approaches to struggle that both unite and divide us as a starting point for overcoming divisions and building greater collaboration, exchange, strategic discussion and action amongst us". In this context of exchange, the Assembly would work towards developing a common analysis of "the current economic crisis" as one rooted in capitalism as well as "alternative visions" that would challenge both "private corporations and the states that back them". Finally, on the grounding of those common elements of analysis and strategic thinking, the Assembly would "identify and develop concrete strategies and organizational forms of struggle which defend working-class people's immediate needs and lay the groundwork for an equitable and democratic alternative to our present economic and political system".[14]

In initiating this process, the SP also convened or participated in a series of preliminary conversations amongst labour and left activists to explore whether others were committed to working together in new ways and on what kind of basis. In retrospect, this was very important preparatory work which both built relationships of trust and demonstrated a democratic style of working. First, adopting the language of the Zapatistas, a series of three "Consultas" explored whether there was a shared desire for a new type of organization, what it might do, and how a conference on that issue should work[15]; what the areas of political agreement and difference were; what it meant to call oneself a socialist or express a commitment to 'class'; and how the relationship between class and other oppressions should be understood.

---

14   Socialist Project Labour Committee, "Solidarity. Resistance. Transformation. Organizing Working Class Communities," First Assembly Call, Toronto, 2009.
15   At the first Consulta in March 2009, SP presented their Assembly proposal to activists involved in a wide array of left, social movement and labour organizations for feedback.

At the same time, the 'Allies' meetings between representatives from Socialist Project, New Socialists, No One Is Illegal, OCAP, BASICS, Black Action Defense Committee, and STOP Community Centre and others were focused on developing joint political education projects, particularly around the economic crisis. The process of developing shared materials brought to the surface crucial political and ideological differences, particularly about attitudes to organizational questions, but participants were able to engage these issues in honest ways.

Finally, during the Fall of 2009, two members of SP and two union leaders[16] convened the 'Progressive Think Tank', three day-long meetings between a small but strategically placed group of left-labour and social movement activists. The goal was to have a deep conversation about the nature of the crisis (both external and internal) and the kinds of political capacities needed to intervene. While the Think Tank process encountered difficulties, not least because of the problems of activist overload, it served to connect with union-based people who had remained outside the first Assembly (see below), and the conversations led a good portion to conclude that a broader organizational form was needed. Ultimately, in these various conversations, and despite persistent differences in political and strategic perspectives, there was a clear common desire to build something larger than the immediate and specific struggles of particular organizations, and that bridged groups focused on organizing different segments of the working class.

The Assembly's Achievements

The first Assembly took place in October 2009, bringing together 100 people over two days in exploratory, small-group discussions focused on the issues posed in SP's call. While there was widespread recognition of the grave need to build something new—new connections, spaces, shared analyses and political/leadership development processes—unsurprisingly, many in established left political as well as community-based organizations expressed skepticism and reluctance to create a new

---

16   The think tanks were organized by Sam Gindin and Stephanie Ross from SP, Michael Hurley, President of CUPE's Ontario Council of Hospital Unions, and former CUPE Local 1 president Rob Fairley.

organizational form that might require the relinquishing of their political infrastructure or a reallocation of time and effort away from important immediate campaigns. While these tensions were noted, the final plenary produced two key decisions: to establish an "anti-capitalist, nonsectarian and democratic network of activists which was militant, effective, multi-racial and working class", and to create a volunteer Interim Coordination Committee with a mandate to organize another Assembly and put forward proposals on the form of this new entity. In the meantime, the relative absence of union-based activists was seen as an important problem to remedy.

The January 2010 Assembly put the organizational question front and centre. Working mostly as a plenary of around 200 people, participants debated proposals from the Interim Coordinating Committee with good will, optimism and excitement, remarkably free of the dogmatism, impatience or grandstanding that often emerges at mass labour/left meetings. The morning session explored what criteria the Assembly should use to decide on which campaigns and actions to adopt, in the knowledge that what the Assembly does will shape what the Assembly is. Based on the work of a fourth Consulta held in December 2009, and eschewing the "activistist" assumption that any action is by definition worthwhile, the Assembly discussed prioritizing campaigns that built sustained collaboration across sectors and communities, that broadened the left both analytically and numerically, that developed internal analytical and organizational capacities, and that balanced short-term and long-term goals. While the issue of campaign criteria was not resolved, it marked the beginning of a crucial political discussion. The Assembly also produced four major decisions on the issue of organization. First, a broad vision statement was adopted, with which people must agree as a key criterion of membership.[17] Second, after an interesting debate over the pros and cons of organizations affiliating to the Assembly, attendees established an individual membership-based organization (rather than a network or coalition of organizations) to which people must commit some time, while maintaining their membership in other organizations. Third,

---

17   Vision Statement of the Greater Toronto Workers' Assembly, January 16, 2010, http://www.workersassembly.ca/vision.

following a debate over how to balance inclusion and accountability in leadership structures, a permanent yet volunteer Coordinating Committee and a set of five sub-committees[18] was formed, tasked with developing proposals for the next Assembly. Finally, the group mandated that the Coordinating Committee organize an Assembly every 12 weeks. As one indication of the extent of support for the Assembly process, 157 people signed membership forms immediately following the day's conclusion.

The third Assembly held in April 2010 worked to operationalize the discussion on campaigns in a debate over which campaigns to adopt. Three specific campaigns were proposed: organizing economic justice sessions at G8/G20 Summit in June 2010, developing a campaign for free public transit, and conducting an educational campaign on the attack on public services that would inform new alliances between service providers and recipients. Although all three campaigns were adopted, interesting debates emerged over the 'proper' scale and site of intervention (for instance, municipal elections versus extra-parliamentary protests against the G8/G20) as well as the means of articulating global and local struggles[19] and the relationship between Assembly initiatives and those of other organizations (see below). Internal organizational questions were also passionately debated. Although some continued to hold that the principle of voluntary participation on the Coordinating Committee is more inclusive and relatively barrier-free, the Assembly adopted by a substantial majority the principle of elected leadership, on the basis that such leadership is more accountable and

---

18   The list of committees adopted in January 2010 included: Finance and Membership Structure, Outreach (which was merged with the first), Campaigns, Internal Political Development and Education, Publications and External Political Education. Additional groups have since emerged, including the Labour Committee (including both union and non-union workers), the Culture Committee, the Feminist Action Committee, the International Solidarity Committee, and the GTWA Flying Squad.

19   While the Assembly did establish both a G20 committee, which later took on organizing support for those arrested before and during the protests, and later an International Solidarity Committee, in practice the scale of the Assembly's activity has been local. Insofar as global issues and the struggles of others have been engaged with and supported, the lens has been to ground such engagement in the struggles and priorities of Toronto's multi-racial working class communities, broadly defined. In that sense, the national and global scales have not been ignored, but rather the Assembly's agency and capacity to intervene have primarily been understood as local.

its (lack of) diversity more transparent to the membership. This was a notable shift from the January Assembly, which voted fairly overwhelmingly to maintain a volunteer leadership for the time being. The Membership Committee was then tasked with creating a proposal for an elected Coordinating Committee, taking into consideration the various goals of accountability, diversity of representation, and inclusivity.[20] The question of dues was also discussed. Both the Coordinating Committee and the Assembly more broadly were closely divided on the issue, with some in favour of a mandatory dues structure that would provide an immediate financial basis for the three campaigns just adopted, while others were concerned about the potentially exclusionary impact a dues structure would have on an organization in its infancy and hoping to reach out to new activists. The Assembly ultimately opted for the development of a plan for a 'voluntary' dues structure, to be presented at the July 2010 meeting.[21] By the end of the third Assembly, membership stood at 217 people from over 40 organizations. One year later, the Assembly had 296 members, indicating its ongoing and growing appeal as a space for creative self-organizing within the context of a broadly shared set of political values.[22]

The Challenges Ahead

Despite these exciting developments, the Assembly's challenges are also enormous. The group stands at the beginning of a long-term political process in which difficult questions, debates and collective efforts are yet to come. Although it has outlived its RTL predecessor by a full year, itself a significant achievement, it remains to be seen what the Assembly will be able to *do* together, and whether it can act in new and more effective ways than existing labour, social

---

20   An elections framework for the Coordinating Committee was adopted at the July 2010 Assembly.

21   As of writing, the GWTA still has a voluntary dues structure, with $5/month set as the minimum and reaching to $50/month. Supporters may also make one-time donations.

22   The GTWA has since held four more Assemblies, in October 2010, February, May, and September 2011, and is currently planning its 10th Assembly. The Labour Committee also organized a conference on "Building the Working Class Movement" in late January, 2011.

movement and left organizations. In order to reach any potential it may have as a new social force in Toronto, and like previous attempts at creating left agency, it will have to confront the following.

The Assembly must first develop a shared political analysis and practice in the context of an ideologically diverse membership with very different traditions, attitudes and priorities. Perhaps sensing how difficult such conversations would be, serious and substantial discussion of key political concepts and their relationship to each other was continually deferred in early meetings. This is understandable, given the need to develop the mutual trust which makes productive debate over difficult issues possible and the need to gather together a critical mass. However, there are risks to leaving these issues unengaged, some of which were observable in the January debate on the vision statement, which produced a 'laundry list' of problems and struggles. Some were concerned primarily to get their particular issue included, while others expressed a *pro forma* commitment to these struggles to get the statement passed. The work of making the connections between particular forms of oppression, and between oppressions and class exploitation, and of developing shared understandings and commitments is still to be done.

That said, the Assembly has been remarkable in creating and sustaining various spaces for such discussion. In October 2010, the Assembly initiated a monthly Internal Discussion Bulletin, which has since dealt with issues ranging from organizational principles and purpose, finances, the political dynamics of volunteer activism, mechanisms to ensure respectful debate, the challenges of working-class electoral politics, the prospects of eco-socialism and workplace takeovers, and the importance of internationalism in left politics. The Culture Committee has also regularly offered a series of very successful coffeehouses featuring themed discussions in a social setting, allowing Assembly members to carry on debate outside of the formal space of a meeting. These initiatives, even if they have not produced 'consensus' on various issues, are crucial to the formation of the Assembly's basis of unity at least as a political community.

A second issue concerns the development of new strategies and tactics in the conduct of campaigns. There is a consensus that *doing things together* is crucial, as it both makes otherwise abstract political discussions concrete and meaningful, and changes how people act with each other. However, the Assembly is faced with the tension between sustaining important existing campaigns, on the one hand, and building and conducting new campaigns that deepen participants' political economic analysis, organizational and democratic capacities for future, more radical interventions, on the other. Participants agree that capacity-building campaigns should anticipate emerging and unifying issues or place new demands on the table, rather than simply react. The Assembly's Free Transit Campaign is a good example of an attempt to push the ideological boundaries of the neoliberal status quo on transit policy, reframing public transit as a right for Toronto's working class, talking to transit users and bringing together segments of that class on a community-wide basis. Although there is an important continuing role for 'fightback' efforts, the tendency to let employers or the state set the agenda for struggle and for activists to remain in a defensive position to preserve what we have has become well ingrained. The work spearheaded by the Assembly's Public Sector Campaign is precisely intended to anticipate the coming attacks against public sector workers and the services they deliver, but it remains unclear whether public sector workers themselves, not to mention their organizations, are taking up the call. Union leaders' view that attacks can only be mitigated rather than opposed has served to undermine many union members' belief in the possibility of alternatives to either the neoliberal world or the *status quo ante* of Keynesianism. Posing such 'radical reforms'[23] will take enormous creativity, but is central to regenerating a sense of real political ambition and possibility.

The question of developing campaigns for radical reforms is linked to another difficult political dilemma, namely whether and/ or how the Assembly should engage in already existing campaigns, designed and led by other organizations. For instance, activists from CUPE Local 1 representing Toronto Hydro workers came to

---

23   Following Ralph Miliband, I take 'radical reforms' to mean those piecemeal changes to current arrangements that also make a "significant indent" in the social order in "democratic and egalitarian directions", but which also develop the desire and capacity for cumulatively more radical changes to capitalist economic and social relations. Others have called these 'transitional demands', although this terminology seems to imply a particular transition to a particular outcome which isn't really known. (Miliband, *Socialism for a Sceptical Age* (London: Verso, 1994).)

the January 2010 Assembly with the proposal that the Assembly 'endorse' their anti-privatization campaign. Although this was not explicitly rejected in a vote, the majority of Assembly participants seemed cool to the idea. Similarly, in the April 2010 Assembly, some opposed the adoption of a 'free transit' campaign for fear this would undermine efforts of other groups in the city, namely the Labour Council and the Public Transit Coalition, focused on maintaining adequate levels of public funding to sustain and expand the transit system (in line with the current municipal administration).[24] However, others insisted that the Assembly should develop its own campaigns, even if they implicitly or explicitly challenge the limits of other existing campaigns, not least because it could serve to pull more moderate campaigns to the left as well as carve out the terrain for new demands that existing organizations can't or find it hard to demand, even if some within their ranks agree with them. However, Assembly members also involved in these other organizations may find it difficult to navigate these tensions.

All this raises a third major issue, which is how to create unity while maintaining the pluralism of the Assembly and preventing particular groups or factions from dominating or driving debates and decisions. This is not so much a problem of 'political capture' as such, although there are some who would like to see the Assembly marshaled for other organizations' purposes and this dynamic has shaped debate at the last two early meetings. Rather, the habits of sectarianism are ever-present, if, for the moment, contained. By 'sectarianism' I mean the politics of organized factions who believe they have already discovered the 'correct' political analysis or approach and who, by 'boring from within' other working-class organizations, attempt to dominate through monologue or recruit to their own group at the expense of building a broader agency of the left/working class. Undoubtedly, organized currents of opinion and analysis exist within the Assembly. Such pluralism is rightly seen as a strength. Moreover, such groups will and do

---

24   This debate over transit strategy took place in the context of Mayor David Miller's Transit City initiative, which would have significantly expanded light rail transit throughout the city, and particularly to the inner suburbs. With the election of Rob Ford as mayor in October 2010, the Transit City initiative was cancelled and service cuts have been implemented, radically altering the terrain for both these campaigns.

caucus, putting forward their vision of the Assembly and working to convince others of its political and strategic merit. However, the motivations and attitudes behind such organizing are crucial: whether these currents are in the open or hidden, whether people are willing to being convinced of other perspectives in the course of debate or irremediably wedded to their 'line', whether people can lose debates and remain committed to the organization and to working with people with whom one disagrees will all determine whether the Assembly can flourish and create something genuinely new on the left.

Avoiding sectarian conflict is related to the creation of a new democratic culture of the left, with procedures, structures and social relations that support and sustain it. Is it possible to create a plenary space like the Assembly that avoids the problems of both formalized processes (like union or party conventions) and structureless improvisation (typical of many global justice movement groups and now the Occupy movements)? Differences over what structural arrangements are 'democratic' have emerged from the outset. As mentioned above, in debates over the constitution of the Coordinating Committee, some have argued that elections are key in establishing accountability relationships in ways that self-selected volunteer leadership does not, as well as ensuring diverse representation. Others preferred a more spontaneous model of leadership, holding that electoral contests are exclusionary by virtue of someone losing and keep out younger, newer participants reluctant to challenge established activists. Similar dynamics are at play around the Assembly sub-committees: while entirely volunteer, and initially drawing more than 80 people to participate, the work of coordination, organization, and liaising with the Coordinating Committee remains vague. Deeply held, often unexamined and conflicting assumptions about the relationship between structure and democracy are involved here, which need to be openly discussed without making a fetish out of process and sidelining the importance of effectiveness as a key criteria of democracy.

Another democratic question is whether the Assembly can develop new methods of debating and deciding that ensure both inclusivity and an effective capacity to act on decisions that participants accept and support, even when they may depart from their particular preferences. There is a danger that, when priorities are established, some people will fall away since, unlike unions, there is no mandatory basis for citizenship keeping people in the Assembly if and when they 'lose' in the difficult debates to come. In other words, in a purely voluntary group like this, can norms and allegiances be created that sustain commitment even when the priorities and strategies adopted are not always universally supported?

The Assembly also must face the issue of how to broaden its social base in the working class, broadly understood, while not diluting the radicalism of its politics. In that sense, the challenge is how to get beyond what has appeared to be only two choices open to left organizations: remaining politically 'pure', radical and small or becoming a mass organization through political moderation. The Assembly is explicitly committed to developing a mass yet anti-capitalist organization, which will require reaching beyond its current, and admittedly fairly narrow, social base. This problem is evident on the level of both organizations and individuals. First, it is worth noting who has and has not been present, organizationally speaking. Many members of various socialist and anarchist organizations, including Socialist Project, New Socialists, International Socialists, the Communist Party of Canada, Socialist Voice, and Common Cause are involved. As well, there has been significant participation from people involved in the social movement/community-based left, such as the Ontario Coalition Against Poverty, No One Is Illegal, workers' centres from Toronto and Montreal, and the Coalition Against Israeli Apartheid, most of whom are young and racialized activists. However, it could be argued that these are already highly politicized groups, and while it is an achievement to bring them together in some provisional unity, that doesn't guarantee that these will be able to reach beyond to new constituencies.[25]

Moreover, the participation of left union activists and leaders—let alone members of the non-unionized working class—has been

---

25   The Assembly's commitment to support and engage regularly with the Occupy Toronto movement through the establishment of "Solidarity Tuesdays", at which Assembly members meet and engage with occupation participants on various issues, brings with it a renewed potential for expansion given the large number of 'new' activists the Occupy strategy has pulled into action, but assessment of this work would be premature.

slow to emerge. The attempt to bring together social movement and union people outside of 'official labour' events was a unique and crucial aspect of the SP's initial motivation to call the Assembly, and the prospect that union activists will not engage undermines many of the important guiding principles built up over the Assembly's first two years and eight months. On a positive note, and in contrast to the October 2009 meeting, January 2010's Assembly produced a significant labour caucus of about 40 people and, in keeping with an expansive understanding of 'working class', explicitly included both unionized and non-union, wage and unwaged workers.[26] In other words, the organizational and ideological space has been created for such participants. However, SP Labour Committee activists had expected greater participation from dissenting CAW activists, with whom they had worked to oppose the CAW-Magna 'Framework of Fairness' and the last two rounds of concession bargaining, and as yet relatively few of these people are engaged. The reality is that both unionized and non-union workers have been so demoralized by thirty years of austerity and left defeat that their belief in the utility of collective action in making things better has been significantly eroded.[27] Instead, left activists mostly based in public sector unions have come forward. While public sector workers' participation is crucial, a broad base in both public and the union movement private sector unions is also important, if fostering greater working-class unity and anti-capitalist perspectives and alternatives in the union movement is ever to be a serious prospect. But the Catch-22 remains: regenerating workers' sense of possibility involves showing that the Assembly is *relevant*, and has the potential to *win* something concrete in the short run, even though that capacity to win is partly dependant on those workers' much greater participation in the Assembly's work.

---

26 It should be noted that, after the Labour Committee's January 2011 conference on "Building the Working Class Movement", divisions over the purpose of the committee, and in particular whether it should be organizing amongst unionized workers or in the broader non-union community, led to its dissolution. Since May 2011, the Public Sector Campaign Committee has taken up part of what was the Labour Committee's work, namely organizing amongst both union and community members to take up a defense of public sector jobs and services. Another group, the Labour Caucus flying squad, provides support for picket lines and other labour actions.

27 Murray Cooke, "To Interpret the World and To Change It: Interview with David McNally," *Socialist Studies* 7, no. 1/2 (2011): 1-36.

If there is one advance over the previous rounds of struggle, it is a renewed attention to the role of organization in fostering capacity for sustained collective action. In that sense, a political 'space' is no longer enough to address the left's analytical, strategic and organizational challenges. Ultimately, however, it remains to be seen what kind of organization the Assembly will become. On this, too, there is much diversity of opinion. Some see this as a pre-party socialist formation, into which existing left organizations should become incorporated with the eventual goal of engaging or contesting state power in some way, via municipal elections, for instance. For others, this is a non-socialist fight-back organization aimed at consolidating existing capacities, and creating new ones, in order to generate more effective forms of resistance against economic and political attacks on the working class. For still others, it is a loose coalition or network of movements which merely expands and supports existing projects. However, at this point, even two years on, such matters remain unsettled, and whether the Assembly can become more than the sum of its parts is still in the process of being discovered. However, despite its challenges, the Greater Toronto Workers' Assembly is a creative and ambitious new organization through which the broad left is attempting to collectively answer these questions, in debate and in practice, and deserves ongoing attention.

CONTRIBUTORS
(in alphabetical order)

David Brons is a long-time community activist who at various times has been active in queer liberation, anti-poverty, anti-imperialist and anti-globalization struggles. He is currently a member of Common Cause.

John Clarke has been active in anti-poverty movements since 1983, when he helped to form the London Union of Unemployed Workers. He has been an organizer with the Ontario Coalition Against Poverty (OCAP) for more than two decades.

Elizabeth Cobbett is a PhD candidate in Political Science at Carleton University. Her research explores the different ways in which global finance seeks profitable opportunities within localized social structures.

Simten Coşar is Professor in the Faculty of Communication at Hacettepe University in Ankara. Her areas of research include political parties and political thought in Turkey, and women in political thought. She is the author of various articles in *Journal of Political Ideologies*, *Contemporary Politics*, *Feminist Review*, *Journal of Third World Studies*, *South European Society and Politics*, and *Monthly Review*.

Carlo Fanelli is a PhD candidate in the Department of Sociology and Anthropology at Carleton University, with research interests in critical political economy, labour studies, Canadian public policy, social movements, urban sociology and education. He has published widely on these themes and is the managing editor of *Alternate Routes: A Journal of Critical Social Research*.

Tim Fowler is a PhD candidate in Political Science and Political Economy at Carleton University. He is researching how the Canadian Autoworkers have responded to neoliberalism and globalization, and has published articles on the CAW and on class and elections in Canada. He is currently co-editing a book (forthcoming from Red Quill) on Canadian labour and the Great Recession.

Alda Kokallaj is a PhD candidate in Political Science and Political Economy at Carleton University. Her dissertation explores the role of multilateral development banks and civil society groups in shaping environmental governance in post-communist transition countries, while her broader research focuses on theorizing nature-society-state relations and their implications for political ecology and democratic ecological governance.

Michael A. Lebowitz is Professor Emeritus of Economics at Simon Fraser University and is associated with the Centro Internacional Miranda in Caracas, where he has been directing a programme on Transformative Practice and Human Development. He is the author of numerous books on socialist theory, including *Beyond Capital: Marx's Political Economy of the Working Class* (Palgrave Macmillan), which won the 2004 Deutscher Memorial Prize, and most recently *The Contradictions of "Real Socialism": The Conductor and the Conducted* (Monthly Review, 2012).

Priscillia Lefebvre is a PhD Candidate in Sociology and Political Economy at Carleton University. She was a union delegate to the Philippines for a Global Justice Worker Solidarity Exchange, and was an election observer with the People's International Observers' Mission in the 2010 Philippines general election.

Greg Macdougall is an activist with Common Cause, the Indigenous Peoples Solidarity Movement Ottawa (IPSMO), Organizing For Justice, and EquitableEducation.ca. He first became involved in activism through the student newspaper at the University of Waterloo, and then by working with the Independent Media Centre network. His writing has been published in various print and online publications.

Aylin Özman is Professor in the Department of International Relations at TED University in Ankara. Her published articles focus on Turkish politics and political thought, and she is currently conducting research on gender and nationalist politics and political opposition in Turkey.

Gülden Özcan is a Ph.D. candidate in the Department of Sociology and Anthropology at Carleton University. She is the co-editor of several books and journals with Red Quill, including *A General Police System: Political Economy and Security in the Age of Enlightenment* (2009) and *Saving Global Capitalism: Interrogating Austerity and Working Class Responses to Crises, Alternate Routes* (2011).

Anupam Pandey is an Assistant Professor of Political Science at Saint Mary's University and also teaches in the International Development Studies department at Dalhousie University in Halifax. Her research has been focused on ecofeminism and the Third World, including the development of an ecofeminist critique of international relations theory.

Justin Paulson is an Assistant Professor of Sociology at Carleton University, where he also teaches in the Institute of Political Economy. He researches social movements and the unevenness of capitalist social relations, and his work has appeared in journals such as *Affinities*, *Cultural Logic*, and *The Socialist Register*. He is an editor of *Mediations* and *Studies in Political Economy*.

Stephanie Ross is an Assistant Professor of Social Science at York University, and Coordinator of the Work and Labour Studies Programme and Co-Director of the Centre for Research on Work and Society. Her research and teaching focus on democracy in working class and social movement organizations, public sector unionism and renewal, the global justice movement in North America, and the links between social justice organizing inside and outside of the workplace. Her work on these themes has appeared in *The Socialist Register*, *Studies in Political Economy*, *Labour, Capital and Society*, and *Labor Studies Journal*.

Susan Spronk is an Assistant Professor of International Development and Global Studies at the University of Ottawa. Her work on anti-privatization struggles in the Andes has appeared in *Latin American Perspectives, Review of Radical Political Economics* and *International Labor and Working Class History.* She is a research associate with the Municipal Services Project, which focuses on policy alternatives in municipal service delivery in Africa, Asia, and Latin America, and is an editor of *Studies in Political Economy.*

Kyle Wark is an Ottawa-based writer and activist. He has been involved in anarchist organizing for most of the last decade, and is currently working on a project to translate anarchist texts from the Mexican Revolution.

www.ingramcontent.com/pod-product-compliance
Lightning Source LLC
Chambersburg PA
CBHW030330270326
41926CB00010B/1566